D0374547

John McMillian is an associate professor of American history at Georgia State University. He is the author of *Beatles Vs. Stones* and *Smoking Typewriters: The Sixties Underground Press and the Rise of Alternative Media in America*, and a co-editor of *The Radical Reader* and *Protest Nation* (both published by The New Press). He lives in Atlanta.

WITHDRAWN

ALSO BY JOHN MCMILLIAN

Beatles Vs. Stones

Smoking Typewriters

Protest Nation (editor)

The New Left Revisited (editor)

The Radical Reader (editor)

AMERICAN EPIDEMIC

Reporting from the Front Lines
of the Opioid Crisis

EDITED BY JOHN McMILLIAN
WITH A FOREWORD BY LESLIE JAMISON

THE
NEW
PRESS

NEW YORK
LONDON

© 2019 by individual contributors
All rights reserved.
No part of this book may be reproduced, in any form, without written permission from the publisher.

Requests for permission to reproduce selections from this book should be made through our website: https://thenewpress.com/contact.

The Damage Done, a series by Beth Macy, © *The Roanoke Times* and republished with permission.
"How's Amanda? A Story of Truth, Lies and an American Addiction" © 2016 by Eli Saslow / *The Washington Post*
"No Family Is Safe from This Epidemic" was originally published in *The Atlantic* magazine by Admiral James A. Winnefeld Jr. (U.S. Navy, retired).

Published in the United States by The New Press, New York, 2019
Distributed by Two Rivers Distribution

ISBN 978-1-62097-519-0 (pb)
ISBN 978-1-62097-520-6 (ebook)
CIP data is available

The New Press publishes books that promote and enrich public discussion and understanding of the issues vital to our democracy and to a more equitable world. These books are made possible by the enthusiasm of our readers; the support of a committed group of donors, large and small; the collaboration of our many partners in the independent media and the not-for-profit sector; booksellers, who often hand-sell New Press books; librarians; and above all by our authors.

www.thenewpress.com

Composition by dix!

This book was set in Garamond Premier Pro

Printed in the United States of America

10 9 8 7 6 5 4 3 2 1

CONTENTS

FOREWORD

This book is built of brutal moments: Two parents overdose at their daughter's softball game while she watches from the other side of a chain-link fence. A mother screams at the police as they take away her son's body: "That's my child! He is not a piece of garbage!" A rehab house manager gets a handwritten note in the mail, folded around a funeral announcement: "my son tried to get into your program and you guys didn't have a bed for him." A married couple walks two and a half hours to reach a Pennsylvania coal town with a robust supply of street heroin. That same couple, a few years earlier, shoots up after their kids' bedtime, then falls down the rabbit hole of that relief into another life entirely: tying off with an orange headband in the bathroom of a Giant Foods while a stranger knocks on the door, impatient to pee, probably wondering if it's *yet another addict* in there, wasting everyone's time with her senseless self-destruction.

This book isn't just about the brutality of addiction, but about the brutality of the industry that has grown up around it. It's about dealers driving around Denver with thirty uninflated balloons of heroin in their mouths and big bottles of water by their sides, in case they get pulled over by the cops; and it's about a woman wearing a surgical mask in a suburban house, taking swigs from a Red Bull and taping glassine bags while her preschool daughter eats cereal a few feet away. It's about a Big Pharma CEO making $89 million a year.

This book is merciless. It's nearly unbearable to read these stories back to back. It's unrelenting, their insistence on *another* and *another* and *another*: another grieving parent, another kid on the phone with 911 after her dad ODs in front of her, another baby crying in a trailer, another box store bathroom, another used syringe marked with eyeliner. But the overwhelming bulk of this accumulation, the *again-and-again* of it, the way that repetition hurts your heart, is part of what this book asks you to confront. It asked me to confront the ways I wanted relief from what it was telling me.

I kept wanting to go numb, to say, *seen it already, heard it already, know it already.* But ultimately, I couldn't take refuge in those dismissals, because part of the force of this book is the way its pieces fight the crutch of that numbness. They bring the story to life again, by giving it a pulse—like a body retrieved from overdose, made human once again. We watch a woman try to pass the days until her Naltrexone shot by playing games on her cell phone, by driving around the suburbs of Detroit, by flipping TV channels—anything to make the hours disappear, anything to fight the boredom and the craving—while her mother hovers, worried sick, worried sick for years, willing to do almost anything to save her. This isn't just another story. This is *their* story.

One addict says the hardest part of an overdose is waking up again, and in this book, you have to wake up again and again and again—to each new piece, each new angle on the tragedy: ordinary days of extraordinary hell in New Jersey, or Massachusetts, or Virginia, or Michigan, Pennsylvania, Ohio, Tennessee, Maryland.

I read this book in stolen pockets of time while my infant daughter was napping in the next room, and her sleeping body was at the core of how it ached for me. The love of parents for their children is the secret soul of this book. When I read about parents willing to do anything for their children, and losing them anyway—to foster care, to the state, to the grip of the drug itself—I knew my love for my daughter was a projection flung onto lives that aren't my own and never will be. But there it was, that love—saturating the pages anyway. That love was alive to these "addicts" as more than just addicted—it was alive to them as mothers, daughters, sisters, sons and fathers and husbands and wives.

The story this book tells is at once primal and specific. On one level, it's another chapter in the ongoing story of our human reckoning with pain itself, physical and psychic: the ways we've tried to blunt it or escape it. But it's also telling a much more concrete story about a particular set of circumstances: the tidal wave set in motion when Purdue Pharma introduced OxyContin to the pain relief market in 1996, actively underplaying its addictive potential and incentivizing its over-prescription, effectively creating an entire population of opioid-dependent users, many of whom ended up eventually turning to street heroin because it was cheaper and more available. As Eric Eyre reported in the *Charleston Gazette-Mail*, more than 780 million painkillers came into West Virginia between 2007 and 2012. What was it like to be a human being caught inside the flood of those statistics? These pieces try to find language for the interior hallways of compulsion, for the elusive swell of relief: "you curl up in a corner and blank out the world." "It's like a warm blanket," "like shooting Jesus," "like a best friend to me now."

Even the structure of this book tells a story about our evolving understanding of the opioid crisis. The articles shift from on-the-ground reporting, tracking the damage when no one could entirely envision its contours, to long-form reportage trying to make sense of the epidemic's causes, mechanisms, and human toll. It shifts from Beth Macy writing articles in the *Roanoke Times* in 2012—about suburban teenagers dealing and dying, everyone shocked at what was happening to them—to Margaret Talbot writing about West Virginia's opioid crisis for the *New Yorker* in 2017, by which point it had already become an "epidemic," when the damage had become eerily normalized, even tiresome: EMTs picking up chocolate milk and beef jerky between overdose calls, or public seminars on how to administer lifesaving Narcan shots in which leaders have to argue for *why* it's worth saving addicts' lives in the first place.

Following the arc of this book feels like watching a monster emerge from the shadowy corners of our collective peripheral vision. But even *that*, the impulse to call the opioid crisis a monster, is part of what the book ends up documenting so acutely: our desperate desire to find or construct villains—addicts as villains, dealers as villains, doctors as villains—when in truth, these charges of villainy almost always reduce or redact the truth in order to invite us to recline on the easier affective furniture of blame or indignation. We might want to blame dealers for killing addicts, but many dealers are simply addicts desperate to kick their own habits.

If any compelling villain emerges from these pages, it's greed. It's Big Pharma making money off the suffering of the folks who got hooked on their drugs. In 2012, the CEO of McKesson, the largest drug distributor in America, was also the nation's highest paid executive. It's nearly impossible to read that statistic without feeling rage. But even that blame doesn't solve the core dilemma of this book: how to get free from the compulsion.

When any individual recovery feels so impossible, like such a ceaseless accumulation of hours, it becomes almost untenable to imagine the scale of collective recovery. And this book doesn't shy away from that question or its complexities. It takes us into recovery meetings, and into the vexed debates around medication-assisted treatment: the importance of medications like methadone and buprenorphine in helping people stay sober, as well as the ways these medications can be abused, and certainly the ways they have been unfairly maligned. The moral of the story is there is no easy moral. No salvation is easy. Every salvation is vexed, tenuous, subject to a thousand contingencies and reversals.

This book is full of glimmers of recovery that are honest in their hope as well as their fragility: a man who gets clean feels wonder at the vast expanse of the Atlantic Ocean, stretching beyond his gaze; another man overdoses in his car on his way to a Narcotics Anonymous meeting to collect his ninety-day chip; a woman speaks at a Cincinnati meeting, three years clean, with her daughter on her lap, remembering how she left the hospital immediately after her birth to buy heroin. There's hope in that moment of confession, but it's a hope that understands its own perilous footing. When a mother and son take their kayaks onto a New England lake, under a blaze of fall leaves, and the mother feels relief—because there is no way her son can relapse out there, on the water—it's relief with an expiration date. Eventually, mother and son both know they will have to return to shore.

Near the end of an article called "Finding a Fix," when reporter

Julia Lurie calls a subject she hasn't spoken to in a while, a man named Dre who'd gotten sober a few months prior, she hears his voice slurred on the other end of the line. He tells her he did some Percocets and now he's nodding off in the bathroom. The last thing he says, before they hang up, is this: "Don't forget about me, okay?"

This book says, *Okay. We won't.*

Leslie Jamison

INTRODUCTION

On the morning of March 2, 2019, I sat down at Aurora Coffee, an eccentrically styled café in Atlanta's Little Five Points neighborhood, which is about half a mile from where I live. I often visit Aurora on Saturday mornings, after my weekly long run. On that particular Saturday, I had arrived specifically to begin writing the introduction to this book, which you are reading now. Spring arrives early in Atlanta, and it was shaping up to be a beautiful day.

Then a strange thing happened. Just as I opened my laptop, and began trying to compose my thoughts, I noticed three people sitting at a nearby table. They appeared to be in their late twenties or early thirties, and they seemed to me a slightly oddly matched group. Two of them were men (one black, one white) and the other was an attractive white woman. And unlike everyone else in the coffee shop, they were not talking, reading, working, or fiddling with their phones. They had not ordered anything, either, not even a cup of coffee or a bottle of water. They were just quietly occupying a table, and their inscrutability caught my attention.

At exactly 9:00 a.m., I overheard the woman say, "It's time." Without another word, they got up and filed out the door.

I wondered about this mysterious group. I had a feeling about them. I watched as they walked along the shabby strip mall—past Savage Pizza, the florist, the nail salon—toward Little Five Points Pharmacy. At that point, I knew.

The woman came out of the pharmacy, only now she was smiling, while holding a small brown paper bag. The group seemed a bit more animate. They had been waiting for the drugstore to open, I am certain, in order to buy syringes.[1] As they clambered into a black minivan, and headed south on Moreland Avenue, I knew they would soon be shooting heroin.

Should I have been surprised? We are, after all, living in the midst of the most gruesome and pervasive drug epidemic in American history. In 2018, drug overdose deaths in the United States set a new record. There were more than 70,000 of them, mostly due to opioids.

Let's put this in perspective. Seventy thousand is far more than the number of Americans who died in 2017 from car accidents (40,100), or guns (39,773), or suicide (47,173). It is more than the number of American servicemen killed during the entire Vietnam War (58,220). It is far more than all of the American deaths from 9/11, the Iraq War, and the Afghanistan War, combined (39,396, as of March 2019). Drug overdoses are now the leading cause of death for Americans under fifty. Life expectancy in the United States has diminished over the past three years—a phenomenon that is unprecedented since World War II.

This book does not set out to comprehensively trace the origins of the epidemic. Three writers have recently done so, expertly. Readers who would like to know more about how regional pain pill abuse metastasized into a gargantuan drug crisis are encouraged to read Barry Meier's *Pain Killer: An Empire of Deceit and the Origins of America's Opioid Epidemic*, Beth Macy's *Dopesick: Dealers, Doctors, and the Drug Company that Addicted America*, and Chris McGreal's *American Overdose: The Opioid Tragedy in Three Acts*.[2] These three books, by accomplished, veteran reporters, cover some of the same material. And while they each have different strengths, they are all outstanding.

Briefly, the problem began in 1995. That is the year the corporate-funded American Pain Society began arguing that doctors must begin considering pain (which can only be subjectively measured) as "the fifth vital sign" (along with body temperature, blood pressure, breathing rate, and pulse, all of which can be objectively measured). Furthermore, they declared that acute and chronic pain were being seriously undertreated. They said the problem could be solved, however, through education, outreach, and product development.

The following year, Purdue Pharma began selling OxyContin, a powerful opiate painkiller that released its active ingredient more slowly than its competitors. ("Oxy" stands for "oxycodone," and "contin" is short for "continuous.") Purdue claimed that OxyContin was less likely to be abused than its competitors. The following statement appeared on the drug's label: "Delayed absorption, as provided by OxyContin tablets, is believed to reduce the abuse liability of a drug."

But Purdue's claim was not based on any clinical studies whatsoever. It was little more than a hunch, a theory, or a hopeful supposition. Purdue's statement may have seemed authoritative, but in fact it was a cunning piece of lawyerly obfuscation. It did not refer to any known evidence, but rather, merely to a *belief* that OxyContin had low abuse potential.

This was a sham. The fact is, *all* opioids are potentially addictive. And OxyContin proved far easier to abuse than its competitors. It carried a much higher dose of its active ingredient than Percocet or Vicodin, but unlike those drugs, it did not contain acetaminophen (which deters abusers, because in high doses acetaminophen can harm the liver). When OxyContin was crushed up and snorted, or dissolved into water and injected, the powerful pills delivered their pure narcotic payloads instantaneously. OxyContin was arguably the most potent, easily abused, and highly addictive drug ever put to market.

At first, OxyContin was mostly widely prescribed in economically distressed communities, in places like southwest West Virginia, Kentucky, and rural New England. Before long, regional authorities—coroners, police chiefs, and doctors—grew alarmed by the rising numbers of opioid deaths they were seeing. In 2000, an estimable West Virginia physician named Art Van Zee went to considerable lengths to inform Purdue, and the FDA, about what was happening. He told them that OxyContin was being overprescribed and abused, and that this was causing addiction and death. He assumed that if the right people knew about the problem, they would act swiftly, and do something about it.

That is not what happened. Although a Justice Department report later proved that Purdue executives knew about the OxyContin abuse shortly after it began, the company did precisely the opposite of what the situation required. Instead of warning us about the risks of opioids, Purdue actually intensified its aggressive marketing campaign.[3]

Between 1996 and 2002, Purdue hosted thousands of physicians, pharmacists, and nurses at dozens of all-expense-paid conferences held at luxury resorts in Florida, Arizona, and California. The company assembled a small army of health care experts, numbering about five thousand, who touted OxyContin's benefits. Its sales representatives earned huge bonuses, often far in excess of their base salary. Virtually the entire thrust of Purdue's exorbitant promotional campaign—which included print advertising, audiotapes for physicians, videotapes for patients, and a "Partners for Pain" website—was that OxyContin carried very little risk of addiction.[4]

This was made possible, in part, because the drug industry had made inroads into the Food and Drug Administration (FDA). The FDA, of course, is responsible for ensuring that the drugs we are given are safe, effective, and appropriately prescribed. Pharmaceutical manufacturers had long complained, however, that the FDA was too slow to approve its new medicines. As the AIDS crisis neared its peak in the late 1980s, many consumers and activists finally agreed, so lawmakers devised a workaround. The Prescription Drug User Fee Act, signed by President George H.W. Bush in 1992, allowed drug companies to underwrite the FDA's drug approval process. It shifted power from the FDA—which is supposed to play a watchdog role—to giant corporations, which have huge financial stakes in putting out drugs as widely and as speedily as possible.[5]

Since then, Big Pharma's influence has grown substantially. Over the past ten years, it has funded lawmakers to the tune of about $2.5 billion. A 2016 report from the Center for Public Integrity found that the pain lobby is eight times larger than the gun lobby. Pharmaceutical industry advocates outspend those who favor stricter prescribing rules by about 200 to 1.[6]

But I digress.

The FDA allowed Purdue to continue making false claims about OxyContin. In 2001, Purdue was permitted to change just a few words on the tiny-print, tightly folded, technically written "patient package inserts" that accompanied its product. Now, Purdue's potent narcotic pills were said to be effective for "daily, around-the-clock, long-term . . . treatment."[7]

As a result, OxyContin—an appropriate drug for cancer patients, and for those needing end-of-life care—was distributed more widely than ever, to people with sore backs, arthritis, and toothaches. Many patients who had merely sought relief from their pain, and who used OxyContin exactly as it was prescribed, found themselves plunged into addiction. Meanwhile, crooked doctors set up bogus pain relief clinics—known as "pill mills"—which did nothing but prescribe opioids. They were drug dealers, selling their wares openly, freely, with the imprimatur of the state.

Initially, Purdue ignored the growing problem. Later, they tried playing it down, telling doctors that their seemingly drug-dependent patients were not suffering from addiction, but rather "pseudo-addiction." When patients who had been prescribed OxyContin began begging for more of the drug, and at higher doses, Purdue claimed that merely indicated that the patient's pain was worsening. (So they needed more of the drug, and at higher doses.)

Once the escalating crisis became impossible to ignore, Purdue responded by viciously stigmatizing the addicts it had created. "We have to hammer on the abusers in every possible way," said Richard Sackler, a member of the family that founded Purdue Pharma. "They are the culprits and the problem. They are reckless criminals."[8]

We have to hammer on the abusers in every possible way. At least no one can deny the success of Purdue's marketing campaign. Sales leapt from about $45 million in 1996 (from 300,000 prescriptions) to a staggering $1.5 billion in 2002 (from 7.2 million prescriptions). That is a 3,233 percent increase in sales, and a 2,300 percent increase in prescriptions, in just six years.[9]

Eventually, Purdue did receive some pushback. Criticisms of the company started accumulating in 2003. That was the year the FDA finally warned Purdue about its specious advertising. The U.S. Government Accountability Office (GAO) also raised concerns about Purdue's marketing strategies, as well as its influence over federal regulators. Also in 2003, West Virginia's attorney general, Darrell McGraw, won a $10 million settlement from Purdue over its dishonest marketing practices. Finally, Dr. Jane Ballantyne, a pain specialist at Harvard—who had initially been enthusiastic about OxyContin—raised concerns about the drug in a co-authored article that appeared in the prestigious *New England Journal of Medicine*. She decried the lack of any clinical trials supporting Purdue's claims, and asked doctors to think twice before prescribing OxyContin long-term.[10]

In 2007, Purdue Pharma pleaded guilty to "criminal misbranding." The company admitted to misleading doctors, patients, and the FDA about OxyContin, and it paid $600 million in fines. Three former executives at Purdue also pleaded guilty, as individuals, to misdemeanor versions of the same crime, and they were fined an additional $34.5 million. Nobody went to jail.

Alas, the story does not end there. (Far from it.) Four years later, in 2011, the Centers for Disease Control and Prevention (CDC) declared that prescription painkiller overdoses had reached "epidemic" levels.[11] By then, the problem had spread from rural America into suburbs and cities. Criminals were pilfering pills from pharmacies. Unscrupulous doctors emptied them into the streets. African American, Latino, and Native American communities were now being hit nearly as hard as white ones. In 2012, in the United States—a country of 314 million people—doctors wrote 259 million opioid painkiller prescriptions.[12]

By 2013, the problem was getting much worse, at an even faster rate. Many of those who were introduced to opioids via prescription painkillers started using heroin, which is cheaper, often easier to procure, and far more dangerous. When traffickers stir fentanyl into their heroin—as they sometimes do, to make their product more potent—they are using a synthetic opioid so powerful that just two milligrams of it (roughly the size of a few grains of salt) would be enough to kill most people. Since 2014, overdose deaths from street drugs have been more common than fatalities from prescription opioids. Most addicts have a particular drug of choice, but they do not always abuse just one drug; they mess around with others, too. When overdoses occur, they typically involve combinations of drugs, such as when heroin is laced with fentanyl, or when people mix opioids, cocaine, benzos, and alcohol. Prescription drug abuse may finally be diminishing, but it has unleashed a larger, more deadly, and even harder to control street drug epidemic.[13]

This is a big part of the reason why public health officials keep reminding us to brace ourselves. In 2017, President Trump declared the opioid crisis a "national health emergency," but policy experts are virtually unanimous in their view that the federal government needs to do far more in order to address the problem.[14]

Know this: However staggering the toll of the epidemic already, it is not yet done. It probably is not even slowing down. The reckoning is far from over.

As recently as a few years ago, the opioid crisis could be referred to as a "silent epidemic," perhaps partly due to its degrading nature. Opiate addiction is often described using images of slavery, or zombie plagues. Those within its clutches are liable to feel hopeless, bereft, and ashamed. No longer, however, is it possible to argue that the scourge of opiate addiction is being overlooked. That is in large part thanks to the writings featured in this volume. In fact, some of the finest and most impactful reporting that has been done in the United States in recent years has been focused on the opiate addiction crisis. The stories in this book are sharply etched, energetically reported, and well-told; the essays and arguments here are spirited, informed, and eloquently written. This volume should serve as a *vade mecum*—a handbook, a guide, an essential introduction—for anyone who is seeking insight into this most deadly and vexing crisis.

A famous F. Scott Fitzgerald quote holds that the "test of a first-rate intelligence is the ability to hold two opposed ideas in mind at the same time and still retain the ability to function." The writings included here may put readers to an even tougher test, by pulling them in numerous different mental directions. Anyone who is familiar with the reportage and literature on opioid addiction—but who is not occasionally conflicted, or uncertain, about how to understand the crisis—is probably a fool. (Or at least their intelligence is not first-rate.)

Consider, again, the culpability of Purdue Pharma, the pain lobby, and the FDA. I've just sketched a grim portrait. I happen to think some people should go to jail. But economists teach us that when otherwise normal people behave badly, they're usually responding to bad incentives. Surely, not everyone who profited from the crisis, or who helped perpetuate it, is a moral monster. They are not all wicked and evil people. Many of them, in fact, were obviously well-intentioned. The opioid crisis is partly a story of unintended and unforeseen consequences, made possible by our capacities for rationalization and self-deception, in an era of corporate and political corruption.

Or let us consider addicts. Specialists tell us that addiction is a brain disease, which can afflict anyone. The roots of addiction are complicated, and poorly understood, but the process often involves childhood trauma, despair for the future, and deficits of meaning, purpose, and connection. Regardless, once a brain gets hijacked by addiction, the sufferer becomes less capable of thinking and acting rationally. Ordinary stressors, and even minor triggers, can send an addict spiraling into relapse. Eventually, the addict pays an enormous price. Who would withhold sympathy from an addict?

But when we say that people are "slaves" to their addiction, we are using a metaphor. A person's free will is never *entirely* extinguished. Every addict who plunges a syringe full of dope into their arm knows what is about to happen. Furthermore, a big part of the reason the opioid crisis keeps growing is because some people who are *not* addicted are either so ignorant, shortsighted, or reckless that they're choosing to fool around with opioids in the first place. When they do so, they don't just put their lives at risk; they may soon become frightening, undependable, and burdensome. They badly undermine the social fabric.

Currently, about 2.6 million Americans suffer from opioid use disorder. Sadly, many of them will not recover. Those who do get better will usually require multiple long-term treatments, which can easily end up costing hundreds of thousands of dollars. This is money that addicts do not have. If policymakers are serious about relieving the crisis, they will need to commit to major investments, over a long period of time, in order to build a new treatment infrastructure. That will necessarily require reform of our broken healthcare system.

But another part of the solution—if we are to see one—will require addicts to take greater responsibility for their own lives. I do not say this from on high. (I am not in a position to do so.) This is not a case of "blaming the victim." Nor is it an uninformed or simplistic viewpoint. Virtually every treatment provider knows that at some level, if addicts are to free themselves, they must take charge of their own recovery. More of them should do so. As long as the message is delivered compassionately, it should not be considered an affront.

What to do about drug traffickers? The United States has an insatiable demand for drugs. This book is titled *American Epidemic* for a reason: We represent less than 5 percent of the world's population, but we consume about 80 percent of the world's narcotics. Drug dealers are a scourge, but surely they cannot be eradicated. It probably does not make sense to subject people to lengthy prison sentences for nonviolent drug offenses. As Michelle Alexander has powerfully shown in *The New Jim Crow*, those who commit relatively minor crimes involving drugs—especially if they are young and dark-skinned—can easily get ensnared in a system that ruins their chances moving forward.[15] Mass incarceration is a hex and a plague in its own right. The question of how to interdict the nation's drug supply without greatly exacerbating related social problems remains unanswered.

As Leslie Jamison underscores in her powerful foreword, this is not an easy book to read. *This book is built of brutal moments.* It was also difficult to organize. The first part of *American Epidemic* features recent on-the-ground reporting and longform essays. The second section explores ideas and debates about treatment and recovery (and not always just for opioid addicts). Anyone suffering from addiction, or who is curious about the challenges it poses, may come away enlightened from this material.

You need not read this book by starting at the beginning. Each piece can, for the most part, be read separately from the others without losing much of its significance. So, you may read it all the way through, or you can pick and choose to read various articles, according to your preference. This book could have been substantially longer than it is, and toward the end of the editing process I was disheartened to have to cut some pieces from the manuscript that I'd planned on including. Nevertheless, when I began compiling this book, I determined to make it something that I would want to read, and in that respect, I have been successful. Put another way, this is in some ways an idiosyncratic collection of writings, which I happen to recommend and find valuable. Obviously, they are not the first—and they surely will not be the last—words on the opioid epidemic.

But *American Epidemic* has a larger purpose, as well: I hope it will stir ethical worry among citizens. It invites readers to summon— even in very small or minor ways—their capacities for kindness, empathy, and connectedness. We are all so depressingly fragmented these days—by race, region, gender, religion, and, of course, our political allegiances. Meanwhile, we are increasingly dislocated and made anxious by change—demographic, cultural, and technological. Without question, the divides that currently plague the United States represent one the greatest and most intractable problems this country has ever faced.

No one knows how this will end. It would be useful, however, for us to begin thinking about the problem teleologically. Someday it *must* end, or we will not survive as a country, or at least not as we have been accustomed. We are all in this together. The opioid crisis, especially, reminds us of this.

John McMillian

Notes

1. Here in Atlanta, the major chain drugstores—mostly CVS and Walgreens—will not sell syringes to anyone without a prescription. To its credit, Little Five Points Pharmacy does not have that policy. Addicts require clean needles, otherwise they run a greater risk of transmitting HIV and other viruses.

2. Barry Meier, *Pain Killer: An Empire of Deceit and the Origins of America's Opioid Epidemic*, Expanded and Updated Edition (New York: Random House, 2018); Beth Macy, *Dopesick: Dealers, Doctors and the Drug Company that Addicted America* (New York: Little, Brown, 2018); Chris McGreal, *American Overdose: The Opioid Tragedy in Three Acts* (New York: Public Affairs, 2018).

3. See Barry Meier, "Origins of an Epidemic: Purdue Pharma Knew Its Opioids Were Widely Abused," *New York Times* (May 29, 2018).

4. Julia Lurie, "A Brief, Blood-Boiling History of the Opioid Epidemic," *Mother Jones* (January/February 2017).

5. McGreal, *American Overdose*, 119.

6. Chris McGreal, "How Big Pharma's Money—and Its Politicians—Feed the US Opioid Crisis," *The Guardian* (October 19, 2017); Julia Lurie, "Opioids Are Ravaging the Country. These Lobbyists Want to Keep the Drugs Flowing," *Mother Jones* (September 21, 2016); Center for Public Integrity, "Politics of Pain: Drugmakers Fought State Opioid Limits amid Crisis," (September 18, 2016).

7. See *60 Minutes*, "Did the FDA Ignite the Opioid Epidemic?" (airdate February 24, 2019).

8. As quoted in Katie Zezima and Lennie Bernstein, "'Hammer the Abusers': Mass Attorney General Alleges Purdue Pharma Tried to Shift Blame for Opioid Addiction," *Washington Post* (January 15, 2019). Sackler made the comment in a confidential 2001 email that came to light in a court filing by the attorney general of Massachusetts.

9. Daniel McGraw, "How Big Pharma Gave America Its Heroin Problem," *Pacific Standard* (November 30, 2015).

10. Jane Ballantyne and Jianren Mao, "Opioid Therapy for Chronic Pain," *New England Journal of Medicine* (November 13, 2003); McGreal, *American Overdose*, 295, 91–93.

11. CDC Newsroom, "Prescription Painkiller Overdoses at Epidemic Levels" (November 1, 2011).

12. Lurie, "A Brief, Blood-Boiling History."

13. Marcia Angell, "Opioid Nation," *New York Review of Books* (December 6, 2018).

14. German Lopez, "Trump Declared an Emergency over Opioids. A New Report Finds It Led to Very Little," *Vox* (October 13, 2018); Caitlin Owens, "Congress Isn't Doing Enough on Opioid Treatment, Experts Say," *Axios* (April 11, 2018). Need I mention that a two-thousand-mile southern border wall would not much help? Heroin is a compact, often odor-free, easily concealed drug—it is not hard to get through border checkpoints. It can also be shipped through the mail. The DEA (Drug Enforcement Agency) reports that the overwhelming majority of illegal drugs come through ports of entry. People who attempt to come into the United States unlawfully, by making risky border crossings, generally do not bring huge quantities of drugs with them.

15. Michelle Alexander, *The New Jim Crow: Mass Incarceration in the Age of Colorblindness* (New York: The New Press, 2012).

Part One

Reporting and Essays

GETTING ADDICTED

Beth Macy

The Roanoke Times, September 2, 2012
First in a three-part series titled *The Damage Done*

Spencer Mumpower stood before them, spilling the secrets of his addiction.

He stashed marijuana inside his computer and guns under his pillow. He stole prescription painkillers from his parents' medicine chest. For a time, he even outfoxed his court-appointed drug testers.

For his entire adolescence, Mumpower managed to outwit any parent, program or police officer that stood between him and his drugs.

But it all caught up to him, eventually.

Scott was dead.

And here Spencer was now, on the eve of leaving for federal prison but talking to these people—parents of teen drug and alcohol users—as part of his atonement.

The moms were especially vocal, one after another asking different versions of the same desperate question:

How'd you pull it off? What could we do differently? What did your mother miss?

His mother, Ginger Mumpower, has thought about those questions a lot.

So has Robin Roth, Scott's heart-broken mom. And though she hasn't been able to forgive Spencer yet, she wants parents of teenagers to listen closely to what he has to say.

Both moms want it known, the story of how two suburban Roanoke families became enmeshed in a growing heroin scene that ended with one son dead and another bound for prison.

In March, U.S. District Judge James Turk sentenced 23-year-old Spencer to serve eight years for his role in Scott's death, beginning Aug. 1. But before he left, Spencer shared his story repeatedly and voluntarily, for reasons that went far beyond judicial penance.

"I do this for karma," he said. "God knows, I've got a lot I need to build back up."

"Like Shooting Jesus"

They met at Hidden Valley High, though both dropped out. They were never best friends, just drug buddies. Both hung out in the basement of a fellow partyer whose dad gave them space to get high and routinely injected heroin in front of them, according to both Spencer and Robin Roth.

A well-known drug user, Spencer was seen amid the Hidden Valley crowd as having good connections. "His mom sent him away to 15 rehabs because she didn't know what else to do," said his counselor Vinnie Dabney, drug court coordinator for Family Service of Roanoke Valley.

But Spencer viewed rehab as Drugs 101. "He would return to the community with better drug connections every time," Dabney said.

He was never a high-level dealer, federal prosecutors say, not connected to the crowd they targeted in 2009, a Northeastern heroin ring known for contributing to a surge in local usage among teenagers and young adults. Police, crime analysts and rehab professionals say opiate usage—heroin and prescription painkillers—has only grown since then.

As of June, Roanoke County police had arrested 66 people on heroin-related charges since 2010, compared with five in 2007. And in the Western District of Virginia, the U.S. attorney's office had gone from prosecuting two people for heroin-related crimes in 2008 to 29 in 2011 and 38 in the first half of this year, most in the Roanoke Valley.

The Virginia Department of Criminal Justice Services estimates that the number of cases in which forensic labs have identified heroin or other opiates seized in the Roanoke area has surged more than 80 percent over the past five years, with notable increases in Roanoke and Pulaski counties and the city of Roanoke.

The problem is urgent enough that Carilion Clinic recently began training psychiatry residents and attending physicians to administer the legal drug Suboxone, a methadonelike substance that helps opiate addicts withdraw from heroin and painkillers without the excruciating torment of becoming "dope-sick."

While some in the 12-step recovery community say Suboxone only replaces one opiate addiction with another, some addicts find that taking Suboxone under medical supervision allows them to live normal lives, according to Dr. William Rea, Carilion's vice chair of psychiatry.

Given the dangers of heroin, Rea believes the benefits of Suboxone outweigh the risks. Teens who become addicts typically begin by snorting heroin—because doing so isn't as stigmatizing as injecting the drug. But they can easily overdose because the purity, while uneven, is on average 10 times more potent than it was two decades ago.

Most young opiate addicts begin the same way Spencer did—by stealing painkillers from their parents' medicine cabinets. "I took pills and snorted heroin before I had my first beer," Spencer says.

They typically transition to heroin because it's cheaper than buying pain pills on the black market and the high is more immediate, said Ron Salzbach, a Roanoke County addiction therapist.

"The biggest rise in the past two years has been users who are middle- and upper-income folks," Salzbach said. "Opiates are all over the high schools now. I have multiple doctors' children addicted to opiates, and their parents didn't have a clue."

That was the case with "Jake," a 23-year-old Roanoke County doctor's son who said in a recent interview that the first time he injected heroin, "it was like shooting Jesus into my arm."

Now a member of Salzbach's opiates support group, Jake asked that his real name not be used because he feared losing his job. He took his first drug at 15, OxyContin tablets given to him by a friend whose brother had them left over from a wisdom tooth extraction. Later, he stole painkillers from elderly people he came in contact with on the job. A good student who played in the Hidden Valley band, he smoked marijuana and drank occasionally, but pills were his passion. By 17, he was hooked.

"Once you start taking pills, it's not that big a leap to snort heroin—it just looks like a crushed-up pill," he said. But within six months, he was deep into the heroin scene and shooting up daily. Strictly a user, he was never caught by police.

He dropped 25 pounds, enough that his father worried about bulimia.

He had bought drugs—marijuana, mostly—from both Spencer Mumpower and Scott Roth, and Spencer sold him pills as well. "Scott was a much less serious user than Spencer," Jake said. "Spencer was doing drugs a lot longer, and he was much crazier."

Jake recalled buying marijuana from Spencer at Ginger Mumpower's house under the ruse of borrowing CDs. "He'd been up for 12 days straight on meth. When we were leaving the house, my friend points out a frog on the ground by his garage, and Spencer just picks it up and smashes it on the ground.

"He was an outlier," Jake added. "The kinda guy, he's got the really good drugs, but you wanna get the drugs and get away from him as fast as you can."

Eighth-Grade Bling

"I was a demon child," Spencer says, conceding that his mother still doesn't know the extent of his drug descent. Those 12 days on methamphetamines? He was having nightmares at the time—someone was trying to kill him—and was terrified of falling asleep.

He wasn't always that way. Asked to assemble pictures of Spencer's childhood, Ginger Mumpower fills a living room table in their brick southwest Roanoke County colonial with mementos—colorful childhood drawings of aliens, class pictures and a telling piece of paper the boy kept in his locker at the private North Cross School, where he attended kindergarten through fifth grade.

"SPENCERS EMERGENCY 45¢" he scrawled in pencil above coins he taped to the paper. Spencer was so nervous about the possibility of forgetting his ice cream money that the spare change was his cure for easing the anxiety. His fear of forgetting to wear a belt—a uniform infraction that earned boys at the school a demerit—was so over-the-top that Ginger placed an extra belt in his locker.

Once, in fifth grade, fearing that he'd forgotten his homework, he became so nervous that he actually passed out. It turned out the homework had been in his backpack all along. His pediatrician recommended a counselor, who said Spencer's anxiety seemed to stem from his perfectionism.

Hellbent on getting a perfect attendance record, one year he refused his mother's offer of a trip to Disney World and insisted on going to school even when he was feverish.

The counselor "reassured me that he was doing OK and remarked on his sense of humor," recalls Ginger, the owner of Ginger's Jewelers, then a thriving chain with five stores and 35 employees. "She said he may need to come back in a few months or years, or he may be fine and never need to be seen in her office again."

Ginger believes her son's anxiety ratcheted up in the wake of her marital problems, which she said began 11 years ago, when Spencer was 12. She and her husband, Roger, separated when Spencer was 14 and divorced when he was 15. Legally, they shared joint custody, but Ginger says the father's visits were inconsistent and rare, the fallout of a drawn-out feud that still stings. Roger Mumpower declined to be interviewed for this series.

"I think self-medication was a big part of what he was doing, trying to fill the void," Ginger says.

She worked long hours while being a single parent to Spencer and his younger sister, Paris, but insists she maintained strict rules and supervision in the home. Paris, a cheerleader and Young Life leader, was voted the most artistic girl at Hidden Valley and is headed to Savannah College of Art and Design this fall.

By eighth grade, the tone of Spencer's school pictures had shifted dramatically. He sported braces, blond highlights and a heavy sterling silver chain around his neck—an awkward teen who looked to be wearing drug-dealer bling. "I was just trying to look cool," he says.

Ginger didn't know it at the time, but he was already using marijuana regularly at 13. He hung around older kids who would supply him with the drug, which he then sold to his classmates. "I'd give [the older kids] money at school, then they'd drop the drugs off down the street in a backpack for me to pick up," he recalls.

He used the money he made selling marijuana to buy pills from classmates, usually the ADHD medication Adderall and other amphetamines.

Spencer used and sold drugs for eight years before his name ever entered a police blotter.

Rehab and Repeat

He was 14 the first time Ginger caught him with marijuana and promptly grounded him for a month. Later that year, she found a huge bag of the drug in his room, which precipitated the first of his three stints at a Florida rehab center called Twelve Oaks.

"She thought rehab was how you fixed someone. You send 'em there, and they're fixed," Spencer recalls.

By then, his drug of choice was cocaine. Older friends had given him his first line to snort along the railroad tracks behind the Tanglewood Mall movie theater. When Ginger suspected he wasn't going to the movies after she dropped him off, she physically purchased the tickets for him.

No matter where his mother sought help for him, Spencer turned it into a drug opportunity.

When she sent him to Grundy to live with her sister and to remove him from the older drug crowd, he found people who taught him to use methamphetamine and to make it, too.

A Christian rehab she sent him to in West Virginia backfired badly when he bolted after two days. He had finally been getting his appetite back after a tough opiate withdrawal—only to be told that the group would be fasting that day.

On the bus ride home, he got drunk with four men just released from state prison in Pocahontas. When he arrived in Roanoke, his mother had him committed to a psychiatric ward.

All told, Spencer went to 15 rehabs in seven years, from Mount Regis in Salem to facilities across the mid-Atlantic; costs ranged from $5,000 to $15,000 each time. While insurance covered a few of the stays, Ginger says she paid for most of the treatments herself, sometimes resorting to melting gold or selling something. "I was always shuffling," she says.

"Ginger has suffered a lot," said the Rev. Quigg Lawrence at Church of the Holy Spirit, where Ginger and Paris, now 18, are regulars. "It's easy to sit on the sidelines and go, 'If only their parents had done X, Y and Z, this wouldn't have happened.' But that's pretty arrogant; that sounds to me like someone who's never had a complex situation dropped in their lap.

"My read is that Spencer's got a really high IQ, some anxiety issues and probably a lot of hurt from not getting as much of his dad's attention as he wanted. Mix that together, and I think you had a perfect storm."

Ginger reached out to Families Anonymous, a 12 step support group for relatives and friends of people with addiction and behavioral problems; counselors; and faith-based support groups, and she met with Lawrence many times. She tracked Spencer's cellphone calls and wrote down the license plate numbers of friends when they left the house, and threatened to call police.

The only professional advice she ever refused? When Spencer was 16, a counselor told her to kick him out if she caught him using again.

In reality, parents cannot legally kick out a minor without turning to a juvenile court to request a Child in Need of Services, or CHINS, petition.

That might have resulted in a court-ordered removal from the home, parent-child counseling and random drug screenings. But Ginger knew nothing of CHINS petitions at the time, and none of her counselors suggested that route.

"It can give a parent more leverage than they would have on their own," says Dabney, the drug counselor. "It maybe could have helped when the behavior was first starting" in his early teens.

Ginger sent Spencer to rehab instead and allowed him to return home in between.

Once he was 18, she refused to let him in the house if she suspected he was using. "I had to protect my daughter," she says.

She gave him no money, only food.

Crackheads and Coaching

As a young adult, Spencer lived off and on in motels and with drug-addict friends, including a group of downtown Elm Avenue crack addicts he'd befriended in rehab. "There's nothing worse than when you're on heroin trying to chill than a bunch of crackheads looking out the window thinking somebody's coming for 'em," he says.

When he could no longer bear the misery, he returned home and begged to be put back in treatment.

One of those times, Spencer showed up high while Ginger's septuagenarian mother was baby-sitting, and she had to turn her grandson away at the front door, tears streaming down both their faces.

Looking back, Ginger wishes she would have pushed him earlier into Young Life, a Christian youth organization that his sister loves. She wishes she could have kept him involved in sports—the only period he was mostly clean during high school was while playing junior varsity football at Hidden Valley his freshman year.

"I wish I had known more about what to do after the rehabs," she says. "What he needed was to be involved and feel important and be engaged."

In his own way, Spencer agrees. "The biggest thing for me was boredom. You can be the boredest you've ever been in your life, and any drug will make it fun and interesting."

The first time he got high? He was 13, and he learned that what adults said wasn't always true.

He'd gone to the trouble of barricading himself in his bedroom. He'd seen how fun using drugs looked in films and admired the characters from "Scarface" and "Fear and Loathing in Las Vegas."

"But my mom had always said drugs make people do crazy things and kill people. And when that didn't happen, I was like, 'They were all lies; this is wonderful!'

"I loved doing drugs, I just hated getting in trouble," Spencer adds. "But I didn't hate it bad enough, and not enough bad things happened."

Not until the night Scott Roth died. And even then, it would take months for Spencer to understand the depths of his trouble.

Addicts' Paths Converge

By the time his path converged with Scott's in April 2010, Spencer was living in the Grandin Village Apartments. His parents were splitting the cost of his rent, per their divorce decree, because he was enrolled at Virginia Western Community College. His grades weren't stellar, but if a course didn't require homework he could pass it just by showing up, even when he was high.

Ginger says she never gave Spencer money—only food—and paid the rent directly to his landlord. "When I came by to visit, somehow he always pulled it together. I didn't understand what was really going on."

Her son was by that time a full-blown junkie who was injecting 20 to 30 bags—more than $400 worth—of heroin a day, courtesy of his dealer Crystal Frost, another junkie who lived with him rent-free in exchange for heroin. Frost was 31 at the time, a convicted felon with numerous drug offenses and five children who were living with relatives.

"We were a couple of low-level junkies getting high in a house with a couple pieces of furniture and a broken TV," Spencer says.

Frost's mother, Deedee Bramlett, says her daughter first became addicted to Vicodin; a doctor prescribed it after she hurt her back while working as a waitress at the New Yorker Deli on Williamson Road. As a teenager, Frost was diagnosed with depression, anxiety and schizophrenia but only sporadically took her medications and refused counseling when she turned 18.

When Frost was in her late 20s, her mother and sister drove her to a Roanoke methadone clinic to help wean her from opiates, but the habit soon escalated to heroin. Bramlett isn't sure when or how.

"She tells me, 'Mom, you don't wanna know,'" Bramlett says. "I think she was self-medicating all along."

Frost kept Spencer "loaded up on heroin in exchange for living there for free and doing whatever it was she felt like having him do," according to Assistant U.S. Attorney Andrew Bassford. Setting up shop in Spencer's bedroom, Frost made him her "walker" to avoid dealing directly with customers (and lessen her culpability), getting him to exchange the cash and foil-packet drugs.

The more emaciated and desperate he got, the more Frost took what she wanted, making him sign over in handwritten contracts his bed and other furniture in exchange for the drugs, Spencer and the prosecutors say.

Spencer says he stopped directly selling drugs in 2009 after being briefly detained by Roanoke County police, who had spotted him and another suspected dealer engaging in a sale. Earlier that year, Spencer twice sold heroin to friends who'd been coaxed by police into becoming wired informants.

He was not arrested on any of those three occasions, according to Lt. Chuck Mason, because doing so could have imperiled the case police were building against a larger drug-dealing network.

"I wish they'd have arrested me right then," Spencer says, referring to the July 2009 stop. He was encouraged to snitch on his friends and dealers but says he refused and tried to keep a low profile instead.

Nearly a year later, a week before Scott Roth's death, police presented evidence against Spencer to the Roanoke County prosecutor, and an indictment was issued, along with a warrant for his arrest. But he was not picked up.

That practice is standard, the theory being that low-level dealers can help authorities build a case against higher-level suppliers in exchange for freedom and/or lesser charges.

"It's a dirty business, and it involves using dirty people to get it done," Bassford said. "If we just arrested everybody who sold a bag of heroin, we would never get" the bigger suppliers.

Roanoke County police finally took custody of Spencer on April 8, 2010, a night that culminated in two overdoses, one death—and a world of trouble for the Grandin Road junkies.

The salvation would come later, for everyone but Scott Roth.

Spencer Mumpower's story may be more dramatic than most, but its genesis is not unusual. Typical heroin addicts do not start out injecting drugs into their veins.

According to local addicts and counselors, most young adults begin the slippery slide into opiate addiction not on the streets or alleyways but in the most common of places: the family medicine cabinet.

"They start out stealing drugs from their parents' or grandparents' medicine chest, and then when they run out they go to the cheapest thing, and right now heroin is rampant up and down I-81," said Kathy Sullivan, a prevention specialist for the Roanoke Area Youth Substance Abuse Coalition.

For that reason, RAYSAC teams up with the Western Virginia Water Authority and other groups to collect unused medications twice a year. This spring, the coalition collected 1,417 pounds of prescription drugs from seven locations, and the next prescription drug take-back is set for 10 a.m. to 2 p.m. Sept. 29.

Of particular concern are the painkillers that are typically prescribed in the aftermath of surgery—oxycodone, codeine, morphine, hydrocodone, fentanyl and meperidine.

It's unsafe to the water supply to dump drugs down the drain, expired or not, Sullivan said. She advises those who want to dispose of the drugs in the interim (between take-backs) to lock them up or otherwise make them difficult to find for relatives and strangers alike.

Drug-seekers have been known to rummage through strangers' medicine cabinets at real estate open houses. Another ploy addicts have employed is to knock on a stranger's door, say their car broke down and ask to borrow the phone—then ask to use the bathroom. One user interviewed for this series described a moving-company job he had that gave him easy access to customers' drugs.

Roanoke substance abuse counselor Ron Salzbach says middle schoolers have been known to bring medicine bottles to school to share with their friends. "It's like a virus that spreads to their friends," he said.

With opiate addicts, the midbrain, which is the emotional pleasure center, holds the forebrain or decision-making center hostage.

"Your forebrain says, 'This could destroy my life,' but your midbrain says, 'This is like shooting Jesus; I'll be OK,'" Salzbach said.

Heroin is difficult to withdraw from because it can take a year of being drug-free before an addict starts to experience pleasure again.

If Salzbach suspected his own child were using opiates?

"I'd be down to CVS buying a drug kit in a heartbeat. Then I'd get myself to the next Families Anonymous meeting."

HEROIN HITS HOME

Beth Macy

The Roanoke Times, September 3, 2012
Second in a three-part series titled *The Damage Done*

The night Scott Roth showed up at Spencer Mumpower's Grandin Village apartment in April 2010, it had been a while since the former schoolmates had seen each other—at a Narcotics Anonymous meeting.

"Dude, I haven't seen you in years," Spencer said.

"What are you doing here?" Scott asked.

"This is my apartment. How about you?"

"You know what I'm doing here," Scott said as he handed Spencer $200.

They were both 21, Hidden Valley High School dropouts and drug addicts. Spencer was living with another heroin junkie, a low-level dealer named Crystal Frost. She bought the stuff in bulk, repackaged it in homemade foil envelopes and made Spencer play middleman.

What happened next would wreck the lives of two southwest Roanoke County families and alert the region to an opiates scourge that has spread throughout Western Virginia without regard to race, position or income.

It would destroy Spencer's freedom, and ultimately, it would save his life.

Spencer walked back to the bedroom he had signed over to Frost in a rent-for-heroin exchange. He retrieved 10 bags of heroin.

Before Scott left, he and Spencer did the only thing they knew to do together. They got high one final time.

"Lighten Up, Rob"

Robin Roth couldn't bring her son to court earlier this year on March 1, so she carried his picture instead. Scott Roth was 21 when he died of a heroin overdose on April 8, 2010.

In a federal courtroom, she stared long and hard at the young man who'd handed Scott his final drug.

"I would like to applaud you, Spencer, for your recovery, and I think that's great," she said.

"However, my son wasn't given that same opportunity to complete his recovery, because of your illegal actions."

Frost had already been handed a 20-year prison sentence, and now it was Spencer's turn. And though Robin Roth's anger has mellowed a little toward Spencer since their day in court, she has her own story to tell.

She told it recently at Panera Bread, flanked by her best friends for support, and pictures of her happy adventure-seeking boy—birthday parties, the beach, snowboarding. She emailed pictures of chef Scott juggling knives and shrimp at Ichiban, a Japanese steakhouse where co-workers nicknamed the rapping cook "Vanilla Rice."

Scott Roth was a blond young man with movie-star good looks and a dry wit. He wore preppy plaid shorts and polo shirts, and he loved the sunflowers his mom grew in their yard. A favorite saying he shared with friends: "I am who I am, and that is something you'll never be. Love me or hate me, I'm still gonna shine."

He called his mom "Rob" and liked to tease her by telling her to lighten up.

His mom will never forget the first time he used that nickname. Seventeen at the time, he came home loopy one night. A registered nurse, Robin suspected drugs and decided to respond boldly.

Rather than buy a drug test at CVS, she took Scott to the emergency room. But her plot backfired when the doctor said Scott had tested positive for drugs but that "it's only marijuana, Mrs. Roth."

It was all the ammunition Scott needed to tell her she was over the top.

"Lighten up, Rob," he said.

But there was reason for concern. The first time he smoked heroin, he confessed later, it was hidden in a marijuana joint. He was at a Hidden Valley party and realized there was something extra soothing about this particular high.

"You think of heroin as seedy street slums, but that's not at all how it started," Robin Roth said. In 2008, she found a needle and a syringe in his room, and, figuring he was already in too deep, she left it there. Afraid he'd resort to sharing needles, she put him into rehab instead.

Kindred Paths

Like Spencer's mother, Ginger Mumpower, Robin was a single mother. Scott's father was a physician she'd met at the Virginia Beach hospital where they both had worked. Though he paid child support, the only time he ever saw his son was during child-support hearings in court. Robin says he made it clear: He had his own family and wanted no part in hers.

Robin believes Scott, an only child, self-medicated in response to his absent dad. Like Ginger Mumpower, she tried myriad ways to sway her son, from admitting him into three rehabs to driving him to weekly drug tests at a doctor's office.

Robin even had every door inside her house removed—including ones to the bathrooms—so he could not hide drug use in her home. She took away his car after an alcohol-fueled fender bender in her driveway, and after he turned 18, she kicked him out of the house whenever she found him drinking or doing drugs.

But when he showed up drunk on a rainy night at 3 a.m., she let him come home. They drew up contracts with curfews and behavior expectations, but when Scott bumped against the barriers they'd agreed on, she often let it slide.

While most parents were driving their 18-year-olds off to college, Robin drove Scott to the Roanoke Rescue Mission to enroll him in its recovery program. "He looked so out of place standing in line to get in wearing his plaid shorts and preppy clothes," she said.

He was kicked out of the program after two months when workers caught him sneaking into the kitchen one night to steal food. He'd learned to cook at the Rescue Mission, and his mother has fond memories of arriving home to find Scott making elaborate meals for his friends—using all the groceries she'd bought for the week.

Robin believes her son had been clean for several months before the night he sought drugs in Spencer's apartment. He was still drinking, she knew, but he was living in his own apartment with friends who weren't drug users, she said, and was working at Ichiban.

Four days before his death, he went to Easter Mass at St. Andrew's Catholic Church with his mom and a friend. Dressed up and clean-looking, "he came because he knew it was important to his mom that he be there," recalled Robin's friend Doug Jones.

Scott wasn't Doug's No. 1 fan, because Doug helped Robin enforce her household rules. Both were trying hard to follow the boundary-setting advice Robin learned from Families Anonymous, a 12-step support group for relatives of people suffering with addiction and behavioral problems.

"We didn't understand how you could go to a recovery group, come home and take a shower, put your best clothes on, and then go out to Awful Arthur's," Robin said. But Scott maintained that only a dummy would not be able to manage drinking a few beers.

Moving the Bar

Looking back, Robin wishes she had set stricter boundaries sooner—and stuck to them.

"I would set the rules and the consequences, and then something would happen and I would stick to them for two weeks," she said. "Every time I'd set the bar and Scott would hit it, the bar would move a little farther back."

As a single mom, she worked long hours, and she still beats herself up for leaving Scott unsupervised after school as a teenager.

"When they're little, you search out the best baby sitters with the best references, but then they hit a certain age, and you think they can be on their own when actually teenagers need more supervision than at any time in their developmental years," she says.

Scott's affable, if mischievous, manner made the rules all the harder to enforce. "He was never mean to me or confrontational. I never took him kicking and screaming to rehab. When you were disappointed in him, it was always, 'I'm sorry. I'll try harder to do better.'"

She's glad she got help via counseling and Families Anonymous but wishes she had followed their tough-love recommendations more consistently.

"You're ashamed, you're embarrassed, you think you've done something wrong," she says, then echoes her grief counselor's response: "But addiction isn't about the parent, and it isn't about how you raised your child. My son had a physical condition called addiction, and it got the best of him."

The day Scott died, Robin didn't find out about it until hours later, when a phone call from his girlfriend startled her awake at 11 p.m. "Something's wrong with Scott," the young woman said without elaborating.

It was a rainy night, and when Robin arrived at Scott's Salem apartment complex, she found throngs of police and crime-scene tape. They wouldn't let her into the apartment, even though she kept insisting she was a nurse and knew CPR.

Police made her wait downstairs as they gathered evidence. Twenty minutes passed, but when Robin Roth watched an empty ambulance gurney leave the apartment, she realized her son was gone.

Though she knew Scott had once been a heroin user, she was floored to learn he'd overdosed on the drug. His roommates found him slumped at the edge of his bed, an empty needle at his side.

"I thought he had been in an accident or become ill," Robin says. "Denial reaches us at every level."

"I'm Still Gonna Shine"

Not long after Scott left the Grandin Village apartment, another junkie friend staying with Spencer and Frost overdosed on the same high-purity heroin. Spencer chucked the friend in the shower, hoping to jolt him awake, and performed CPR. He begged Frost to call 911, knowing he'd likely be arrested on the spot.

When police arrived, they learned there were outstanding arrest warrants against Spencer and Frost, and took them to jail—Frost for an earlier probation violation and Spencer for 2009 heroin possession/distribution felony charges in Roanoke County.

It was days before Spencer finally learned Scott had died and months before he realized he was on the federal hook for handing his former schoolmate the drugs.

For six months solid—including a detox so painful that his jailers put him on IV drugs—Spencer begged his mother to bail him out of jail. He lied that he'd been stabbed, and worse.

"A friend told me the media would get a hold of it if I didn't bail him out, but I said I'd rather my son be on the front page of the newspaper than in the obituaries," said Ginger Mumpower, a well-known jewelry retailer. "I honestly knew it was the only way to keep him alive."

Robin Roth didn't get that choice. For Scott's funeral Mass, she requested friends bring sunflowers and place them on the altar. She dried them, saved the seeds and, though she was too depressed to plant them last year, her behind-the-fence neighbor tilled up a garden plot in her side yard this spring.

Last month, hundreds of Scott's sunflowers were blooming in her yard.

A few feet away, a wicker rocker sat in the shade of the apple blossom tree Robin and her only child planted long ago. The tree was laden with the wind chimes she buys and hangs when she's feeling blue.

When the wind whipped down Sugar Loaf Mountain and wended through her subdivision, the sunflowers swayed and the chimes banged out a bittersweet noise.

COMING CLEAN

Beth Macy

The Roanoke Times, September 4, 2012
Third in a three-part series titled *The Damage Done*

Spencer Mumpower had fattened up so much that the judge marveled: "You're a little overweight now, aren't you?"

He had gone to jail two years earlier, in April 2010, a scrawny 21-year-old heroin junkie and amphetamine addict who weighed 135 pounds. His eyes were bruised and sunken, and there were chickenpox-like scabs on his face—from amphetamine itch.

He'd bulked up during an 11-month jail stint on state heroin charges that happened to begin the night of Scott Roth's death.

And now here he was in federal court, about to be sentenced for his role in the death of Roth, 21, a former Hidden Valley High School schoolmate who had died of a heroin overdose.

Spencer had put on 90 pounds, and he was drug-free for the first time in a decade. He told U.S. District Court Judge James Turk that he planned to become a drug counselor in honor of Roth.

Turk sentenced Spencer to eight years in a low-security federal prison in Petersburg, a reduction of the usual 20-year minimum that reflected his cooperation in helping prosecutors nab a dealer higher up the chain.

A personable jurist who shakes every defendant's hand and brings his dachshund mix, Baby Girl, to court, Turk seemed to take a personal interest in the case. He encouraged Roth's grieving mother, Robin, to meet with Spencer.

"I think it would help you," he said.

Too angry at the time, Robin Roth declined from the witness stand, saying she wasn't yet ready to forgive.

But if Spencer's turnaround is genuine, she said recently, she wants parents and teenagers everywhere to heed his words—in his talks to troubled teens, at karate classes and 12-step meetings, even in the Kroger checkout line.

As he prepared to report to prison this summer, Spencer Mumpower wanted to make amends to his family, to his community—and when she's ready for it—to Robin Roth.

Hitting Bottom

Six months of jail time, from early spring to late fall 2010, passed before Spencer finally hit bottom. Six months of pleading with his mother—in letters and phone calls and during video-monitor visits—to bail him out of jail. Six months of lying that he was being stabbed, threatened and worse.

Six months before Spencer accepted that he could no longer do drugs.

"People were giving me a hard time about how skinny I was, and one day I realized I could touch these two fingers around my forearm," he said.

"It meant I was a junkie."

He remembered the way Crystal Frost and other dealers treated him—putting him totally under their control—and he thought: It doesn't have to happen again unless I let it.

The pleading calls had taken a toll on Spencer's mother, Ginger Mumpower, recalled defense lawyer Tony Anderson.

"She'd call me up crying," he said. "But she ultimately understood that the best thing for Spencer was to stay right where he was."

Ginger Mumpower could have bailed Spencer out at any moment. Instead, she encouraged church friends and relatives to write to him, as did his sister, Paris, 18, who mailed poems, drawings and handmade cards. Ginger sent him inspirational song lyrics, information on jewelry-making and copies of pages she'd marked from the Bible and "The Purpose-Driven Life."

She'd been thinking about running for office and wrote Spencer to ask for his blessing before she began her campaign against Greg Habeeb for a House of Delegates seat—an election she would lose in January 2011, a month before her son's release from jail.

"I talked about Spencer in my campaign speech because I think having gone through this makes me more knowledgeable about the drug epidemic," the prominent businesswoman and jewelry retailer recalled. When the results came in, they were on the phone together—him in jail, her at a restaurant thronged by campaign volunteers.

Spencer was beginning to realize just how lucky he was. Unlike most of the other inmates, he had a mom who put money in his jailhouse account for toiletries and extra food. He used the goods like currency, trading ramen noodles and bags of coffee for his cellmates' quarts of milk.

In the fitness magazines his mom sent, he studied how to build muscle via protein and for months drank one carton of milk every hour.

Spencer made a plan. It began with a picture in a magazine. If he couldn't transform his surroundings, he could at least transform his body—and eventually, he hoped, the rest would follow.

He stole trash bags and filled them with water from the sink. He cut bedsheets into strips and wrapped them around the heavy water sacks, transforming them into hand weights.

For several hours a day, he lifted the makeshift weights. The drug-addicted shell that landed in jail the night of Scott Roth's death was growing stronger by the week.

After nine months of incarceration, Spencer stopped begging his lawyer to get him freed.

"He was a solid 200 pounds," Anderson said. "His hair was groomed nicely, and his color was good."

As Anderson describes it, Spencer turned to him and said, "I like being clean. I like being sober. I like being able to talk to my mother and she talks to me, and I get what's going on here."

Two months later, he was remanded to intensive counseling and regular drug screenings courtesy of the Roanoke Valley 23rd Judicial Drug Court Program, as a condition of his state probation. By the time he met with counselor Kevin Thompson, the turnaround seemed genuine.

Thompson had met the old Spencer the first time he entered drug court at 19, a probation condition stemming from a petit larceny conviction. Spencer had stolen a DVD player from his dad, with whom he'd lived very briefly. Spencer says his dad had him charged partly to get him off the streets and into treatment and partly to get him out of his house.

"He was young and defiant and didn't trust the system or the interventions," Thompson recalled. But after Roth's death and his time in jail, Spencer "was waking up to some of the damage he was causing his family."

"His mother became very important to him, and the federal case was forcing him to look at his behavior and, finally, hold himself accountable," Thompson said.

Vinnie Dabney, another drug court counselor, agreed. "Fifteen rehabs couldn't convince Spencer that it was not in his best interests to get high. It took time in jail and a friend dying before he could decide he wanted to change."

Spencer now has two years and more than four months clean. Dabney, a recovering heroin addict himself, said he tells newly recovered addicts that the real proof is in long-term sobriety. Until that happens, he tells them, "I believe nothing of what you say and only half of what I see you do."

Scaring Them Straight

Before a recent drug-awareness seminar for parents of troubled teens, Hidden Valley guidance counselor Bonnie Rourke pulled Spencer aside. The last time he spoke to the Saturday class, his delivery had been too flip, she said, worrying that it made for a watered-down message for some participants. "Some people thought you were glorifying it almost," Rourke warned.

In a freewheeling talk full of advice and drug-detecting techniques that was half "Scared Straight" and half "American Gangster," the 23-year-old had parents alternately laughing, wincing and crying.

He displayed the needle-mark scars down both his arms and the teeth once ruined by amphetamines. ("I've had 40 hours of dental work to get 'em fixed," he said.) He showed off his jailhouse tattoos, fashioned with burned Vaseline mixed with VO5 shampoo and applied with a staple squirreled away from a jail-account receipt. (He has had those neatened up recently, too.)

He discussed the dangers of black-market Adderall, an ADHD medicine and amphetamine he once took hourly for eight days straight. He recited a list of places where as a teen he'd hidden his stash—inside computers, emptied Sharpie markers and socks and in the pockets of gym shorts he secretly wore under his jeans. ("My mom made me empty the pockets of my jeans, but she didn't know about the shorts.")

Among his tips to parents: Rid your medicine cabinets of anything with "-codone" in the name. Set rules and hold kids accountable when they break them.

"The problem with me was, the trouble had to outweigh the fun," he said.

In the past eight years, he's lost 12 friends to drug-involved deaths, and every dealer he's known is now dead or in jail. He recounted the warped reasoning behind his decision to quit selling drugs after being targeted by Roanoke County police in 2009.

His compromise? He'd allowed his heroin dealer to live with him in exchange for the drugs. When Scott Roth showed up at the apartment to buy drugs from her, Spencer played go-between, a move that resulted in death by overdose for Roth and prison for Spencer and his roommate dealer.

"I thought I'd stay out of trouble by not being the one who sold anymore, and now I'm in more trouble than I've ever been in my life," he said. "If you're in the same room with somebody who's caught with drugs, the police charge everybody. If somebody dies, you're an accessory.

"The biggest thing for me now is just staying away from everybody" associated with drugs. "I look at them as they've got a contagious disease."

Spencer said he was 22 before he found an activity he enjoyed as much as drugs—martial arts. To ease anxiety, his kenpo karate teacher Rikk Perez coached him on deep breathing and meditation techniques before his federal sentencing hearing, and Spencer took group and private lessons at Perez's Vinton studio almost every day.

"Staying busy is really the best thing to do, because boredom is huge, and smoking weed is like having an amusement park in your back yard."

A few days later, Spencer described the talk he gave to the teens that followed his presentation to their parents. Most were in some legal trouble, while others had been caught with drugs or alcohol at home or school.

"I told 'em about jail—about the awful food, about the predators. Some were looking down like they were bored, but a lot seemed like really good kids who were ashamed.

"Hopefully I put a thought in at least one kid's head."

Karate and KFC

Before he left for prison on Aug. 1, Spencer's friends were mostly guys from karate class—many of them middle-aged men, a few who helped with his mother's campaign. With Ginger Mumpower's help, they took turns giving him rides to karate and to his mother's Smith Mountain Lake store, where Spencer worked part time.

They ate out together after monster two-hour workouts. If they went anywhere that alcohol was served, Spencer made the required call to his probation officer to let him know.

The first time Spencer showed up at Perez's studio, he was still on house arrest and wearing an ankle bracelet.

"He told me the whole story, everything," recalled Perez, 45, a Long Island, N.Y., native and cabinetmaker who's a fifth-degree black belt. "My attitude was, 'We're here to develop a new future, a present and a future.' He's one of my few students that's training physically, mentally and spiritually at the same time."

When Spencer got upset, Perez reminded him, "Write it down. Don't think, write." Kenpo comes from the Chinese for "fist law," a vigorous karate form that targets street-level self-defense, discipline and respect.

To prepare him for prison and to make him feel safer when he got there, Perez demonstrated exercises he could practice in his cell—slow foot taps, for instance, that progress up a cinder-block wall. But just as important, Spencer said, the practice was a tonic for his anxiety and anger, and for the first time since he was a child, he had healthy friends he could trust.

At a nearby KFC earlier this summer, the karate guys inflicted damage on the lunch buffet, each returning three times for more chicken, veggies and biscuits. Spencer showed off a sauce he concocted in jail that involves packets of ketchup, Tabasco and barbecue sauce.

Down from 225 pounds in jail, he weighed 186.

"He's like a son to me," Perez said. "I'm looking at this as one of my kids is leaving for college."

Spencer chuckled and nodded. "Yeah, I'm tired of saying I'm going to prison. From now on it's, 'I'm going to college.'

"I just wish it was a coed school."

The men cackled.

They talked about last year's setback, when Spencer's community service coordinator turned him in for "noncompliance" following a verbal disagreement. He was immediately kicked out of drug court and remanded to jail for seven weeks.

(Spencer's drug court counselors say it was a misunderstanding,

adding that Spencer was one of a few people in the court's history to
be reinstated after such an offense.)

"I spent hours working on my kicks and punches in there," Spencer said. "We made boxing mitts out of toilet paper rolls and socks."

He's made amends with his father, with whom he and his sister
have been intermittently estranged, and Spencer met him periodi-
cally over the summer for lunch.

His dad even attended Paris' Hidden Valley High School graduation in June and sat next to Spencer, though he was not invited to
the family meal.

(Roger Mumpower declined repeated requests to be interviewed
for this story.)

At Sakura, where the family gathered, Spencer and Ginger gave
Paris a new cellphone for graduation but tricked her by wrapping it
in a Ginger's Jewelry bag. Art school-bound Paris doesn't care for
jewelry and buys her clothes at Goodwill.

("She's a completely different kind of kid," Spencer said.)

At least once a week over the summer, Spencer spontaneously
hugged his mom and told her he was sorry for the hurt he caused.

Belated Sympathy Card

They were working on letters to Robin Roth, who had said she was
not quite ready to heed Judge Turk's advice. She wasn't prepared to
meet with them—yet—but she would welcome a letter mailed to her
grief counselor, who said he would give it to her when she was ready.

When Ginger found out Robin was willing to hear from her, she
was sitting in her well-appointed living room amid stacks of letters
and cards Spencer kept from jail—enough to fill a garbage bag.

She sobbed.

The next day, she sought advice from a family friend, a former
nanny who had helped raise Spencer and Paris and had lost a 10-year-
old child herself. Then she wrote and rewrote and rewrote.

"I'm going to share the challenges of being a single mom and dealing with addiction and how close Spencer has come [to death] so many times," she said. "And while I can't imagine the depth of her pain, she's always in my thoughts and my prayers.

"I'm going to tell her that I hope Spencer will take all the wrong things he's done and all the bad choices, and try to work for good to help other families and to honor Scott's memory."

She wants to design Robin Roth a necklace, something like the piece she created during Spencer's darkest times, called "When Life Falls Apart." It features a cross held loosely by magnets that falls into a zigzag but can be easily repositioned into a cross—a metaphor for God's love.

Not long after Spencer's talk to the troubled teens, a Kroger grocery bagger approached him, saying he'd been in the class because of a recent DUI conviction.

The young man had been thinking about Spencer's tale. He hadn't been there to preach to the kids, like some droning drugs-are-bad character being mocked on "South Park."

"If you're gonna continue to use, get used to s____y jail food and put on some weight because you're gonna need to fight," Spencer says he told them. "There's only one thing you don't have to do so you can have a great life and do what the hell you want: Don't do dope, steal stuff or act like an idiot."

His face red with embarrassment, the young man thanked Spencer and asked to carry his grocery bags.

"I'm not going down that road again," he told him and shook Spencer's hand. "I promise you that, man."

Beginning of Closure

The week Ginger took her son to prison, Robin Roth said his incarceration brought her no pleasure.

"I hurt as much today as the day my son died," she said, choking up. "I pray for Spencer every day, that he'll be strong. My heart's breaking for that kid. But it's the only shot he has at a normal life—to get some accountability."

A few weeks later, Turk's instincts proved correct after all when Robin Roth received Ginger's card. She didn't share its contents but said Ginger expressed deep sympathy without making excuses for her son. Word by word, Robin's anger began, finally, to thaw.

"It brought some warmth into my heart," Robin said. "This card made my heart feel closure that a mother understood what I've lost."

She hopes they can meet and maybe work together to help other families struggling with addiction.

"Any way that I can support her and her son and their journey toward healing, that's something I'd certainly be willing to do," Robin said.

She stands amid Scott's sunflowers, grown from seeds saved from his funeral spread. She still regrets her lack of consistency, still wishes she'd have enforced more of the rules. But, she knows her son felt the vastness of his mother's love.

She senses his breezy presence amid the sunflowers, which are so tall now they envelop her.

"Hang tight, Rob," she imagines him saying. "We'll be together again some day."

A RISING DEATH TOLL OFFERS TRAGIC PROOF OF HEROIN'S REACH ACROSS NORTH JERSEY

Rebecca Davis O'Brien

The Record, May 5, 2013
Part of a series titled *Suburbia's Deadly Secret*

After several arrests and stints of sobriety, a baby-faced 22-year-old man vowed last August he was "gettin' straight." A month later, he died of a heroin overdose in his grandfather's Paramus home, Bergen County's 12th fatal overdose in three months.

On Feb. 8, a 21-year-old volunteer firefighter from Glen Rock died under his parents' roof, just 24 hours after he had left rehab.

And in March, two months after being arrested on car burglary charges, a 20-year-old self-trained magician died of a heroin overdose in his father's Montvale home.

Since the beginning of 2011, heroin has claimed at least 50 lives in Bergen County. It has its grasp on hundreds more.

Once, they were talented athletes, promising students, happy siblings. Now they drive into Paterson, a hub of the regional drug trade, several times a week to buy bundles of heroin, risking violence, arrest and death to sustain $300-a-week addictions.

They snort or inject it on highway shoulders, at home in towns such as Wyckoff, Ringwood or Fair Lawn. Many young addicts live with their parents, dependent on the family's money and shelter as they stash hypodermic needles and slender glassine bags of heroin in their childhood bedroom.

Most got hooked through pills—prescription painkillers such as

OxyContin and Opana—procured legally through a doctor, swiped from bathrooms or shared by friends. But heroin, at $5 per bag, is far cheaper, potent and widely available.

"It is an absolute epidemic," said Bergen County Prosecutor John L. Molinelli, who led a multi-jurisdictional task force to crack down on North Jersey's heroin trade over the past four months. "These kids have no idea what they're getting into."

Public health data confirm what local authorities across the United States have known for several years: Heroin use is on the rise, particularly among suburban youth. Between 2007 and 2011, the number of heroin users nationwide increased dramatically, from 373,000, to 620,000, according to federal data, while the number of heroin-dependent young adults more than doubled, from 53,000, to 109,000, between 2009 and 2011, according to the National Survey on Drug Use and Addiction.

In New Jersey, a wave of heroin addiction in affluent communities has been accompanied by a spike in reported overdoses and drug-related crime and death. Bergen County is no exception: In 2011 and 2012 combined, the Prosecutor's Office counted 130 heroin-related overdoses, 38 of which were fatal, a steep increase from prior years.

The recent increase in heroin use in New Jersey has many layers, officials say. The state's massive ports and highways are conduits for South American heroin. The drug flowing onto New Jersey streets is at least five times more pure than it was several decades ago, which makes ingestion easier—it can be snorted—and addiction more rapid.

But above all, heroin addiction is believed to have its roots in what public health officials have called an "epidemic" of prescription pain-killers, which are readily prescribed and highly addictive. Chemically and metabolically, painkillers based on oxycodone are nearly identical to heroin, to such a degree that they are often conflated in emergency room reports and public health data.

"Heroin is much more commonplace than it's been in years," said Ellen Elias, director of the Center for Alcohol and Drug Resources in Hackensack. "We see it all around. It seems like the population in which heroin is most prevalent is that 18- to 25-year-old population."

Last October, the Bergen County Medical Examiner's Office reported "an alarming spike" in heroin-related deaths. But trouble had been brewing for months: Police blotters in quiet towns have been thick with drug arrests, young adults caught with hypodermic needles and bags of dope. In the past few months alone, six arrests of Wayne residents. Five of Garfield. Two of Fair Lawn. And many, many more.

In Paterson, a strained police force struggled to keep pace with addicts pouring into the city, across the Passaic River, to buy heroin. Paterson cops reported arresting a Bergen County resident "every other day," according to an internal report from the Bergen County Prosecutor's Office.

The war on drugs is waged not just in the homes of affluent Bergen County families, but in the streets of Paterson, where effects of heroin demand take the form of gang activity and criminality.

"The drug trade has successfully destroyed, ravaged, our community and communities across our nation," said Laquan Hargrove, director of the Paterson Youth Services Bureau. "The war on drugs, we are losing it."

Hargrove said he has seen the reach of gangs extend in recent years to nearly every corner of the city, nearly every age group. "These kids are exposed to the whole spectrum of the gang lifestyle," Hargrove said. "Its crime, its violence, they are exposed to the drug trade, they are exposed to it all."

On a recent afternoon in Paterson, heroin was being sold openly on the street mere blocks from a public school. In March, Bergen County detectives arrested a midlevel dealer after he dropped his child off at school, part of his morning routine.

Most of the gang activity reported by the Bergen County Prosecutor's Office was attributed to the Bloods, a national gang with strong offshoots in Newark, Camden and Paterson.

Paterson's needle exchange program, intended to provide junkies with clean needles to lessen the spread of disease, has reported a steep increase in 18- to 28-year-old members. So has the Bergen County homeless shelter, as young addicts—having exhausted the patience and resources of their parents and local police—are kicked out of their homes.

Police across Bergen County have seen spikes in shoplifting, home invasions, burglaries and armed robberies, "localized crimes" to get money for drugs. Addicts were showing up at open houses hosted by real estate agents, scouring strangers' medicine cabinets for prescription pills.

"Even if you're not seeing the use, you're going to see the crime from it," said Detective Brian Huth of the Ramsey police. "The faces that are getting arrested for heroin, they pop up in commercial burglaries all through our areas. We are all affected by it."

As a father and a police officer, Huth has been alarmed by what he said is a cavalier attitude teenagers take toward prescription drugs, from Ritalin to Ambien to oxycodone.

Eric Richter, a 20-year-old from Franklin Lakes who now lives in Kinnelon, got addicted to heroin through oxycodone. "It started with pills," said Richter, who was arrested in February on possession charges. "It slowly progressed."

Richter vowed he would never do heroin, but his pill addiction was too expensive to sustain. He was soon spending hundreds of dollars a day just to function. "Heroin was already around me, because there were a lot of people I know that did heroin." By the beginning of 2013, he was snorting several bags a day.

Officials say parents are often unaware of the risks of prescription drug abuse and are loath to admit that their child has a heroin habit. In February, an 18-year-old from Ramsey died from the effects of Ambien, Xanax and carisoprodol, a muscle relaxant.

"Everybody has a hand in this," Huth said. "They are just normal kids that just fall into this lifestyle. I see them start a lot younger."

In March, Paramus police arrested a 14-year-old girl after she bought heroin at a local house known for drugs and parties—she had asked her mother to drive her to "a friend's house" at 1 a.m., police said, claiming to have left behind her hat. Questioned by a detective, she shrugged and said, "It makes me feel good."

"It is not getting better," said Deputy Police Chief Ken Ehrenberg in Paramus, which has seen five overdose deaths from heroin or Oxy-Contin in the past 16 months. "It's starting to ramp up."

Local police departments see death coming before the families or the addicts do.

Huth knows certain addresses by heart, the houses of frequent burglars who steal to feed their habit or where emergency respond-ers have revived unconscious addicts with shots of Narcan, which counteracts the effects of opiates. Cops watch as mischievous 18-year-olds become tattered, desperate 20-year-olds, and they know it is only a matter of time.

"The kids using oxies in high school will sustain for a while, then they fall off," Ehrenberg said. "It starts as snorting, ends as shooting. And then there's a good chance they're dead."

There was the 24-year-old former Don Bosco baseball player caught shooting heroin into the arm of a former Ramsey football captain in the back seat of a car in Elmwood Park. The 24-year-old granddaughter of a former Bergen County judge. The 23-year-old son of an Allendale doctor. A 46-year-old former local cop, who sus-tained an injury on the job that led to an addiction to pills, which soon gave way to heroin.

In contrast to the dealers, many of whom were arrested in "buy and grabs" in Paterson, or swept up in nighttime raids, most of the addicts were brought in for what detectives call "interdiction"— tough-love intervention sessions with Prosecutor's Office detectives. Parents were often called, even for non-juveniles. In stark, window-less rooms in the detectives' bureau, as users began to go through withdrawal, the shakes and sweats of "dope sickness," addicts and families often confronted the reality of their addiction for the first time.

Some of those arrested became confidential informants— introducing undercover detectives to dealers who have been swept up in arrests throughout Paterson. Others detoxed at Bergen Regional Medical Center in Paramus; a few headed to private rehabs out of state.

But many relapse almost immediately. In February, a 21-year-old from Franklin Lakes sneaked out of her family home and was back on the streets of Paterson less than 24 hours after she was arrested, detectives in the Prosecutor's Office said.

"People don't understand the drive behind that addiction," said Lt. Tom Dombroski, a leader of the Bergen prosecutor's task force. "There's something in their brain, and once that drive is there—there will always be triggers that put them back in the need mode. Heroin is like medicine for some of these people."

Lyn, a 24-year-old heroin addict from Tenafly, says she cannot function without her daily doses of the drug.

"The one time you try it, you get sucked in," Lyn said. She started experimenting with pills two years ago; after a month in rehab last spring, she turned to heroin. She was recently arrested on possession charges, but continues to inject up to 10 bags a day, worth $40—for this reason, she asked to be referred to only by her middle name.

She has exhausted her parents' patience, and her own savings; she has sold off cameras and laptops, and has shoplifted, "anything to get money so I can buy the drug."

Heroin addiction is a constant state of unfulfilled need—an addict will forever be "chasing the dragon's tail," the elusive reclaiming of that first experience, a rush of euphoria and analgesia. It is a deeply physical, private drug, not what you take to go party, but what you take to escape.

"You used to think of heroin user in a dark alley with a needle sticking out of his arm," said Special Agent Doug Collier with the New Jersey office of the Drug Enforcement Agency. Back in the 1970s, Collier said, street heroin was maybe 6 or 8 percent pure— today, the DEA data show heroin purity levels in New Jersey at 40 percent, down from a 2005 peak of 70 percent.

"Heroin has never gone away," Collier said, "Now, you can snort it, and it's chic, it's in vogue, it's fueled by opioids. The stigma of a needle is not there. We have seen 18- to 25-year-olds hooked because of trying a narcotic painkiller, and when that source runs out, why not buy a bag of heroin?"

THE GRIM LIFE OF
SUBURBAN ADDICTS

Rebecca Davis O'Brien

The Record, May 6, 2013
Part of a series titled *Suburbia's Deadly Secret*

At 21 years old, Graham Dooner has the same wit and easy charisma that kept him on the edge of trouble as a student at Ridgewood High School. He cracks jokes, he drops lines like "ipso facto" into conversation, he could talk for hours about the history of the labor movement in Paterson.

But nearly two years of intravenous heroin use have consumed the body of this 6-foot, 4-inch former varsity athlete. His pale arms are lined with track marks, slender yellow bruises from daily injections. Beneath his Knicks cap and a mop of reddish hair, Dooner's handsome face is gaunt and clammy, haunted by a bluish pallor and spotted with sores. His yellowed teeth are worn along the edges.

"With shooting heroin, people say it is something they would never, never, ever do," Dooner said. "But, I mean, things change in a flash, especially when you are addicted to opiates. Your levels—your 'I won't go past that line'—they quickly diminish.

"It's sad. It really is," Dooner said. "Eventually, it becomes you need it just to be yourself, you know what I mean?"

Like many addicts in and around North Jersey, Dooner has experienced a near-fatal overdose, fights with drug dealers and police, and multiple arrests.

Dooner's latest arrest was in March. Between mid-January and mid-April, he and 89 others were arrested in Bergen and Passaic counties and charged with heroin possession, as part of a large task force operation led by the Bergen County Prosecutor's Office. That figure, roughly one arrest per day, does not include repeat offenders— Dooner was arrested twice in the same week. The addicts flocked to Paterson from towns across Bergen and Passaic counties, from as far south as Princeton and as far north as Rockland County, N.Y. More than two-thirds of those arrested over the past four months were under age 30, with high school degrees and middle-class families.

Most told the same story: A casual relationship with pills, particularly painkillers, in their late teenage years led to a full-blown heroin addiction, a need that tugged on their every cell, demanding every waking moment.

They include a 25-year-old from Tenafly who has shoplifted and sold off her belongings to support her addiction; a 20-year-old from Franklin Lakes, who hid his painkiller and heroin habit from his fiancée for years; a 21-year-old woman from Rockland County whose addiction was so powerful she found her way to Paterson on Christmas Day, looking for a high.

Most, including Dooner, now face third-degree possession charges, which can later be expunged. They are unlikely to see jail time.

Dooner and his friends experimented with drugs in high school, mostly marijuana and the occasional pill. But his troubles really started, Dooner said, with a lacrosse injury his senior year. He was prescribed Percocet, then stronger painkillers. Once those stopped, he stole the drugs prescribed to his mother after she had back surgery.

"At that point, I was playing sports again, and I was taking opiates just to get through ballgames," Dooner said. "None of my friends knew. It was a coping thing, a maintenance thing. It was almost mental—I thought I had to do this, to play in my games or to perform."

For several years, the widespread abuse of prescription painkillers has alarmed public health experts and law enforcement officials. Prescriptions for OxyContin, Percocet and other popular brand-name drugs based on the painkiller oxycodone have soared in recent years:

In 2009, 257 million prescriptions for opioid painkillers—derived, like heroin, from the opium poppy—were dispensed nationwide, almost one per person, according to a 2011 White House report.

In New Jersey in 2010, enough prescription painkillers were dispensed to medicate every state resident—there are nearly 9 million—at standard dosage rates for a month, according to data from the Centers for Disease Control and Prevention.

"It's easy to get your hands on some sort of opioid," said Ellen Elias, director of the Center for Alcohol and Drug Resources in Hackensack. "I think that many parents may be unaware of what the risks are in terms of how kids are accessing these pills. I believe prescriptions are written too frequently."

These painkillers are, for many, a gateway to heroin, their chemical cousin. Heroin addicts in North Jersey tend to start their addiction stories with variations on the same line: "In my town, pills are everywhere." They describe a suburban teenage culture that treats pill-popping the way many in their parents' generation treated marijuana—casual, commonplace, a rite of passage.

Ramsey has seen several fatal heroin overdoses in recent years, Detective Brian Huth said. Like many, he placed some of the blame on pills.

He recalled picking up a 21-year-old Allendale woman—a heroin addict, he said, whom River Edge cops had caught several times hawking stolen goods at the local pawnshop. "She told me, 'My generation sees pills differently than you do,'" Huth said. "That stuck with me. She's absolutely right. They all started seeing the pills as OK."

Dooner graduated from high school in the spring of 2010 with an addiction to painkillers and admission letters to several colleges. He chose the drugs.

OxyContin has for years been the nation's most popular oxycodone-based painkiller, bringing in at least $3 billion in annual sales. In 2010, responding in part to costly legal cases and public pressure, Purdue Pharma introduced a new version of OxyContin that was more difficult to abuse: The new Oxies could no longer be crushed or dissolved and were slower to take effect.

The change appeared to stem abuse of that drug, but it also had unforeseen consequences—it soon became clear that addicts were simply substituting other opioid painkillers, particularly heroin, which was cheaper and widely available. A study published in 2012 by the New England Journal of Medicine showed that heroin use among surveyed OxyContin addicts nearly doubled after the 2010 reformulation.

"When they changed the formula to something that was abuse-proof, the pills started disappearing from the streets," said Eric Richter, 20, whose heroin addiction began last winter after years of prescription drug abuse. Richter, who is from Franklin Lakes but now lives in Kinnelon, said he used to buy pills from a dealer on Route 46. "They were weaker, you couldn't crush them."

It was easier to find "blues," 30mg Roxicodone (known as "roxies"), Richter said—but they cost up to $30 a pill, and he needed more of them to "feel something." Every day, Richter hid his daily dose of five or six pills in strategic places around the Franklin Lakes home he was then sharing with his fiancée, Jessica.

Richter held down a job at the family business, but was often late. "I wouldn't be able to wake up in the morning," he said.

"When you first start doing something, you think you're just having fun," Richter said. "Then you're like—I need this. That's basically how it starts."

Richter said in April that he had never injected heroin and was now clean, taking college courses online. But the addiction cost him dearly: Between the pills and the heroin, Richter estimates he had spent more than $45,000 on drugs over the past year and a half. He and his fiancée, who said she only found out about his addiction after his February arrest, have moved back in with his mother.

Changes in pharmacology weren't the only thing that accelerated Graham Dooner's addiction. In 2011, Dooner and his mother and brother left Ridgewood for Fair Lawn. He was now within just a few miles of abundant, cheap heroin.

"What really helped the progression to street drugs, to heroin, was moving to Fair Lawn," Dooner said.

Route 4 cuts through southern Fair Lawn, turning into Broadway before it goes over the Passaic River into neighboring Paterson, one of many access points along a porous border.

Not that anything could stop an addict. "If Paterson was flooded, they'd swim," said Lt. Tom Dombroski of the Bergen County Prosecutor's Office. "The geography is not good. It's like a gambler living in Atlantic City."

Shortly after moving to Fair Lawn, Dooner said, he snorted heroin for the first time with a friend of his older brother. A few months later, Dooner's girlfriend, who was an intravenous user, shot him up. It felt like a "warm blanket," Dooner said, an embrace of contentment.

"The first time I shot up, it's kind of like the first time you ever did the drug, which is really what everybody is after—they're after that first time," Dooner said.

But the first high was followed by a first arrest, in October 2011. "Once that happens, you know, I start getting down on myself," Dooner said. " 'What kind of kid am I?' It almost becomes easier to keep doing it once you get arrested because you get so down on yourself."

For young users, coming to terms with addiction and a first-time arrest can seem insurmountable.

"I just think of all the things I could have done at this point in my life," said A.C., a slender, doe-eyed 21-year-old from Rockland County.

A.C. was arrested in March, in Elmwood Park, after buying a brick of heroin in Paterson—50 bags, roughly a gram, the amount of powder in a packet of Sweet'N Low.

Sitting in a stark interview room in the Bergen County Prosecutor's Office with a detective and a reporter, A.C. was beginning to get sick: It had been several hours since she sniffed some heroin, and she was going through withdrawal. Makeup was smeared under her eyes, and she was sweating, itchy and nauseated. A.C. crossed and uncrossed her legs, played with her cellphone, and avoided eye contact with Sgt. David Borzotta, who was seated across from her wearing a sweatshirt and jeans.

"I never, ever thought this would happen to me," said A.C., who asked that her full name not be used because she hoped to cooperate with the police as a confidential informant.

"My group of friends—my real friends—they don't know anything," A.C. said. "My drug friends are acquaintances." A.C., who dropped out of high school because of her pill addiction, said she knew several people who died of pill or heroin overdoses.

Since turning to heroin a year and a half ago, A.C. had not gone a day without it, and was snorting around 20 bags a day, roughly $80 worth of heroin. She swore she would "never, ever" inject it, but Borzotta raised an eyebrow incredulously—injecting brings a much faster, powerful high.

A.C. said, with an embarrassed smile, that she had driven to Paterson to buy heroin on Christmas Day. She pleaded with Borzotta not to call her parents.

"If you're not addicted, you don't understand," A.C. said.

"I've spoken to about a thousand of you," Borzotta said, shaking his head. "I understand. This is not a life.

"Here's the deal with heroin," Borzotta said, leaning forward to look A.C. in the eyes. "It leads to jail or death. This was your first arrest. There will be more. And some cops won't be nice. You have got to get control of this."

A.C. nodded.

As he left the room, Borzotta sighed.

"Sometimes, I feel like I'm talking to dead people."

A handful of those arrested for possession by the county task force were students, often taking online classes or attending nearby community colleges. Others held down full- or part-time jobs, or worked freelance—particularly in food services and construction.

A large number of them lived at home with parents who provide security and financial support, and were neither working nor in school—like A.C., who said she and her mother fight about her drug habit.

"Kids get bored," said John, a 20-year-old from Rockland County. "A huge factor is boredom."

John was arrested with A.C. in March. The two used to date, and remain close friends, he said. John started using pills at age 14, stealing OxyContin from his terminally ill father, and has been using heroin on and off for more than two years.

John was sweating, too, but was not as sick as A.C., in the neighboring interview room. He was animated, swearing with abandon as he spoke about the thrills of having sex on heroin, and his determination to quit.

"When I get home tonight, I'm going to drink a few Mike's Hard Lemonades, take a ZzzQuil, and watch some television," John said. "I'm going to make up an excuse for where I was, to tell my mother."

John lives at home with his mother, who thinks he is clean, he said. She gives him cash, though John also said he has savings from odd construction jobs and inheritance. He estimated that he spends $30,000 a year on heroin, not including the cost of gas for daily trips between Rockland County and Paterson.

John said his habit worsened after local jobs ran dry.

"Typically, when you have recessions, people resort to other things to entertain themselves, just like alcohol use grows in recessions," said Jerome King, who heads the Well of Hope center in Paterson.

The center's syringe access program—which provides free, clean hypodermic needles for drug users—has a membership of roughly 2,500 and the numbers are climbing, particularly among young women from the Passaic and Bergen suburbs, King said.

When the program started five years ago, women made up just 10 percent of the members. Now, that number is nearly 40 percent, even as use among men continues to climb.

"Most women who use heroin are introduced by their boyfriends," King said.

Of the 90 names released last Thursday by the Prosecutor's Office for heroin possession, 17 were women. Police also say young women are increasingly using heroin.

Lyn, 25, was among them. After her arrest in February, she continued to inject heroin, and for this reason asked to be identified by her middle name.

When Lyn began experimenting with painkillers two years ago, she was taking classes at a local college and living with her parents in Tenafly. Among her friends, pills were widespread—she knew two kids with sickle-cell anemia, Lyn said, who sold their painkillers to peers—and Lyn was soon addicted.

One day last spring, Lyn said, she came home to find her mother in the kitchen with a police officer. "'They said, 'You're going to rehab, or you're going to jail,'" Lyn said.

The 30-day stint in rehab got Lyn off the pills, but it poisoned her relationship with her mother.

"My mother is a definite trigger for me," she said.

She moved out of her parents' home and stopped going to school. Then she began using heroin, she said. "I just wanted to have that feeling again," Lyn said. "I was around people who were doing it, so it was hard, being around those people. I should have distanced myself, but I didn't."

Heroin, like other opiates, dulls pain—it brings a trance-like calm, along with a rush of euphoria. For this reason, users say, heroin is a solitary drug. Lyn called it "a relief."

Now, she can't get out of bed without it. When she uses, she feels healthy, she showers, she puts on makeup, does her nails, she said.

"A lot of people want to get away from the troubles and problems they're having," Lyn said.

She said she wants to quit. "It's a miserable life, a miserable existence," Lyn said. "Two years have gone by, and where did they go? Once you abandon yourself, that drug will never give you a rest."

Withdrawal from heroin, which can begin within hours of last use, comes with intense physical symptoms: cold sweats, aches, extreme discomfort. The fear of detox, Lyn said, "would push me to continue to do it, to go to Paterson at night, and do those things that in my right mind is not a good idea."

Lyn drives down to Paterson with her fiancé, who is also an addict—the two live together in Elmwood Park. "It's definitely not a safe scenario," she said. Her fiancé has been shot at, she said.

This is not an uncommon occurrence, police say. When addicts run out of cash, they hand over electronics or jewelry as temporary payment to their dealers. If they return later to retrieve their goods, there can be violent confrontations.

Dooner has twice had a gun drawn on him, he said with a small amount of pride. He said he also takes pride in the fact that he has never stolen anything to support his habit—"I've always been a little more business-minded," he said.

When Dooner started shooting heroin in 2011, he said he was working nights at a bar in downtown New York City, bringing in hundreds of dollars a week.

Every hour, he slipped into the bathroom to shoot heroin, sometimes mixed with cocaine, he said. His boss knew, Dooner suspects, since trickles of blood sometimes ran down his arm, "if I got sloppy."

He would take the train home to New Jersey in the early morning hours, stopping in Paterson to buy drugs.

Dooner became close with high-level dealers in Paterson, and eventually began to cut pure heroin and sell it for them in Bergen County, keeping some cash for himself. His addiction accelerated. By the time he went to rehab, last October, he said he was injecting 30 to 40 bags of heroin a day, roughly two-thirds of a gram, which is—he readily acknowledges—an "insane amount" of heroin.

Despite the agony of withdrawal (he said he would "rather cut off a toe" than go through it again), Dooner liked the structure of rehab; he wrote daily in a journal and was happy with the "clarity" of his thoughts.

He was surprised to find that most of the people in his group were young heroin addicts like himself; many seemed to live a double life, with addict friends and "real" friends.

But he picked up heroin again shortly after he got out. "You wake up and it's just this urge, this voice in your head, telling you, you need this to be normal," Dooner said.

One night last December, Dooner shot up at home while waiting for a friend to come over for a Knicks game.

His friend found Dooner unconscious on the sofa, a needle sticking out of his right forearm.

Dooner has been arrested three times, but he's talked his way out of at least five other "tight spots," he said. "Once you get to that level, you are a master at deception, a master at manipulation."

Richter, in April, was seeing a therapist, working full time, and going to meetings, he said. His fiancée, Jessica, said she was "watching him all the time."

"I have clarity," Richter said. "You feel better. You're not depressed."

Dooner, like Lyn, said he "can't see myself" as a junkie at age 30.

"I've always had this feeling—I think everything is going to work out just fine, as much as what has happened to me should tell me otherwise," Dooner said.

"I still tell that to myself. Sometimes, I don't want to admit how much work it takes."

He plans go back to school in the fall. But before that can happen, he has to deal with his addiction—and the charges he faces for drug possession.

HEROIN'S POISONOUS PATH TO NEW JERSEY

By Rebecca Davis O'Brien and Tom Mashberg

The Record, December 22, 2013
Part of a series titled *Suburbia's Deadly Secret*

The case began on a quiet suburban street in North Bergen, in the attic of a vinyl-sided Cape Cod, where in October 2008 investigators discovered 6 kilos of pure, uncut heroin wrapped with white packing tape, concealed in a blue Reebok duffel bag. Scattered throughout the Cottage Avenue house—above the refrigerator, tucked inside a love seat, in the master bedroom closet—was more than $2.7 million in cash. The man renting the house was Mario Villaman-Puerta, a 32-year-old Mexican citizen who had been deported several years earlier after a cocaine distribution conviction in Illinois. He was arrested along with another man.

Five years later, that investigation, dubbed Operation Shut Down by the Drug Enforcement Administration, has reached from the suburbs of North Jersey to the poppy farms of Colombia, exposing a 5,000-mile international narcotics network that connects the Cottage Avenue stash house to a Colombian drug-trafficking organization that supplies Mexico's powerful and violent Sinaloa cartel with cocaine and heroin for distribution in the United States.

Ten days ago, the head of that Colombian organization, Jorge Milton Cifuentes-Villa—considered one of the world's most powerful drug kingpins—was extradited to the United States to face charges stemming from Operation Shut Down, a DEA official confirmed. Authorities say the Cifuentes family has close ties to Joaquín "El

Chapo" Guzmán Loera—the notorious and elusive leader of the Sinaloa cartel, which dominates drug trafficking in the Western Hemisphere. Guzmán's criminal network brings hundreds of tons of cocaine, heroin, crystal methamphetamine and marijuana into the United States each year.

A large quantity of these drugs ends up in New Jersey, which is confronting a dramatic rise in addictions to prescription painkillers and their opiate cousin, heroin. It is no coincidence that New Jersey has the most potent street-level heroin in the country— a typical dose, sold for $5 in waxy glassine envelopes, is about 50 percent pure, 10 times as potent as heroin was in this area three decades ago.

In 2012, nearly 800 people died from overdoses involving heroin, morphine or opiate painkillers in New Jersey, according to the state Medical Examiner's Office. Heroin alone accounted for an average of one death every day. Officials say that number could be rising. This year, Ocean County alone has reported 100 heroin and opiate overdoses.

Two dozen deaths in Bergen County in 2012 involved heroin; 25 others involved morphine and opiate painkillers. Figures for 2013 are not yet available. Across North Jersey, towns from Allendale to West Milford have reported a sharp increase in heroin overdoses, drug-related crimes and deaths.

"Look at where we are located—we are the crossroads of the Northeast," said Gerard McAleer, former special agent in charge for the DEA in New Jersey and now chief of detectives for the Middlesex County Prosecutor's Office. At least 90 percent of New Jersey's heroin comes from Colombia, officials said, an increasing amount of it traveling overland from Mexico in tractor-trailers, dozens of kilos at a time. With more than 13,000 trucks crossing into the U.S. from Mexico every day, according to federal transportation statistics, along with 62.7 million personal cars each year, authorities say stopping so much contraband is nearly impossible.

"Look at the numbers for border crossings, how many trucks come through," McAleer said, expressing a frustration echoed by city, county, state and federal officials. "It is the proverbial needle in a haystack."

While it is possible to connect a single fatal overdose to a local dealer, connecting the source of that heroin up the chain of distribution and production to drug-trafficking organizations takes years. Such a case requires coordination among multiple authorities, reliable informants, wiretaps and, of course, luck.

After starting in North Bergen, Operation Shut Down led to one of the largest seizures of heroin on U.S. soil—75 kilos, along with 84 kilos of cocaine, seized at a Palisades Park warehouse in July 2009. That raid led to the discovery of 8.3 tons of cocaine in Ecuador and finally to the arrests of several members of the Cifuentes crime family of Colombia.

Operation Shut Down is still open, and Guzmán remains at large with a $5 million bounty on his head. But interviews with law enforcement officials and investigators familiar with the case, along with an examination of court documents, DEA material made available for review, and dozens of similar cases, show how modern heroin traffickers derive millions by delivering the drug, as the DEA saying goes, "from the farm to the arm."

Six years before the breakup of the North Bergen stash house, Mario Villaman-Puerta, a heavy-set man with a furrowed brow and a heart-shaped tattoo on his arm, was deported to Mexico after serving several years in prison for a 1997 cocaine distribution conviction in Illinois, according to court documents. In May 2008, Villaman-Puerta reentered the United States illegally and took up residence at 7306 Cottage Ave. in North Bergen, a modest house with a detached garage.

There, around the corner from North Bergen High School, authorities said, Villaman-Puerta directed a large-scale drug trafficking and money laundering operation that extended into New York City and down the East Coast.

The operation was tied closely to New York City, drawing regular traffic to the Cottage Avenue home, which soon caught the attention of the DEA's Newark office. In October 2008, agents set up surveillance on the house, joined by a camera crew from the Spike TV network filming the second and final season of its reality series "DEA," which followed federal drug investigations in Detroit and New Jersey.

The agents suspected the home was being used to keep cash for the operation and did not expect to find drugs—it is unusual to keep the supply and revenue in the same place.

"You target the money because it's like punching somebody in the throat," one agent told the cameras. "They can't breathe. It shuts everything down. Dope, marijuana, heroin, cocaine, it all grows in the ground. You lose a shipment, you just grow some more."

But losing money upsets the entire supply chain.

Agents had been monitoring the Cottage Avenue home for days, but things began to heat up in the early evening of Oct. 29 when a white Ford Windstar minivan with New York plates stopped at the house, lingered for an hour, then headed to the Bronx. There, on the corner of Jerome Avenue and 183rd Street, a man waved down the van using a lighted cellphone, exchanged backpacks through an open door and quickly darted into the subway while the van sped off.

The next day, agents followed Villaman-Puerta and an associate as they drove from Cottage Avenue to Union City to have lunch at El Mole Poblano, a Mexican restaurant on New York Avenue. But the men picked up the tail and began driving in circles, trying to get away.

Agents detained Villaman-Puerta and his associate and searched the van. Finding nothing, the agents returned to Cottage Avenue with a search warrant. That's where they found the 6 kilos of heroin in the attic, more than $2.7 million stuffed in duffel bags and concealed throughout the house, two vacuum sealers and shoeboxes filled with rubber bands and plastic for packaging drugs.

Caught cold with drugs and money, and given his past, it seemed likely that Villaman-Puerta was headed for a long-term stay in a federal prison.

But nothing is simple in the world of drug prosecution, and pieces don't always fall into place. For one thing, agents and prosecutors are always looking to turn lower-level conspirators against those above them. And seemingly minor elements of an investigation can lead to unexpected consequences.

Federal prosecutors in Newark had decided early on that they would not pursue cases captured on the Spike TV series, in part out of wariness about the live filming of drug investigations, but also because the show's producers would fight efforts to turn over outtakes that lawyers needed to present the full case.

That put Villaman-Puerta in state court, where he pleaded guilty to a minor drug charge. The only federal charge brought against him was an immigration offense for illegal reentry. He pleaded guilty to that charge as well.

If it weren't for a pre-sentencing report that described the nature of his crimes, Villaman-Puerta might have faced only a two-year sentence on the immigration charge.

"The government will note that Mr. Puerta is the luckiest man in this room right now," Assistant U.S. Attorney Eric Kanefsky told the court at the sentencing, explaining his office's policy when dealing with Spike TV.

The luck was short-lived.

U.S. District Judge Joseph Greenaway expressed "outrage" that "someone who was involved in a drug transaction of that magnitude [and] is here illegally, is subject to a penalty that in my judgment appears minor."

Greenaway ignored the sentencing guidelines and sent Villaman-Puerta away for 75 months on the immigration charge, noting that he had indicated to his probation officer that he would likely return to the United States if deported again to Mexico.

"Looking at Mr. Villaman's past drug involvement, his current drug involvement, his desire to return to the United States yet again, if he is deported, leads one to come to the conclusion that he is literally incorrigible," Greenaway said. Villaman-Puerta is currently in federal prison in Virginia.

Perhaps the most important outcome of the Villaman-Puerta case was not his six-year sentence, but the exposure of a wholesale heroin and cocaine distribution network reaching from New York City to North Jersey to Georgia to the Southwest and eventually into Mexico and South America. It is unknown whether anyone involved in the North Bergen stash house provided information to the authorities, but the cash, the pedigree of the drugs, along with wiretaps and the other evidence gathered in the bust provided road maps that led further into the international operation.

In the months after the North Bergen bust, Rafael Villagrana-Arreola, known as "Raffa," emerged on investigators' radar.

Sent to North Jersey from Georgia by a Mexican cartel in 2009, Raffa found a home in Woodland Park, according to an investigator on the case. He also bought a car that was built by a body shop on Dyckman Street in Manhattan—complete with hidden compartments to conceal drugs, court records show.

"There's body shops that these certain guys go to" that specialize in outfitting cars with concealed compartments, or traps, said Lawrence Williams, a detective with the New Jersey State Police. "They'll pay between $5,000 and $10,000 for a good trap."

Raffa then went to work, using a false identity to set up a warehouse in an industrial area of Palisades Park, where he could receive shipments of drugs from Mexico, DEA records and court documents show.

Setups like this are increasingly common as Mexican cartels seek to make inroads into the U.S. drug market and create their own internal distribution networks to better control the pipeline and keep a tighter grasp on profits. Kilos of heroin are smuggled directly from the border to cartel-run mills in New Jersey, which cut and package it for delivery to local criminal groups, including gangs like the Bloods and Latin Kings, who sell it on the street.

One widely cited Department of Justice report from 2011 said Mexican cartels had "transnational criminal operations" in more than 1,000 U.S. locations in 2010. That figure has since been disputed, but state investigators said it was unusual, and alarming, to see Mexican cartel operatives on the ground in New Jersey.

Soon, Raffa made contact with Rafael Vargas-Aguilar, who lived in the Los Angeles area, to make arrangements for a shipment of drugs from Mexico, according to a DEA report.

In July 2009, investigators followed Raffa from his Palisades Park warehouse, a nondescript building on Commercial Avenue with loading bays, to the Ramapo service plaza on the New York Thruway, a few miles north of the New Jersey border, where he met with Vargas-Aguilar and Alberto Nieto Jr., another Southern California native, DEA investigators said.

The two men had arrived in an old motor home, which they had driven from California, according to an investigator who worked on the case. Raffa got into the motor home and, with Nieto, drove to the Commercial Avenue warehouse; investigators watched as the pair began to open a compartment in the vehicle, then moved in on them, the reports said.

Nieto and Raffa were arrested at the scene; Vargas-Aguilar, who left the service area separately, was captured later that day at a New Jersey motel.

Concealed in compartments in the motor home were nearly 160 kilos of what investigators at first believed to be cocaine. Days later the lab results came back: it was 84 kilos of cocaine and 75 kilos of nearly 100-percent-pure South American heroin. The heroin, valued by authorities at $62,000 a kilo, was worth nearly $5 million wholesale; the cocaine, valued at $32,000 a kilo, an estimated $2.7 million. On the street, the drugs would have been sold for much more.

It was the largest drug seizure in New Jersey history and the fourth largest nationally. The three men were indicted on federal distribution charges in September 2009, in New York's Southern District.

The following month, acting on information gathered during the investigation, 8.3 tons of cocaine was seized in Ecuador, and the packaged drugs, which were on their way from Colombia to Mexican traffickers, matched the cocaine seized in Palisades Park, according to a DEA investigator involved in the operation. The investigator said that some of that 8.3 tons was likely heroin—not all of the packages were tested and heroin is often packed along with cocaine shipments from Colombia, the investigator said.

Raffa pleaded guilty; court records indicate he was released from federal prison in April. Nieto pleaded guilty and was sentenced to 84 months in jail, plus supervised release. Vargas-Aguilar's case was not prosecuted, according to court documents, without explanation.

The vast majority of the heroin that arrives in New Jersey and New York is grown and processed in Colombia. The remote, mountainous poppy fields that produce the raw opium, federal and international officials say, are the domain of guerrilla groups and armed cartels that combine brutal violence with farming and creative smuggling tactics to feed the American appetite for heroin.

Years ago, most South American heroin was brought to the northeastern United States through the Caribbean, several kilos at a time, by plane or boat. Human carriers are still common: They wear the heroin in their shoes, strapped to their bodies, or take the risk of ingesting packaged heroin to avoid detection on airplanes. "Swallowers" are trained by cartels to swallow up to 60 10-gram packages of pure heroin, squeezed into the fingers of rubber surgical gloves or condoms that are sealed with hot wax. These pellets are coated with olive oil or cooking oil and tied tight with waxed dental floss to insulate them from stomach acids.

But today, much of New Jersey's heroin follows a well-worn route overland from Mexico. Mexican cartels use the U.S. highway system to channel their goods in wholesale batches, concealed in hidden compartments in tractor-trailers or in legitimate shipments, to a ready network of regional distributors.

Vehicles bearing 20 kilos of heroin at a time have been stopped in the Northeast, federal and local officials say. Trucks have several routes: some take Interstate 95 north, others travel across the country from Southern California or hole up in Chicago, a major hub of narcotics trafficking, before heading to New Jersey.

New Jersey arrest records from the past decade show that men of Dominican descent make up the vast majority of suspects arrested for possession of a kilo or more of heroin. International drug trafficking organizations often make use of local distribution networks, particularly organized crime groups within immigrant communities—the large Dominican population in North Jersey, the Bronx and northern Manhattan, officials say, is home to some of this criminal element. Dozens are facing indictment, dozens more have been sentenced and investigators say a large number have escaped major jail time or simply been deported home after becoming confidential informants.

Stopping it all from crossing into New Jersey "just isn't possible," said Carl Kotowski, special agent in charge of the DEA's New Jersey division. The state has one of the busiest turnpikes in the nation, enormous amounts of freight arriving at its northern ports by sea and air, and bridges and tunnels linking it directly to parts of New York City, where heroin is also plentiful.

Seizures of heroin along the Southwest border increased 232 percent between 2008 and 2012—1,855 kilos in 2012, up from 558 in 2008, according to federal seizure data.

The 8.3 tons of cocaine seized in Ecuador—tied to the July 2009 bust in Palisades Park—was en route from Colombia to Mexico, for distribution in the United States, officials said.

Investigators began to close in on the Cifuentes family, a Colombian drug trafficking and money laundering organization, and in particular its leader Jorge Milton Cifuentes-Villa. In 2011, the U.S. Treasury Department froze his assets under the federal kingpin act.

In 2008, Cifuentes-Villa had met with several co-conspirators, including a DEA informant, in Ecuador to discuss "transporting tons of cocaine to Mexico, and eventually to the United States," according to a 2011 federal indictment in New York.

The Cifuentes family has long been entrenched in Colombia's drug trade—Jorge Milton's brother was a pilot for Pablo Escobar, the Colombian drug lord who died in 1993—and in recent years the family has served as the main supplier of cocaine and heroin to the Sinaloa cartel, with direct ties to Guzmán, officials say.

After the Ecuador bust, Cifuentes-Villa's sister, Dolly Cifuentes-Villa—suspected of laundering money for the organization—was caught on a wiretap discussing the seizure with a co-conspirator, according to the 2011 indictment, which names both siblings.

Dolly was arrested in 2011 and extradited to the U.S. a year later. Jorge Milton, fleeing authorities, lived in disguise for more than a year in a Venezuelan village—he even married a local woman, according to Colombian news reports. Local suspicions were aroused after he made multiple calls a week at a village phone—Colombian investigators later said they traced the calls to Guzmán's Sinaloa cartel, the largest drug organization in the world. Cifuentes-Villa was arrested in Venezuela in November 2012.

Ten days ago, Cifuentes-Villa was among a group of prisoners extradited to the United States, where he is expected to face charges in New York's Southern District, a DEA official confirmed.

The extradition connected links in a chain that began in the nondescript house in North Bergen and reached across multiple borders, involved millions in illicit trade and drew in conspirators like Villaman-Puerta, Raffa, Vargas-Aguilar and the Cifuentes siblings.

But the greatest prize of all is Guzmán, who continues to elude authorities.

There are multiple unsealed indictments in U.S. federal court for Guzmán, including cases in New York, Texas and Illinois. In July 2009, a grand jury in New York's Eastern District indicted Guzmán as part of a vast cocaine trafficking conspiracy. The indictment outlined an operation of tremendous reach and power, involving corrupt local police and politicians in Mexico and South America, "a large-scale narcotics transportation network" that brought "multi-ton quantities of cocaine from South America, through Central America and Mexico, and finally into the United States."

A Chicago indictment, which covers a period from 2005 through 2008, implicates Guzmán and the Sinaloa cartel in a wholesale heroin and cocaine distribution scheme that brought thousands of kilos of drugs up from Colombia through the interior of Mexico to Chicago, where it moved to other parts of the country, including New York and New Jersey.

Operation Shut Down opens one window into the underground drug trafficking networks that have made New Jersey a mecca for pure heroin. According to state and federal statistics compiled by

The Record, more than 1,000 kilos of heroin have been seized in New Jersey since 2004.

The seizures result from lengthy investigations with operation names like "Dismayed," "Honeycomb," "4th Down" and "Jumpstart." They involve multiple state and federal agencies, generate splashy press releases, and have led to hundreds of arrests, indictments and prison terms. But investigators acknowledge that they make barely a dent in the New Jersey pipeline—they don't even know how much heroin gets into the state.

"We only know what we get," said Timothy P. McMahon, a special agent with the DEA's New Jersey division.

In fact, traffickers may see the loss of heroin through seizures, busts, thefts by rivals and the occasional ghastly accident—like a heroin pellet breaking open in the digestive tract of a human carrier—as an inevitable inconvenience.

"The shippers are making so much money that even when we catch them, it's a write-off to them, it's the cost of doing business because of the greater demand," said Bergen County Prosecutor John L. Molinelli. "We continue to try to get those big cases because they tend to have a greater impact from a long term, as a greater deterrent. You continue to do it because you have to. There is always somebody ready to step up."

Still, at the end of the day, major local suppliers like Mario Villaman-Puerta know that when they get arrested in operations like Shut Down—and lose large batches of heroin go to the police—they and family members are in debt to cartel leaders and their criminal networks. This adds urgency and violence to an illicit trade, amid a growing epidemic of addiction.

In cities like Paterson, diminished police forces struggle to keep up with the steady flow of suburban addicts driving into blighted neighborhoods for heroin, let alone manage the drug trade and the gang activity that thrives alongside it. Parks there are often littered with used needles and empty heroin envelopes.

But in places like Fort Lee, Elmwood Park and North Bergen, where heroin mills have begun to pop up, residents "don't realize there are so many illegal guns and so much heroin" in their communities, said Steven Cucciniello, chief of detectives for the Bergen County Prosecutor's Office.

And while the supply may be hard to quantify, demand is terrifyingly easy to measure. Some users can go through dozens of $5 doses a day. A street dealer can burn through several kilos a week.

Sgt. Brian Polite of the New Jersey State Police put it simply: "There is certainly enough demand to soak up that supply."

INSIDE SUBURBAN DRUG MILLS, A GRIMY, LUCRATIVE BUSINESS

Tom Mashberg and Rebecca Davis O'Brien

The Record, December 23, 2013
Part of a series titled *Suburbia's Deadly Secret*

New Jersey drug agents have seen plenty of bizarre sights when busting heroin mills, the sunless, foul-smelling assembly lines where laborers spend hours on end grinding up raw heroin and spooning it into $5 street bags.

They've seen trash bags filled with coffee grinders that fried out after being used thousands of times to pulverize the drugs into sniffable powder; they've confiscated tens of thousands of tiny glassine envelopes stamped with cheeky brand names like Barack Obama, DEA and Lady Gaga; and they've seized Build-A-Bear stuffed animals sliced open at the belly to reveal freshly smuggled wads of the raw narcotic. They've walked in on middle-aged drug packagers clad only in underwear—to prevent stealing—and surgical masks—to keep them from getting high from the airborne powder.

But for local investigators, one case stands out: an April 2011 raid on a new suburban two-family home on Grandview Place in Fort Lee, a quiet green cul-de-sac near the George Washington Bridge, less than 1,000 feet from a school. There, investigators found a woman at a kitchen table, stamping glassine bags filled with heroin while her preschool-age daughter sat nearby eating cereal. She was among a dozen Dominican immigrants who had been bused in from New York City overnight by minivan to work the 12-hour shifts needed to meet what cops call "a ravenous demand" for opiate drugs.

"They can make a lot of money doing these jobs," sometimes up to $500 a day to work at a table, said Lawrence Williams, a top state police detective who oversees North Jersey's anti-drug unit. "The people who run them are very smart and organized and they like steady workers."

Heroin mills have become a major focus of the state police and other law enforcement officials who are trying to get drugs off the streets of North Jersey. But the micro-factories are relatively easy to set up and often difficult for authorities to identify. In recent years, more and more have cropped up in quiet suburban neighborhoods around North Jersey, in places like Fort Lee and Ridgefield Park and Maywood, a development that alarms the authorities, who believe the best way to disrupt supply is to kill off the mills.

They are the linchpin of the heroin trade, where a cartel's raw product meets local distributors. It is there where the stakes are the highest, because there is so much product and so much cash. A kilo of raw heroin worth $70,000 wholesale, received by a local cartel contact in the United States, is processed at mills into at least $140,000 worth of doses, parceled out in bulk to mid-level distributors, whose workers sell it on the streets. It is a delicate supply chain and while the return on investment is great, so is the risk.

Breaking a drug mill like the one on Grandview Place takes weeks of coordinated work by multiple law enforcement agencies, according to Williams and a dozen other drug investigators interviewed. Participants include the state police, Drug Enforcement Administration agents, detectives from Bergen and Passaic counties and sometimes out-of-state groups like the Pennsylvania State Police, or the Office of the Special Narcotics Prosecutor for New York City.

Such was the case when the red-brick Grandview Place site was blitzed on April 29, 2011. The leads that led to the raid were generated on the Manhattan side of the George Washington Bridge, according to New York officials. The bridge has become a key artery for New York heroin wholesalers looking for quiet places in the North Jersey suburbs to set up mills and process their wares.

Leads often come from confidential informants looking to bargain their way out of long prison terms by turning on confederates. From time to time, a tip comes from a rival mill operator looking to put a competitor out of business.

And sometimes tips are pure chance. One former federal agent recalled a case in which a trash collector told investigators about a house where dozens of coffee grinders were regularly put out with the trash. Sure enough, the house was a heroin mill.

The Grandview Place mill was first identified after New York agents saw a minivan routinely collecting Dominican immigrants from a street corner in the Washington Heights section of Manhattan. Investigators followed the van to Fort Lee and watched as it pulled into the garage of a clean-looking, three-story house with windows covered by black trash bags.

In the raid that followed, 10 workers were arrested, including the mother of the young girl eating cereal, who was charged with child endangerment. Agents seized 5.5 pounds of unprocessed heroin, $50,000 in cash and all the usual trappings of a small-scale heroin processing operation.

The presence of Dominican mill workers was not unusual. When Colombian cartels began funneling heroin and cocaine into the United States, through the Caribbean, some Dominicans in the U.S. were brought into the drug trade. Today, even as more of North Jersey's heroin comes over the border from Mexico, drug trafficking organizations continue to recruit heavily among large Dominican populations in the suburbs of North Jersey and in Manhattan.

Bridget G. Brennan, the special narcotics prosecutor for New York City, said mill operators hire from the Dominican communities because they would be unlikely to break the code of silence, for fear of retribution against them and their families.

"This keeps the operation very tight," she said.

Heroin processors choose nondescript rented residences like the Grandview Place home because they can comfortably run 24-hour-a-day operations without drawing the attention of neighbors or police for several months before moving on to a new space.

Inside, workers sat at a 6-foot-long table methodically folding thousands of glassine envelopes filled with heroin and taping them shut. Cans of Red Bull energy drink were near at hand to keep them going during hour after hour of the tedious work, authorities said.

At a separate table, the men in charge of the mill used sieves and pestles to stir ground heroin with milk powder. Two men with tiny spoons filled the empty glassine envelopes with a minute dose—enough for a high that will last about an hour. The bags were stamped with logos from McDonald's, Adidas, Best Buy and Budweiser, authorities said.

While Paterson remains a hub for heroin processing and sale, authorities say more mills like the one on Grandview Place are invading the suburbs. And it's not just a matter of convenient geography and cheap, secure real estate. The trend is intimately connected to the recent sharp increase in opiate addictions among middle-class New Jersey residents. The demand is there, and the supply has followed.

Until a few years ago, state police in North Jersey were focused more on cocaine than heroin. Then, in 2007—as prescription pill addiction and heroin abuse began to rise nationally—a heroin mill was uncovered in a residential area of Elizabeth, a two-family home operating as a full-scale assembly line. It was "emblematic," Williams said, signaling a shift in heroin packaging to the suburbs.

State police and New Jersey DEA agents have broken up more than 50 mills over the past decade—about half of them in suburban locations—and seized a combined total of about 1,000 kilos of raw heroin, according to an analysis of data provided by both agencies.

Generally, pure heroin arriving in New Jersey is collected by a distributor, often with ties to Mexican or Colombian syndicates and to local criminal elements, who bridges the divide between South American producers and dealers.

"Once it comes into New Jersey or New York, the heroin will be parceled out to table-top operations," said Gerard McAleer, who led the Newark's DEA office from 2006 to 2010 and is now chief of detectives for the Middlesex County Prosecutor's Office.

Given limited resources, New Jersey officials have made breaking up the table-top operations a priority. More and more this means going beyond the streets of Paterson, a hub of regional heroin trafficking, to the small-town streets in Bergen, Hudson or Essex counties, where the idea of a heroin mill next door is as unimaginable as it is chilling.

Handfuls of these mills are uncovered every year in North Jersey:

In December 2005, DEA agents seized 4.5 pounds of heroin and $150,000 in cash from an apartment in Ridgefield Park.

In June 2010, a kilogram of heroin and paraphernalia were found in an Elmwood Park house where 10 workers packaged the drug for street sales.

In January 2011, five men were arrested and 2 kilos of heroin were seized from a mill in West New York.

In December 2011, investigators found a heroin mill in Belleville operating under the oversight of an Elizabeth street gang and seized 2 kilos.

In December 2012, officials found $6 million worth of heroin and crystal methamphetamine in a suburban home in Cliffside Park, less than 1,000 feet from an elementary school. A New York man was arrested with 2 kilos of heroin packed into the soles of his shoes and strapped around his waist, and 16 more pounds of the drug were found inside ready to be milled.

In May, a tiny mill on South Elm Street in Maywood was raided and a backpack-toting heroin dealer arrested as horrified neighbors watched. Inside the tidy ranch-style home, investigators seized 85 bricks—more than 4,200 doses—of heroin.

"Our philosophy here is to target the source of the supply," Williams said. "It's like gasoline. It comes into this country in different ways—on barges, trains, trucks. We hit the refineries of the heroin trade. If you knock out a refinery, there's going to be a supply issue."

But table-top operations like the one on Grandview Place in Fort Lee are nimble, well-managed businesses run on tight budgets with an eye for security.

"You have to know what you're doing to set up a mill," Williams said.

The goal is a consistent product that addicts can depend on.

"If you put a beat package out there on the street, you will go out of business," Williams said. "It is the purest form of capitalism."

Peddling heroin in New Jersey is "astonishingly profitable," as one law enforcement official put it. A mill operator can make a $40,000 to $60,000 profit from 1 kilo.

Here's how, according to police experts:

A kilogram of pure heroin, straight from South America, is worth $60,000 to $80,000, wholesale; in heroin mills, this pure kilo is ground to a fine powder, cut with diluents such as baby formula or milk powder and measured into individual doses.

Most heroin sold to users in New Jersey is about 50 percent pure, 10 times as strong as it was several decades ago.

Once diluted, a kilo makes about 50,000 single doses, or "decks," weighing 0.02 gram apiece—about what would fit on a salt spoon—and packaged in small glassine envelopes.

Those decks are folded into thirds, stamped with a brand mark, and organized into groups of 10, called "bundles." Five bundles make a "brick," and each brick is wrapped with colorful magazine pages to make the product look sexy.

The process results in 1,000 bricks—or 50,000 doses—of street-ready heroin from the original kilo. The owner of the table then sells the bricks wholesale for $125 to $150 a brick ($2.50 to $3.00 a deck) to a large-scale heroin distributor who, in turn, sells smaller amounts of bricks to street dealers.

A mill operator who sells all of his bricks rakes in $125,000 to $150,000. Factoring in his original $60,000 to $80,000 investment, plus $10,000 for labor costs, $10,000 for items like rent and gasoline, and $1,000 for materials still leaves a profit margin of $39,000 to $64,000 per kilo.

"If a good-sized mill puts out 2,000 bricks a week . . . you are talking an easy $100,000 of profit a week for the mill owner," one state official said.

Mill work is far from glamorous. Police describe raids on apartments where the air is saturated with the stench of heroin and sweat.

The materials generally include a handful of electric coffee grinders—Krups is the brand of choice, considered more durable, according to state police. Tables often have glass tops, so nobody can slip product into their pockets. Then there are the small glassine envelopes, stamps, scales, sealable plastic bags and magazines to wrap their bricks in.

Heroin stamps change frequently, but they are usually names with cultural currency—like LeBron James or Versace. There was a time when stamps identified a brand, a certain dealer or mill. But now mills, like the one on Grandview Place, will have 20 stamps at a time: It is part of the business model and for security. This makes it hard to find the source of a cache of drugs, or even the source of a single fatal overdose.

"You have to have street criminal intelligence," said Bergen County Prosecutor John L. Molinelli, whose office has pursued murder charges against people who supply heroin to somebody that results in death. "You couldn't do it based merely on the stamp, because stamps are so common now."

Key to the trade is anonymity: Local processors use false names and third-party cars. The sites are temporary places of business, managed by somebody with connections to the cartel and to local criminal networks, and staffed by part-time workers working 12-hour shifts. Some mills go the extra mile, providing their staff with showers, cots and takeout.

Mills keep ledgers, scrawled in haphazard code, detailing the supply, the workers, who enters and leaves, who owes what to whom. Inside, the workers have distinct jobs: one measures the heroin with a small spoon, a "stamper" brands each package.

Mill workers, often poor immigrants, earn $300 to $500 a day, depending on their task or experience level.

"It's dangerous and unhealthy just going into these places," a police official said.

Take, for instance, heroin extraction labs found in Roselle in 2006. There a chemist used methylene chloride, a volatile and toxic industrial solvent, to extract heroin from the plastic lining of luggage sent from Colombia. The heroin was converted into a semi-liquid form, passed through a strainer, then put into an oven and cooked into a solid. Afterward it was ground into powder.

Once the heroin has been packaged, it is sold in large quantities to criminal organizations, including street gangs, for sale in cities and suburbs. This is the level of the drug trade most familiar to Americans—local drug lords, corner hustlers and their clientele. It is also where the vast majority of arrests take place.

Several recent busts demonstrated the scale and nature of these drug organizations.

Between 2010 and 2011, Passaic County, Paterson police and the DEA arrested more than 170 people as part of a sweep of gangs in Paterson—including members of the Fruit Town Brims, a branch of the Bloods street gang that operated in the 4th Ward of Paterson. They had weapons, all sorts of drugs and cash. According to the 2012 indictment, the Fruit Town Brims were selling roughly $50,000 a week worth of heroin, cocaine, ecstasy and marijuana in the city's 4th Ward.

In October, a Paterson investigation uncovered a drug ring run by members of the Sex Money Murda branch of the Bloods; many of the street-level dealers arrested had hundreds of bags of heroin and abundant cash reserves on them. The police also arrested 17 buyers, mostly young adults from the surrounding suburbs.

Paterson is a regional hub for the drug trade, drawing customers from New York and Pennsylvania as well as Bergen and Passaic counties. Thousands of bricks, each made up of 50 doses, are sold on the streets of Paterson each week.

"You'll see street-level and mid-level distribution, selling 200 bricks at a time," said Hector Carter at the Bergen County Prosecutor's Office.

The city's 4th Ward is also a hub of gang activity, with branches of Bloods, Crips and Latin Kings, sometimes doing business together. Gangs still run much of the street-level sales of heroin in Paterson. But the control is often loose: there are independent dealers, freelancers, seasonal workers, officials said. Some people might be merely affiliated with a gang, others might be freelancers.

In November 2012, state investigators dismantled an organization that pumped millions of dollars' worth of heroin out of mills in Paterson. The investigation, called "Operation Dismayed," uncovered a network led by Segundo Garcia, 36, of Prospect Park and Wilfredo "Willie" Morel, 39, of Paterson. The two men obtained heroin in large quantities and oversaw its processing—supplying kilos of the drug each week to other suppliers and large-scale dealers in North Jersey, New York, Pennsylvania, and Washington, D.C.

During the bust, investigators searched several houses in Paterson, seizing 3 kilos of bulk heroin, a kilo of cocaine, another kilo of heroin packaged for sale, and $255,000 in cash, according to authorities.

The state Attorney General's Office estimated that the group "moved" or sold 2 kilos of raw heroin each week. Garcia, a Dominican national, served five years in federal prison for drug dealing beginning in 2000—he was deported, but reentered the U.S. illegally and allegedly established his distribution network in Paterson.

That network had roots in Paterson, Prospect Park, Jersey City and New York, according to the July 2013 indictment. The raw heroin was manufactured into doses at mills for local distribution on a "routine and almost daily basis," according to the indictment. The heroin was then transported using two taxi drivers, who also moved members of the enterprise and packages of cash around New Jersey, according to the indictment. So-called "managers" then distributed the heroin to street-level dealers.

Garcia pleaded guilty to first-degree possession charges this month and faces up to 15 years in prison; he had originally been charged with the first-degree crime of leading a narcotics trafficking network, which carries a possible life sentence.

Once the drugs get to the street level, it is up to the local dealers to move their product. Dealers send out blast text messages to their regular customers from disposable "booster" phones, devices purchased without a contract that can be discarded. Or they simply wait for the line of cars coming in from the suburbs.

Some come to Paterson to buy in bulk, returning to their suburban towns to resell the heroin and turn a profit. In Paterson, one brick will go for around $140.

In Hackensack, Englewood and Teaneck, a brick can go for more than $200, Carter said. Or entrepreneurial dealers might buy in bulk in Paterson, then sell in the suburbs of North Jersey—Tristan Rodas, an 18-year-old from Glen Rock, was arrested twice this year for allegedly selling Paterson heroin to local users, taking a profit. Carter said some suburban distributors have gang affiliations.

As state officials noted in a July report called "Scenes From an Epidemic," advances in technology and the growth in demand among suburban users means that "a bag of heroin is now only a text message away."

ADDICT. INFORMANT. MOTHER.

Susan Dominus

New York Times Magazine, May 11, 2014

One day last summer, Ann and her husband, Tom, walked two and a half hours to reach Hazleton, a onetime mining town in eastern Pennsylvania. They had lived there until July, when they were evicted and moved in with Ann's mother in Sugarloaf, a more affluent township nearby. There was not much to miss about Hazleton, with its decaying downtown and its fading homes spotted with satellite dishes, but to Ann and Tom the town held a shimmering appeal: It had heroin, a lot of it. They had called the usual friends for a ride, with no luck, and their own car had been repossessed. So at midday, the two left Ann's mother's condominium by foot and followed the asphalt out of the valley all the way to Hazleton. Eventually they turned onto Alter Street, where, especially in summer, heroin dealers greeted customers outside a packed barbershop and a busy pawnshop, clustering around them, competing for business. Sometimes Ann and Tom joined other users they knew behind a building, where someone had left a tattered couch. Sometimes they got high in an abandoned garage on a side street. Though the walk that day to Alter Street was long, it was worth it to them both: Tom, especially, loved heroin, and Ann loved Tom, and the march to Hazleton was as much about need as it was about love.

Months later, when downtown Hazleton's streets were lined with piles of dirty, crusty snow, Ann (who along with Tom asked that they be identified by only their middle names) thought about that walk with something like nostalgia. It wasn't the kind of nostalgia she felt for the days when she was a new mother, taking care of two small children, going to a job at a warehouse, fussing over car seats and relaxing over lunch with co-workers. That was a nostalgia for the person she had once been; this was a nostalgia for someone else—Tom—and a less lonely time.

Now her husband was in jail, and she knew she needed a plan to avoid ending up there too. She tried a rehabilitation program in the fall and managed to get off heroin for 18 days, but within hours of getting out, she was holed up with a new friend she made at rehab, as high as ever. Now, at 25, she was trying a different way to save herself. She was working with the police, who had told her she was going to be charged with possession. If she wanted to stay out of jail, they told her, she would have to help them. All she had to do was set up her best dealer.

On a frigid day in early February, Ann hurried into the back seat of a red Honda waiting outside her father's small home near Hazleton. She said a quick hello to the people in front: Carol Davenport and John Brennan, longtime narcotics agents, who were taking Ann to buy heroin from someone who had sold to her many times before.

"He actually is a very nice guy," Ann told Davenport and Brennan as they drove. "He's just in the wrong occupation." Unlike everyone else in her life, her dealer, whom she considered a friend, seemed to trust her: For the past month, he regularly fronted her three or four bricks of the drug worth $150 each. She could easily sell one brick—50 bags—for $200 or 10 bags at a time for $60. Either way, she could pay her dealer what she owed him and keep at least a brick for herself, which would supply her for about two days. Ann was flattered when the dealer originally approached her to suggest that they might work together, which seemed to imply a certain faith in her general competence. He was sweet, in Ann's opinion. Once, she told him that her mother might kick her out, and she half-joked that she might have to live with him. "No problem," he told her. Not that he would tell her where he lived. Not that she even knew his real name. He had moved to Hazleton from New York. She thought he was Dominican, like a lot of dealers in town. He was about her age, good-looking, with blue-black hair. He made a nice living, was professional. After they made a deal, they always hugged.

Davenport twisted around from the front seat to look at Ann. "If you think this guy is a nice guy, you need to re-evaluate your idea of the quality of a good person," she said. Davenport had raised a daughter, who was about Ann's age, as a single mother. Forty-five and trim, she had long hair that fell in waves around a face that no dealer could refuse, no male dealer at least. One dealer Davenport had worked with for months wept when he realized Davenport had been gathering evidence on him. "I liked you," he said when they met after he was arrested. "I took care of you."

Ann wore a black hoodie over a T-shirt with a hot pink sequined star and black leggings tucked into black boots. Davenport patted her down, poking around inside the fake fur of the boots, to confirm that she wasn't hiding money or drugs. She smelled of shampoo, and her eyes were carefully made up. "I don't even know if I want to ask you if you've been clean," Davenport said. Ann said she'd been off heroin for three days and gone through withdrawal, which she describes as "the flu times 100." Now she was even beginning to eat again: "My mom says she's starting to see the old Ann." Brennan and Davenport were not sure whether to believe her; she did not seem high, but some users were like that. Tom, who started out with prescription pills like Percocet, managed to hold down a welding job while he was using and drove a forklift under the influence; he had even been promoted twice at an Amazon warehouse. He was about to be hired full time when he failed a drug test.

The plan that day was to drive to the parking lot of a nearby convenience store called Sheetz. The police had given Ann $400 that she was to give to the dealer. She owed him that money, and she would get another two bricks to sell. "How are you going to let us know you have it?" Brennan asked. She told him she would text him one word: "Good."

Brennan was sturdy, 57 years old, with horn-rimmed glasses that seemed at odds with the hoodie he usually wore. He put four children through Catholic school, solid kids, every one, and Ann's mother trusted him implicitly, frequently turning to him for advice about how to deal with her daughter. He spoke to Ann with the deep, confidence-inspiring voice of a successful coach.

Brennan was based in Philadelphia, where he worked as a narcotics agent for the state attorney general on long-term cases—getting warrants for wires and aiming for dealers who trafficked in kilos, not bricks. He was in Hazleton as part of a 10-person task force called the Mobile Street Crimes Unit that was designed to rotate in troubled towns throughout the state. Near the intersection of I-80 and I-81, Hazleton, a town of around 30,000, has long been a convenient distribution hub for drug traffickers. In the late '90s, officers in Hazleton considered cocaine and crack the town's biggest problems; but about a decade ago, they started seeing an influx of heroin. The town's police force of 38 could hardly stem the tide. Hazleton had developed a reputation as a town where users from surrounding areas knew they could find heroin; Alter Street had become the kind of overt drug market linked to crime and social decay. "An open-air drug bazaar is the ultimate broken window," Mark A. R. Kleiman, a professor of public policy at U.C.L.A., says.

The Pennsylvania attorney general, Kathleen Kane, intended the task force to provide towns like Hazleton—there were easily a dozen around the state—with a temporary blitz of manpower. By locking up Ann's dealer, Davenport and Brennan knew they were probably only creating a business opportunity for someone else; but there they were anyway, trying to at least keep things from becoming worse.

In the car, Ann was cracking her knuckles, pink fingernails digging into her palms. "I don't want him to know it was me," she said.

"He won't," Brennan said.

Ann got a text. There had been a misunderstanding; the dealer was coming all the way from Philadelphia. He said it would be an hour and a half, but that probably meant at least two, maybe more. Davenport slapped her leg in irritation: "Ann—this guy exhausts me."

Brennan and Davenport dropped Ann off at home and told her they would see her in an hour. Neither felt particularly hopeful about the plan, but they came back around 6 and settled in at the parking lot. The two detectives had spent more hours than they cared to consider killing time in the parking lots of dollar stores and fast-food restaurants in downtown Hazleton, waiting for deals to go down. Now they drank coffee and talked about Brennan's low-carb diet and Davenport's quinoa recipes. Texts from the dealer dribbled in. "Do you want your money or not?" Ann texted, impatient. "Yesss," he texted back. "Waittt."

At 6:40, Ann went inside the Sheetz to wait, occasionally popping out into the cold air. Her phone was dying—what if she couldn't text Brennan "good"? She ran back to the car to charge it, which made everyone edgy: The dealer could pull in at any minute.

Inside the Honda, Davenport and Brennan were fending off boredom and anxiety. Forty-five minutes went by. An hour. Brennan, staring out at the snowbank in front of them, started dreaming about summer, a coming James Taylor concert. Then he and Davenport were singing: "I've seen fire and I've seen rain/I've seen sunny days that I thought would never end. . . ." No one mentioned it, but Taylor has said the song is about praying for deliverance from the pain of heroin withdrawal: "My body's aching and my time is at hand. . . ."

Inside Sheetz, Ann was on the phone with her dealer. He was telling her he was in the parking lot, but she couldn't see him or his white van. In the middle of this confusion, Ann's phone died. In a panic, she asked to use the store phone, dialed three, four, five times. Finally the dealer picked up. He was at the wrong Sheetz, about 15 minutes away. He said he would come to the right one soon.

Hearing his voice unnerved her. For the first time that day, Ann was tempted to try to abort the plan. It was hard to betray a friend— hard, also, to commit to cutting herself off from a steady supply of heroin. She could tell Brennan and Davenport that he had called to say he wasn't coming, and they would all go home. But there was that problem of the $400 she owed him. She was broke.

She ran to the Honda to update them, then ran back. And finally there he was, in a baseball jacket, with that blue-black hair, driving a white van. Ann got in, and they drove up a street near her dad's house to make the exchange, the way they always did. The deal was a blur: She had bought from him dozens of times but never felt this nervous. When they pulled back into the parking lot, Ann hugged him goodbye and got out of the van. She didn't even have time to text "good" before she realized what was going on.

"Police! Don't move!" she heard men yelling. There were 10 officers surrounding the van, their handguns drawn. Ann took a step, and no one stopped her, so she kept moving. If she looked back, she would have seen the dealer splayed on the ground. Go to John's car, go to John's car, she thought, willing herself toward Brennan's Honda. She threw herself into the back seat, breathing heavily, and rested her head on the headrest.

"Why did you do it like that?" she said. Ann had not asked for or been given too many details that day, but she assumed the police would arrest the dealer some time later, so her involvement would not be apparent.

"We had to, Ann," Brennan said. Just a few days earlier, another agent saw Ann getting into a car with the dealer without alerting them. They had no reason, really, to trust her, and she didn't know how much to trust them.

"I don't feel good," she said. "I'm shook. I got scared—they were coming right at me." But it was worse than that: Her dealer had to know she set him up; it was obvious, he knew, he knew, he knew.

"You did good," Brennan told her. "Just relax—you don't have to worry. And now you can't get dope."

"I hope so," she said. "I want to be done. I want to be over with it." The ride back to Ann's mother's home was quiet. Davenport suggested she find herself a new set of friends, make a clean break. "You did a good job," Brennan said. "Here's $50, O.K.?" He stopped her before she got out of the car. "And, Ann—stay off that stuff."

When it was all over, Ann walked into her mother's apartment, a small two-bedroom intended for an empty-nester, now packed with

Ann's belongings, her children's toys. She explained to her mother, Lucy, how the evening unfolded, and Lucy focused on the aspects of the story she considered hopeful: Maybe this was the beginning of the end of it all—the late-night phone calls, the strange cars pulling up to her condominium.

For a long time, Lucy (her middle name), a medical technician, managed to ignore the signs that her daughter was using heroin. When Ann started asking for money about a year and a half ago, Lucy assumed it was Tom who was blowing their income on drugs— Tom, who always had that empty look in his eyes, who once nodded off right in the middle of one of the big Sunday-night family dinners Lucy used to host. If Ann and Tom's apartment was suddenly disheveled, and the kids looked a little ill kept, that was only because Ann was exhausted, Lucy told herself. By the time she was 24, Ann had two children and was working the 11-to-7 night shift at the Hershey plant, getting by on almost no sleep during the day. She knew Ann was not perfect—she could have a mouth on her, was never much for schoolwork—but this was the girl she'd accompanied to Girl Scouts and watched play field hockey. When Lucy and her husband divorced, Ann, who was 18, chose to live with Lucy. The two were like girlfriends.

It all came out in the fall. Tom, who had been charged with possession, went to jail. But even after he left, Lucy found syringes around the house and demanded that Ann show her arms. She knew then that Ann was shooting up, but it still took time for Lucy to appreciate just how far gone her daughter was. One day, her 4-year-old grandson came running into Lucy's bedroom, telling her to hurry—"Mommy's shooting drugs." Lucy found her daughter in the living room, needle in hand. Not long before that, Lucy realized that her gold jewelry was missing: her grandmother's rings, the diamond pendant a young man had given her just before leaving for Vietnam. Only Ann would have known where to find all those velvet boxes.

Lucy went round and round in her head about what had gone wrong. She had done everything for her daughter, from buying every

Barbie she wanted as a girl to co-signing a car loan when she was grown. Maybe that was it—maybe Lucy had done too much, spoiled her.

Now she was simultaneously housing her daughter and trying as hard as she could to put her in jail. At least in jail, Lucy believed, she would get clean. "Couldn't you just put her somewhere where she couldn't get drugs for like a year?" Lucy once asked Brennan.

"Like kidnap her?" Brennan told her. "That's not how it works."

Ann sometimes accused her mother of plotting to get control of her grandchildren. "You think I wanted to be raising two toddlers at 63?" Lucy would respond. "You think that was my plan?" But Lucy was grateful for the grandchildren: If she had nothing to do but worry about Ann, she would have collapsed from all the strain.

Not long after Brennan and Davenport dropped Ann off, they called her again: They needed to deal with some paperwork about the $50 Brennan had given her. When the car pulled into her mother's parking lot she noticed another police car behind it and felt uneasy.

She went outside. Brennan told her to get in the car. He asked her to show him the $50, then grabbed it out of her hand. "Where's the money?" he wanted to know. "Where's the $400, Ann?" Brennan, gentle Brennan, was cursing at her, his coach's voice booming. When they searched the dealer, they didn't find the $400, and he claimed Ann never gave it to him.

"I didn't take it," she said. "I swear on my life—I swear on my kids!" A cop she didn't know handcuffed her in the back of the car; someone told her she was being charged with theft. She turned to Davenport: Didn't she believe her? "I want to believe you," Davenport told her. "But I get lied to every day."

"I know I'm a junkie," Ann said to Brennan, wildly, a self-description that pained even him to hear. "I know I'm a junkie—but I wouldn't do that." Brennan and other officers went inside the house and tore through a pile of shopping bags and hampers where Ann was storing her clothing. As he tipped up a couch, Ann's young son tried to help, putting all his weight behind it. Lucy, exhausted, in pajamas and glasses, shook her head. "Just lock her up, John," she told him.

Brennan did not find any money. And Ann could not have left

and bought drugs already, that much seemed clear. Then a call came in: Someone had searched the dealer one more time. The $400 was in his coat pocket all along.

Brennan, stricken, looked at Ann. "I'm so, so sorry," he told her. The handcuffs were off by then, and Ann started to cry.

As February wore on, Brennan started to feel tired of the snow, of the small-town desperation, of the sense that no matter how many dealers they locked up, others would take their place. He expected the endless supply and demand in Philadelphia but not in a town of Hazleton's size.

The Drug Enforcement Administration considers prescription-drug abuse, not heroin, to be the country's fastest-growing drug problem: 2.4 million Americans used prescription drugs nonmedically for the first time in 2012, according to the most recent National Survey on Drug Use and Health. Many of those people abuse opiates like OxyContin and Percocet. Some small percentage of them, unable to afford expensive pills or finding their tolerance too high for those drugs, seek out heroin as a cheap, potent fix. Increasingly they find it with some ease. For all the billions the U.S. government has spent fighting drug trafficking over the years, Mexican gangs have been flooding the market. The resulting competition among dealers has made heroin cheaper and purer than it ever has been. From 2007 to 2012, the number of people who reported using heroin in the previous year grew to 669,000 from 373,000, a statistic that represents a tiny percentage of the population but a significant rate of increase.

One week after Davenport and Brennan arrested Ann's dealer, Attorney General Kane arrived in Hazleton to oversee the last days of the mobile unit's work there. A few dozen extra officers were brought in, and about 30 small-time dealers and users were rounded up over three days, in addition to the 90 or so who were arrested over the preceding six months. That Wednesday, the attorney general held a news conference to talk about the unit's success. "I will tell you that this Mobile Street Crimes Unit is about street fighting," she said. "I'm a street fighter. . . . That's what we do—we are down on the ground. . . . We're not think-tanking. We're not talking about concepts. We are out on the streets, on raids."

But David Kennedy, a professor at John Jay College of Criminal Justice, questions the approach of these sorts of task forces. "The people on the ground are doing the best they can do. But the level of effort is never remotely equal to the work that remains to be done. If they stayed there forever, it wouldn't change."

An agent for the special-operations group, brought in to help with the roundup, cheerfully accepted the futility that he understood to be an integral part of his job. "This," he told me, gesturing at the 50 or so officers there to help clean up the town, "is a Band-Aid on a gaping wound."

By Friday, most members of the task force, including Brennan, had returned to their own corners of the state. The drug trade on Alter Street had at least temporarily quieted, no small step for a town trying to dispel its reputation as a drug hub, but Ann had no problem finding heroin elsewhere in town. She was still using despite what she told Davenport and Brennan. That night, she was inside a Giant Food Store, reveling in the privacy of its bathroom. It was big and bright, a cathedral of a space, where she could comfortably kneel down and find peace. The chain stores in Hazleton—Giant, Turkey Hill, Rite Aid—all represented refuge to Ann.

Right out of high school, Ann fell in love with cocaine, which she snorted on lost weekends in the Poconos with friends. But she stopped cold when she became pregnant at 20. For years, she was good, as she put it—a good girl, a good mother—everyone said so, even her mother's friends. But then a friend of Tom's persuaded him to try heroin, and their family life changed—suddenly, he was gone, either out with his friends getting high or home but stoned out of reach. Ann was lonely and tired and more than a little bored: Night after night, at the Hershey factory, she placed little wafers in little molds—God, she hated Kit Kats. Her lunch break came in the early-morning hours. A co-worker started offering her cocaine. At first she resisted—"I'm a mommy, I spend time with my kids," she told him—but she had not forgotten how cocaine once made her feel. Finally she took him up on his offer.

It was easy, then, to move to heroin, to share with Tom, after the kids went to bed, that rare euphoria: "Our time," they called it. At first, Ann only sniffed the drug; Tom refused to shoot Ann up, afraid of where the needle would take her. But soon she could no longer feel the effects of the heroin she snorted, and she eventually figured out how to shoot up.

In the bathroom of the Giant Food, she went to work. Out of a floral makeup bag, from underneath a mound of compacts and mascara, she pulled out a bright orange stretchy headband, a medicine bottle, three small glassine envelopes and a single Q-tip, which she would use as a filter. "My mother got rid of my cotton balls," she said—Lucy knew what she used them for. Ann gently poured the contents of the bags, a pale powder, into the cap of the medicine bottle. She pulled water from a plastic bottle into her syringe, then ejected it into the heroin and stirred. Gripping the syringe in her mouth, she ripped off a tiny bit of the Q-tip. She placed it in the cap, where it soaked up the solution, and then she dipped the needle into its cottony softness. She extracted the drug, leaving a brown ring around the interior of the bottle top.

She took off her hoodie, pushed up the sleeve of her shirt and knelt down. She wrapped the orange headband three times around her arm until it was tight. She massaged a vein on her left arm, gently, as if to coax its cooperation. Then the needle went in, slowly. She failed to connect with a vein, tried again, failed again: Scar tissue was probably starting to get in the way. In and out, in and out. She breathed audibly, sometimes twirling the syringe. A small, dark stream of blood congealed on the pale underside of her arm.

A knock on the door. "Is there someone in there?" Ann did not look up. "Just a minute," she said. Her concentration was complete. Five minutes went by; she switched arms, switched again. "Here's one," she said tenderly, setting her sights on a faint blue, slender line beside the main one in her arm. Finally: "There you go," she said. She sat motionless for a moment.

Ann always described it the same way—first, a feeling in the back of her throat, then the rush, that cosseting, warm feeling barreling its way through her blood.

She cleaned up, marking her syringe with eyeliner so she would know that it had been used. She put her jacket back on, washed her hands, checked her face in the mirror. Three bags was not necessarily so much that she would nod off, falling into the semisleep of addicts who can hang and sway even when standing; it was just enough to get her right in some way. In its comfort, she seemed to find new strength to imagine giving up the drug, especially since it took her so long to hit a vein. "I can't hit anything," she said, as she wiped the blood off her arm with a fresh piece of toilet paper. "It must be God saying, 'Quit.'"

Ann talked about quitting all the time. She imagined herself going to school—maybe taking some classes in criminal justice, a subject she thought about pursuing after high school. For several days, Ann had been carrying around with her a single pill—her sub, she called it, short for Suboxone. Suboxone, like methadone, is a drug that is dispensed to help ease the symptoms of withdrawal. Unlike methadone, Suboxone can be administered outside a clinic by prescription. For all the concern about crime in Hazleton, the town had never been able to muster enough support for a methadone clinic, one of the few measures proven to reduce criminal activity among drug users. And Ann said the waiting lists at the local doctors who prescribed Suboxone were three to four months long.

One Suboxone seemed unlikely to get Ann anywhere close to full recovery. Even on the other side of withdrawal, the satisfactions of a sober, adult life might prove elusive. Recovering addicts report a kind of emotional dullness that can linger for months, even years, a result of compensatory changes in the brain that only slowly reverse. Downregulated by overstimulation, the reward system for the ordinary pleasures in life limps along, an unreliable, rusted-out machine; the stress system, by contrast, works in overdrive, with a ruthless, hair-trigger sensitivity. Even after they have not touched drugs for a year, addicts, studies find, are more sensitive to hot and cold. And amid all that psychic ache, one memory shines exceptionally bright: that unnaturally exquisite reward.

Still, Ann carried around the Suboxone pill, almost as a totem of possibility. She even showed it to her mother, as proof that she really was going to stop.

By Monday, Ann was hurting. She had no money, and she had exhausted any favors her friends owed her. She had no drugs to sell, no buying power. She knew it was stupid, but she kept calling her dealer, whom she heard was out on bail, her need so strong she could not heed her own common sense. He never called back.

At 3 that afternoon, Ann was working the phone outside a convenience store, texting and calling around town for help. She said she had not used since the day before; and now she was starting to feel those first symptoms of withdrawal: hot, cold, hot, cold. She was sighing, over and over again. She was trying to make something work. "All right," she said to someone who had just turned her down. "You don't want a trader?" All she had to offer was Seroquel, an antipsychotic, that she said was given to addicts in withdrawal to help them sleep.

She called someone else—voice mail. "Why can't I get ahold of anyone?" she said. Her voice was small. "I'm in agony." She started to tear up. "I'm all out," she said. "I'm going to die." She called someone else. "Listen, listen, listen—I wanted to ask you. What can you give me for one? 'Cause I'm sick. I just need one," she said, just one bag. Someone texted someone to see if he would make a trade for the Seroquel, give her something she could sell to someone else. She waited; she heard from a friend that a guy who owed her would meet her outside the AutoZone in Hazleton. So she headed there and waited, charging her phone inside the store. Forty-five minutes went by. She walked on wobbly legs into the Japanese restaurant next door, desperate for a bathroom. She vomited and then walked out, still wobbly. She couldn't wait any longer for that guy at the AutoZone. "It's so time-consuming," she said at one point. "It should not be this hard to get drugs."

In parts of Europe, government and medical officials have decided that there's some sense in what Ann said: That the difficulty addicts have obtaining drugs accounts for much of the crime problem. In Switzerland, Germany and the Netherlands, the most entrenched heroin addicts can turn to prescription heroin, safe heroin administered at medical sites, an approach that has been found to reduce crime even more than methadone clinics and to improve addicts' family lives and employment stability.

Ann called someone else who owed her. The best he could do, he said, was offer her some headphones that she could pawn. Maybe they were worth $20, which was, at that moment, a king's ransom. She took them, but the pawnshop gave her only $5. Maybe she could scrounge up some change in her purse. Ten minutes later, Ann emerged from a home near Alter Street with a bag of heroin; just holding it in her hand, she seemed revived. It was something, but she had a 20-bag-a-day habit, and this would not get her through the night. When she got home, she would start working the phone again.

Three days later, Ann was scheduled for an arraignment on the charges of theft of her mother's jewelry. Ann's father accompanied Ann and Lucy to court, and as the three of them bickered and shushed one another, Ann seemed bolstered by the normalcy of family life—her father stern and finger-wagging, her mother by her side.

Lucy had been under the impression that Ann was very likely to be escorted directly from the courthouse to jail. Instead the judge told all the defendants to plead not guilty and gave them court dates when their cases would be heard. "What a joke," Lucy muttered.

Ann was relieved. She could go home with her mom, spend time at the house where her father and brother lived; her father would watch the kids during the day. Things would go on, somehow, with some semblance of what she now considered normal: her children around her, the endless hustling for heroin, the usual daily grind.

But then Lucy told her she had to move out: Social Services, which granted Lucy temporary custody of her grandchildren after Tom was arrested, had said Ann could not stay at the apartment, for the good of the kids.

So Ann left. From that point on, her life didn't resemble anything that had come before. Lucy caught only glimpses of it, which was about as much as she could take. Ann ran out of minutes on her phone and rarely called. A few weeks out, Ann came by Lucy's work to ask for money, for contact lenses, she told Lucy. Her face was black and blue. She had had a fight with another woman, also a user, over a guy—not so much over the guy, but over who was going to get a ride from him. Ann needed to be driven to a hearing that would determine whether Lucy's custody status would shift from temporary to permanent; the other woman wanted a ride to get a fix. Ann didn't make it to the hearing.

She was staying at a motel with friends, she told her mother, playing it off as if that were fine, although Lucy knew what kind of motel it was, a rathole where she would be afraid to seek out her daughter. At some point, Ann reached out to Davenport, who was now working in a nearby town, asking for help finding a place to stay. She and Davenport arranged a time to talk, but Ann didn't show up. The detective felt for Ann, but she could not make it her business to try to save her. "I am so swamped with cases," she texted me. "There are hundreds of Anns out there."

At night, Lucy was dreaming about dire phone calls and strange cars pulling up to her door. She could not reach her daughter but knew that she had a second court date, on March 26, for another theft charge; her father accused her of stealing a sander and a hand weight from his home and selling them to a junk shop for $4 and change. He, too, pressed charges and got the state police involved: The girl had to learn there were consequences. Lucy took time off from work to try to see her daughter at the hearing at the magistrate's office.

When Ann showed up, the strains of the past month were visible on her body, which had wasted away, and on her face, which was tinged with gray. Just the night before, the police told Lucy, Ann was picked up for shoplifting several hundred dollars' worth of clothing at a Walmart next door to the magistrate judge's office.

Now Ann was panicked that the judge might not let her remain free before the trial, which was customary for small offenses. Shaking with nerves and exhaustion, she sat down on a chair in the waiting room and fumbled with her purse. Her eyes were dry and lined with red. She had not taken out her contact lenses in weeks for lack of a case.

The two Walmart security guards who apprehended Ann the evening before were also crowded into the tiny waiting room, there for someone else's hearing. They looked away from Ann, and she avoided their eyes, busying herself with her phone and applying concealer and lipstick with a trembling hand.

"I did some shady things, I have to get my act together," Ann said under her breath. "But it's been very, very hard. Very." For weeks, she had been catching sleep, along with a crowd of other users, in motel rooms that a new dealer friend let them use when he didn't need them for business. Every day, the crew woke up and started the same routine: What could they buy? Where could they buy it? Who had the cash? How would they get there? She was using crack, was sleepless and agitated; her nails were lined with dirt, and she had a broken finger that she thought was infected, its splint grimy.

Eventually a public defender came out of the courtroom, a tall, balding man with a baby face and a reassuringly adult suit. He could not represent Ann, he explained, until she filed the appropriate paperwork, but he could give her some advice: Don't lie. Try to sound calm. Volunteer to go straight to rehabilitation therapy as a condition of bail. Ann was praying the hearing would be postponed until she had a public defender assigned. She was terrified of jail.

Tom had tried to warn her this day was coming. The one time she visited him in jail, Ann was high, and now that he wasn't using drugs anymore, he couldn't bear to see her that way. He told her she had to get off heroin. "I can't," she told him. He knew he would have said the same thing months before: Tom was the one with the 50-bag-a-day habit, the one who had overdosed on a mix of heroin and Xanax, only to rush out of the hospital so he could go back home and shoot up. In jail, he had no choice but to stop using, and in a strange way, he was grateful. "I've had a lot of time to think it over," he said, when I visited him in the Luzerne County Correctional Facility. "It's not all about me. I've got two kids, and they're suffering." Loose-limbed, with a steady gaze, Tom said he was resolved to stay off drugs when he got out, though he looked wary as he said it: He knew how hard it would be. He could not say what his future would hold with Ann, but he felt responsible for where her life had gone. "To be dead honest," he said quietly, "it's all my doing."

Once she was seated in front of the magistrate, a tidy-looking man with dark hair, Ann reached deep into the recesses of memory and pulled out an earlier version of herself: the passable student teachers liked, who used to go shopping for clothing with her mom, who showed up for a steady job with manicured nails, who changed her son's diapers and gazed into his crib with pride. "I don't want to live like this anymore," she told the judge. "I really don't. If possible, if I could get into something today?" She was asking for some kind of a treatment program. "I was on heroin," she told him, "but I haven't used in the last two weeks."

Ann's father had known the magistrate since he was a boy: He and the magistrate's father had worked together at a local coal mine. Now Ann's father sat in the back of the courtroom, arms folded in disgust at the state of his daughter. The magistrate listened carefully to Ann, then set the bail at $10,000. The public defender had gently tried to warn Ann that the judge might set a high bail—given her obvious drug problem, given that even previous arrests did not seem to deter her from committing more crimes. But Ann was nevertheless shocked: "I'm going to jail?" she asked, incredulous. Many months down the road, Ann could be referred to treatment court, where her record would be expunged if she underwent a prolonged period of treatment with clean drug tests. But all of that was an abstraction; now she was filled with the immediate fear of the humiliations of jail, the utter loss of control. Tom went to jail, and he was still there, six months later.

She started pleading with the magistrate. "I don't have a chance to do anything at all?" she asked. The magistrate was now looking down at some papers, ready to move on to the next hearing, but Ann argued on, trying frantically to lay blame elsewhere. She had just put a deposit down on an apartment, she claimed. "So I finally have a place to live," she shouted, panic rising in her voice. "I explained that to my mother, but she doesn't believe me."

She put her head in her hands and cried. Ann suddenly looked very small in the courtroom. The magistrate took a small breath, as an officer of the court moved in to cuff her hands. "If you want to blame somebody, don't blame your mom," he told Ann. "Blame yourself."

And then, hands shackled, she was escorted toward the courtroom exit. "Can I just have my phone?" she asked. It had all her connections. "I just need to be able to call someone," she said, "someone who could help me."

DELIVERED LIKE PIZZA

Sam Quinones

Excerpt from *Dreamland: The True Tale of America's
Opiate Epidemic* (Bloomsbury, 2015)

Denver, Colorado

In 1979, a young man fell into a job at the Denver Police Department. He was new in town, fresh from a broken engagement in his
native Pueblo, Colorado.

Dennis Chavez never meant to be a cop. His family traced its
roots back to a seventeenth-century Spanish conquistador. Four centuries later, Chavez's father was a steelworker in Pueblo.

Chavez, a big guy, played football at the University of Colorado
for a couple years in the 1970s before leaving the school. He worked
construction. Then a friend recently hired on at Denver PD told him
the work was fun and urged him to take the entrance test. Chavez
passed it and within a few months was at the Denver Police Academy.

Early into his first year on patrol, however, a training officer told
his friend that Chavez was failing, probably the dumbest in the new
recruit class and almost certain to wash out before the year ended.
That irked. Chavez put in extra time studying laws and the munici-
pal code, exercising and adding new energy to his street work.

In time, his interest in sports channeled into power weight lifting.
He cut his hair in a flattop, with lightning bolts cut into the sides and
his badge number on the back of his head. Steroids were legal then.
He would buy bodybuilding dope from a doctor who visited the
gym where he lifted. Soon he was spending twelve hundred dollars a

month on steroids and supplements. He was six feet four, 250 pounds, and muscles bulged from him as if his body were a squeezed balloon. Dennis Chavez was a ferocious cat back then, shaking hands with an iron grip, clubbing friends on the shoulders when he saw them. He arrived at every 911 call like a pit bull, pulling for action. When he barked, "How you doing?" at friends, it sounded like a cross between an interrogation and a command. Even cops tried to avoid him.

He was obsessed with his job, which he took to mean arresting bad guys. A lieutenant once criticized him for not writing enough tickets. As training officer to new recruits, the lieutenant said, Chavez wasn't showing them enough balance to his police work.

"That's not what I do," Chavez told the lieutenant. "I find felons."

He spent his first years on the force learning from a cop named Robert Wallis. Wallis was the department's version of a supercop. He made major arrests all the time. He and his partner were involved in more than a dozen shootings, which to Chavez meant that Wallis was always getting in the way of the worst bad guys. Wallis was a guy he wanted to emulate. Wallis taught him about prison tattoos, and recognizing the look of a guy on the lam in line at a downtown shelter. From Wallis, Chavez learned early on that most crime is connected to illegal drugs, so understanding that world was crucial to good police work.

Heroin particularly interested Chavez. Back then, Mexican American families controlled the trade in Denver. But as Chavez worked them and arrested them, he heard they were being supplied by men from a place in Mexico called Nayarit. The name meant nothing to Chavez, but for years it kept coming up. The Nayarits sold a substance he hadn't seen before. Heroin in Denver up to then had been all light-brown powder. This Nayarit heroin, however, was dark and sticky and looked like Tootsie Rolls or rat feces. They called it black tar and Chavez heard stories they cut it with boiled-down Coca-Cola.

As the years passed, meanwhile, what Dennis Chavez realized he loved most about his job was the deduction of crime. It was the immersion in it, finding the thread of a criminal and his MO. Once, a serial rapist was striking across Denver. Chavez had taken the statement of the last victim, a high school girl, who, in tears, grabbed his hand and made him promise that he would catch the guy. Victims said the rapist held a Buck knife to them as he assaulted them. Chavez charted the rapist's attacks—his times, dates, locations. He staked out the southeast Denver neighborhood where he thought the guy would hit next. One night he saw a man walking down an alley and just knew it was the guy. Then the man jaywalked. Chavez stopped him and arrested him for carrying a concealed Buck knife in his pants. Victims came to the station house that night and identified Chavez's arrestee as their rapist.

A few years into the job, Dennis Chavez woke one morning unable to see, his heart pounding like an overheated piston. His girlfriend took him to the hospital. A doctor told him he was going to have a stroke if he didn't let up.

"You can die young and good-looking, or years from now fat and happy," the doctor said.

Dennis Chavez opted for the latter. He backed off the steroids and coffee, and stopped power lifting. He took up aikido and long rides into the Colorado mountains on his Harley. Later, he founded a club of officers who rode motorcycles and raised money for charities.

He mellowed. His police work changed, too. His affinity for sleuthing didn't flag. But no longer the pit bull, he had to develop other skills. Among these was the cultivation of snitches and, with that, a personality that other people wanted to be around. Finding informants was not hard, really. He'd arrest a guy and tell him he could work off the case by setting up others. Eventually that could lead to cash payments to the informant. What was hard was managing the relationship, particularly when the informant went from working off his case to making a salary from it. The best snitches were the ones who stayed in it and would do anything for their handlers. These relationships required finesse and a soothing personality that let an informant know that Chavez liked him and would protect him. It meant going against the book from time to time—accepting Christmas presents, for example, and giving them in return.

Informants became particularly important when, in 1995, Dennis Chavez joined the narcotics unit of the Denver Police Department. He was bequeathed his first long-term informant by a sergeant leaving the unit. The sergeant introduced Chavez to a man immersed in Denver's Mexican heroin underworld.

Chavez never had much connection to Mexico. His father had forbidden Spanish in the house so his children wouldn't speak accented English. But Chavez could see the Denver drug world changing. Mexican American dealer families were going to prison, dying, moving away. Mexicans stepped into the void, and when that happened, Chavez began hearing about the state of Nayarit all the time. The heroin in Denver was all black tar now.

In the late 1980s, he saw guys from Nayarit walking around downtown selling heroin to anyone who'd walk up to them. He arrested many of them, and found Nayarit on a map, but it still didn't mean much. He saw them move into cars and drive it around to customers. Mexicans were arrested at the bus station with backpacks and a kilo or two of the drug. But Chavez still had no sense for how this fit together, if it did at all.

Until one day, when his informant said to him, "You know they're all from the same town, right?"

I met Dennis Chavez at a Mexican restaurant in north Denver, where he told me the story of how he began tracking the Nayarit heroin connection. He said he was intrigued by what the informant told him—that all that he was seeing related to heroin in Denver originated in one small town in Mexico. He prodded the man for more.

What Chavez had been seeing on the streets, the informant said—the dealers, the couriers with backpacks of heroin, the drivers with balloons of heroin—all looks very random and scattered, but it's not. It's all connected.

They're all from a town called Xalisco. Ha-LEES-koh—he said, pronouncing the word. Don't confuse it with a state in Mexico pronounced the same way, but spelled with a *j*. The state of Jalisco is one of Mexico's largest and Guadalajara is its capital. This town, he said, spells its name with an *x*. The informant had never been there, but believed it to be a small place.

All these guys running around Denver selling black tar heroin are from this town of Xalisco, or a few small villages near there, the informant told Chavez. Their success is based on a system they've learned. It's a system for selling heroin retail. Their system is a simple thing, really, and relies on cheap, illegal Mexican labor, just the way any fast-food joint does.

From then on, Chavez sat with the informant, at bars and in a truck outside the man's house, as the informant talked on about these guys from Xalisco and their heroin retail system—which was unlike anything the informant had seen in the drug underworld.

Think of it like a fast-food franchise, the informant said, like a pizza delivery service. Each heroin cell or franchise has an owner in Xalisco, Nayarit, who supplies the cell with heroin. The owner doesn't often come to the United States. He communicates only with the cell manager, who lives in Denver and runs the business for him.

Beneath the cell manager is a telephone operator, the informant said. The operator stays in an apartment all day and takes calls. The calls come from addicts, ordering their dope. Under the operator are several drivers, paid a weekly wage and given housing and food. Their job is to drive the city with their mouths full of little uninflated balloons of black tar heroin, twenty-five or thirty at a time in one mouth. They look like chipmunks. They have a bottle of water at the ready so if police pull them over, they swig the water and swallow the balloons. The balloons remain intact in the body and are eliminated in the driver's waste. Apart from the balloons in their mouths, drivers keep another hundred hidden somewhere in the car.

The operator's phone number is circulated among heroin addicts, who call with their orders. The operator's job, the informant said, is to tell them where to meet the driver: some suburban shopping center parking lot—a McDonald's, a Wendy's, a CVS pharmacy. The operators relay the message to the driver, the informant said.

The driver swings by the parking lot and the addict pulls out to follow him, usually down side streets. Then the driver stops. The addict jumps into the driver's car. There, in broken English and broken Spanish, a cross-cultural heroin deal is accomplished, with the driver spitting out the balloons the addict needs and taking his cash.

Drivers do this all day, the guy said. Business hours—eight A.M. to eight P.M. usually. A cell of drivers at first can quickly gross five thousand dollars a day; within a year, that cell can be clearing fifteen thousand dollars daily.

The system operates on certain principles, the informant said, and the Nayarit traffickers don't violate them. The cells compete with each other, but competing drivers know each other from back home, so they're never violent. They never carry guns. They work hard at blending in. They don't party where they live. They drive sedans that are several years old. None of the workers use the drug. Drivers spend a few months in a city and then the bosses send them home or to a cell in another town. The cells switch cars about as often as they switch drivers. New drivers are coming up all the time, usually farm boys from Xalisco County. The cell owners like young drivers because they're less likely to steal from them; the more experienced a driver becomes, the more likely he knows how to steal from the boss. The informant assumed there were thousands of these kids back in Nayarit aching to come north and drive some U.S. city with their mouths packed with heroin balloons.

To a degree unlike any other narcotics operation, he said, Xalisco cells run like small businesses. The cell owner pays each driver a salary—$1,200 a week was the going rate in Denver at the time. The cell owner holds each driver to exact expenses, demanding receipts for how much each spent for lunch, or for a hooker. Drivers are encouraged to offer special deals to addicts to drum up business: fifteen dollars per balloon or seven for a hundred dollars. A free balloon on Sunday to an addict who buys Monday through Saturday. Selling heroin a tenth of a gram at a time is their one and only, full-time, seven-days-a-week job, and that includes Christmas Day. Heroin addicts need their dope every day.

Cell profits were based on the markup inherent in retail. Their customers were strung-out, desperate junkies who couldn't afford a half a kilo of heroin. Anyone looking for a large amount of heroin was probably a cop aiming for a case that would land the dealer in prison for years. Ask to buy a large quantity of dope, the informant said, and they'll shut down their phones. You'll never hear from them again. That really startled the informant. He knew of no other Mexican trafficking group that preferred to sell tiny quantities.

Moreover, the Xalisco cells never deal with African Americans. They don't sell to black people; nor do they buy from blacks, who they fear will rob them. They sell almost exclusively to whites.

What the informant described, Chavez could see, amounted to a major innovation in the U.S. drug underworld. These innovations had every bit the impact of those in the legitimate business world. When, for example, someone discovered that cocaine cooked with water and baking soda became rock hard, the smokable cocaine known as crack was born. Crack was a more effective delivery mechanism for cocaine—sending it straight to the brain.

The Xalisco traffickers' innovation was literally a delivery mechanism as well. Guys from Xalisco had figured out that what white people—especially middle-class white kids—want most is service, convenience. They didn't want to go to skid row or some seedy dope house to buy their drugs. Now they didn't need to. The guys from Xalisco would deliver it to them.

So the system spread. By the mid-1990s, Chavez's informant counted a dozen major metro areas in the western United States where cells from tiny Xalisco, Nayarit, operated. In Denver by then he could count eight or ten cells, each with three or four drivers, working daily.

As I listened to Chavez, it seemed to me that the guys from Xalisco were fired by the impulse that, in fact, moved so many Mexican immigrants. Most Mexican immigrants spent years in the United States not melting in but imagining instead the day when they would go home for good. This was their American Dream: to return to Mexico better off than they had left it and show everyone back home that that's how it was. They called home and sent money constantly. They were usually far more involved in, say, the digging of a new well in the rancho than in the workings of the school their children attended in the United States. They returned home for the village's annual fiesta and spent money they couldn't afford on barbecues, weddings, and quinceañeras. To that end, as they worked the toughest jobs in America, they assiduously built houses in the rancho back home that stood as monuments to their desire to return for good one day. These houses took a decade to finish. Immigrants added to their houses each time they returned. They invariably extended rebar from the top of the houses' first floors. Rebar was a promise that as soon as he got the money together, the owner was adding a second story. Rods of rebar, standing at attention, became part of the skyline of literally thousands of Mexican immigrant villages and ranchos.

The finished houses of migrant Mexico often had wrought-iron gates, modern plumbing, and marble floors. These towns slowly improved as they emptied of people whose dream was to build their houses, too. Over the years, the towns became dreamlands, as empty as movie sets, where immigrants went briefly to relax at Christmas or during the annual fiesta, and imagine their lives as wealthy retirees back home again one day. The great irony was that work, mortgages, and U.S.-born children kept most migrants from ever returning to Mexico to live permanently in those houses they built with such sacrifice.

But the Xalisco heroin traffickers did it all the time. Their story was about immigration and what moves a poor Mexican to migrate as much as it was a tale of drug trafficking. Those Xalisco traffickers who didn't end up in prison went back to live in those houses. They put down no roots in this country; they spent as little money in America as they could, in fact. Jamaicans, Russians, Italians, even other Mexican traffickers, all bought property and broadcasted their wealth in the United States. The Xalisco traffickers were the only immigrant narcotics mafia Chavez knew of that aimed to just go home, and with nary a shot fired.

Denver became a Xalisco hub as their operations expanded, and probably no cop in America learned more about them than Dennis Chavez. By the time I met him, hundreds of arrests and sweeping federal indictments had not stopped them. They had spread like a virus, quietly and unrecognized by many in law enforcement, who often mistook Xalisco franchises for isolated groups of small-time dealers.

"I call them the Xalisco Boys," Chavez said. "They're nationwide."

HOW'S AMANDA? A STORY OF TRUTH, LIES AND AN AMERICAN ADDICTION

Eli Saslow

The Washington Post, July 23, 2016

She had already made it through one last night alone under the freeway bridge, through the vomiting and shakes of withdrawal, through cravings so intense she'd scraped a bathroom floor searching for leftover traces of heroin. It had now been 12 days since the last time Amanda Wendler used a drug of any kind, her longest stretch in years. "Clear-eyed and sober," read a report from one drug counselor, and so Amanda, 31, had moved back in with her mother to begin the stage of recovery she feared most.

"Is this everything I have?" she asked, standing with her mother in the garage of their two-bedroom condominium, taking inventory of her things. There were a few garbage bags filled with clothes. There was a banged-up dresser she had put into storage before moving into her first abandoned house.

"Where's my good makeup?" Amanda asked.

"Maybe you pawned it with the jewelry," said her mother, Libby Alexander.

"What about all of my shoes?"

"Oh, God. Are you serious?" Libby said. "Do you even know how many pairs of shoes you've lost or sold?"

Amanda lit a cigarette and sat in a plastic chair wedged between the cat food and the recycling bins in the garage, the only place where she was allowed to smoke. This was the ninth time she had managed to go at least a week without using. She had spent a full decade trying and failing to get clean, and a therapist had asked her once to make a list of her triggers for relapse. "Boredom, loneliness, anxiety, regret, shame, seeing how I haven't gone up at all in my life when the drugs aren't there," she had written.

She had no job, no high school diploma, no car and no money beyond what her mother gave her for Mountain Dew and cigarettes. A few days earlier, a dentist had pulled all 28 of her teeth, which had decayed from years of neglect. It had been a week since she'd seen her 9-year-old twin sons, who lived in a nearby suburb with their father, and lately the most frequent text messages coming into her phone were from a dealer hoping to lure her back with free samples: "Got testers," he had just written. "Get at me. They're going fast."

In the addicted America of 2016, there are so many ways to take measure of the pain, longing and despair that are said to be driving a historic opiate epidemic: Another 350 people starting on heroin every day, according to estimates from the Centers for Disease Control and Prevention; another 4,105 emergency-room visits; another 79 people dead. Drug overdoses are now the leading cause of injury-related death in the United States—worse than guns, car crashes or suicides. Heroin abuse has quadrupled in the past decade. Most addicts are introduced to heroin through prescription pain pills, and doctors now write more than 200 million opiate prescriptions each year.

But the fact that matters most for a chronic user is what it takes for just one addict to get clean. The relapse rate for heroin has been reported in various studies to be as high as 97 percent. The average active user dies of an overdose in about 10 years, and Amanda's opiate addiction was going on year 11.

She believed her only chance to stay sober was to take away the possibility of feeling high, so she had decided to pursue one of the newest treatments for heroin. It was a monthly shot of a drug called naltrexone, which blocks the effects of opiates on the brain and makes getting high impossible. But the shot came with dangerous side effects if she still had opiates in her system. Doctors had told her that first she needed to pass a drug test, which required staying clean for at least two weeks, which meant her appointment for the shot was still four days away.

"Soon you can breathe. You can start getting your life back," Libby said. "That's all just days away."

"Days are forever," Amanda said. "Do you even know how hard it is to go for one minute?"

She had been trying to occupy herself with coloring books and cellphone games, anything to keep her hands busy. Now she picked up a hand-held mirror and began reapplying her makeup for the second time that morning, even though she hadn't left the house in a few days. She had worked as a model in high school, but now her gums were swollen and her arms were bruised with needle marks. She tugged down her sleeves and put away the mirror. Shame was a trigger. Regret was a trigger. She grabbed her phone and looked at the dealer's latest text message. She wondered if her mother was still locking her car keys in a safe. She wondered if she could find a ride into Southwest Detroit for one last $10 bag: the euphoria when the drug entered her bloodstream, the full-body tingling that moved in from her hands to her chest, erasing pain, erasing fear, erasing sadness, erasing anxiety and feelings of failure until finally the tingling stopped and the only thing left to feel was blissful numbness, just hours of nothing.

One minute—she could make it one minute. She watched a video on her cellphone. She sorted her nail polish and lit another cigarette. Libby came back into the garage, setting off the burglar alarm she had installed a few years earlier, after Amanda had helped a boyfriend steal $5,000 worth of guitars from Libby's husband.

"I hate that sound," Amanda said. "It brings everything back. It's a trigger."

"I'm sorry," Libby said. "It's our reality."

"Yeah, I know," Amanda said. "And reality's a trigger."

Their condo was tucked away in a small development surrounded by pine trees and occupied mostly by retirees: no loud noises, no solicitors, no unauthorized visitors allowed beyond the guard shack after 8 p.m. Libby was usually in the living room with the TV on mute. Amanda's stepfather was in the study, playing chess online. It was a place so quiet that Amanda could sit in the garage and literally hear the clock tick. Seventy-two hours left until the shot. Seventy-one. Seventy.

"No way I'm going to make it," she said. She was sweating and picking at her nail beds, and when she said that she might know of a few clinics where she could get the shot right away, Libby agreed to drive her.

They drove out of the exurbs, through the suburbs and into the city. Libby tucked her purse against the driver's side door, where Amanda wouldn't be able to reach it. She relocked the doors as she drove and cupped her hands over the car keys, remembering a time when Amanda had grabbed her keys and refused to give them back unless Libby paid her. For most of the last week, she had been requesting time off from her job as a beautician, afraid of what could happen if she left Amanda alone.

Amanda sat in the passenger seat and stared out the window as they came into Southwest Detroit, passing the overgrown lots and decaying houses where she had spent so much of her adult life. Her first opiates had been a prescription for 120 tablets of Vicodin, offered by a doctor to treat a minor snowmobiling injury in high school. The pills chased away that pain and also the anger left over from her parents' divorce, her depression, ADHD and self-doubt, and soon she was failing out of high school and becoming increasingly dependent on pills. Just one or two to make it through another shift at work, a pawnshop where she stood behind the counter and gave addicts their $25 loans. Just two more to pass the time spent alone watching TV while her husband, a truck driver, was traveling. Just three or four to get going with the twins in the morning, to feed them, to sing to them, to feed them again, to sit and play all day in a lonely trailer out in Macomb. Just five when it started to feel like she was suffocating, 24 years old, divorced and already so stuck. Just a dose every five or six hours throughout the day to quiet the noise in her head, so why wasn't she numb? Why was 15 pills each day still not enough? If only there was something cheaper, stronger, and so in 2012 a boyfriend had introduced her to heroin, and she had been injecting it into a vein in her forearm twice a day ever since.

Now they drove past the boarded-up trap houses where she'd met dealers and learned how to buy a $10 bag, until her tolerance grew and she needed five or six bags each day. They continued past the corner where she'd panhandled; and the blocks of abandoned houses where she'd learned how to strip out copper wire and sell it for scrap; and the motel where she'd worked from 4 a.m. to 4 p.m., shooting up before and after each shift, the only housekeeper in a 31-room motel where the rooms were rented in three-hour blocks and the best tips were drugs left behind by customers.

They continued past a decaying apartment tower and then a small Victorian with busted windows. It reminded Amanda of a vacant house where she'd squatted for a while with a dozen other users, a rat-infested place without heat or electricity. She'd tried to make it feel like home, scrubbing the floors with Pine-Sol and hanging a poinsettia wreath on the boarded-up bedroom door. She'd met a girl there who had become like a little sister—a young runaway from Tennessee who was always using too much at once and risking an overdose.

"I want to go find Sammy," Amanda said now, turning to her mother.

"What? Who's that?" Libby said. "What about finding a clinic?"

"This is more important," Amanda said, and so she began to explain how Sammy reminded her of herself, and how they had looked out for each other in the abandoned house. "If she sees I'm doing good, maybe I can convince her to go into rehab."

"This better not be some kind of scheme," Libby said, but she also remembered this side of her daughter from before the addiction—selfless, determined, enterprising, sometimes sneaking extra cash into the loans she handed out to desperate customers at the pawnshop. Maybe helping someone would boost her self-esteem.

"Okay," Libby said. "Tell me where to go."

"Up there," Amanda said, pointing to a two-story building with no windows, no door and trash spilling out from the entryway. Libby pulled over and Amanda jumped out. "How long?" Libby said. "Not long," Amanda told her, and then disappeared into the building. Libby tapped her hand against the steering wheel and stared out the window. She could see a sleeping bag and a needle near the building's entrance. She saw something moving on the second floor. "Come on, come on," she said, until a minute or so later Amanda stepped out.

"She's not in there," Amanda said. "Try that next one," and so Libby pulled up to another decrepit house, where a few people were sitting on the porch and others were pacing outside. One of the men waved to Amanda. "Be back in a minute," she told Libby, and then she hurried out of the car.

Libby checked the clock on her dashboard and thought about all of the other times she had watched Amanda disappear. Once she had stolen Libby's car and run off for a week; another time she had gone out to buy a Mountain Dew and then called a few days later from Florida. "Let Go and Let God," was the advice some other mothers had repeated in Nar-Anon group meetings, but instead Libby had gained weight from stress, developed insomnia and started losing her hair. How many times had she filed a missing persons request? How often had she called the police station, and then the hospitals, and then the morgue to ask again for Jane Doe and to describe Amanda's birthmarks and her "Wild At Heart" tattoo?

"This was so stupid. This was a mistake," she said now, banging her fist against the steering wheel. She checked for her keys. She felt for her wallet. It was all there, but Amanda had been gone for seven minutes. Libby sent her a text message.

"This doesn't look good at all," she wrote.

"I'm about to walk back," Amanda responded.

Libby drove around the block and pulled closer to the house. She saw a man digging into his pockets. She saw other people walking up to that man carrying cash. Twelve minutes Amanda had been gone now. Libby drove around the block again, drumming her hands against the steering wheel, possibilities racing through her head. Was

Amanda using? Where had she gotten the money? What had she done to get it?

She felt again for her wallet. She checked again for her keys.

"This is bullshit," she texted to Amanda, but there was no response.

"Come on," she wrote, and still nothing.

"So over this."

"Come on right now."

She started to circle the block for a third time, and then suddenly there was Amanda, walking down the sidewalk and opening the passenger door.

"What the hell was that?" Libby said.

"What do you mean?"

"Where the hell were you? Where's Sammy?"

"I found her, and we called her parents, but she decided she didn't want help," Amanda said, and to prove it she handed Libby her phone and showed her a seven-minute call made to a number in Tennessee.

"So that was it?" Libby said, staring at her daughter. Her eyes were clear. Her hands were steady. She looked the same as she had when she'd left the car. Another 79 opiate addicts dying every day, but today her daughter wouldn't be one. A 97 percent chance to relapse, but at the moment Amanda looked clean.

"Okay," Libby said. "Let's get the hell out of here."

She had been an admitted opiate addict for 11 years, five months and 14 days, and on almost every one of those days she had promised to quit. She had tried therapy and group counseling, inpatient and outpatient. She'd run up thousands of dollars in credit-card debt to pay for a wellness retreat in the woods, and she'd slept on a cot in the hallway of a Medicaid addiction center. She had tried flushing away her supply; and erasing every number in her phone so she couldn't contact dealers; and waiting again on the long list to get into the city's free medical detox; and showing up at the hospital psych ward to say that she was suicidal. She'd searched for God at 12-step meetings and instead found new dealers. She'd tried methadone and Suboxone, two synthetic opiates used to treat heroin addiction, but instead wound up abusing those synthetics to get high.

She had even tried an earlier version of the naltrexone shot a few years back, and it had helped her stay clean for five months until she relapsed. Maybe this time it would last. Nineteen hours now until her appointment. She lit a cigarette and sat down in the garage. The air was still and the neighborhood was quiet. A group of retired women walked by in visors and spandex, making their usual morning loop.

She had been warned by a doctor that it was normal in the first year of sobriety to feel "bored, flat, depressed, blah, tired, anxious"—a change in brain chemistry that exacerbated so many of the longings that made heroin appealing in the first place. "I'm not seeing what's so great about being clean," Amanda already had told her mother once, and in an effort to feel better she had started thinking back to a time when she was 19, hopeful and sober.

For most of that year she had traveled with her husband as he drove long-haul loads. They had made it to 48 states without ever planning beyond the next week. Maybe they would stay for a while in Texas. Maybe they would move up to the Rocky Mountains in Colorado. All that sky. So many possibilities. And then eventually the job had gone away and the road had led them back to Michigan—to the trailer, to the pawnshop, to the pills, to the twins, to a dissolving marriage and a courtroom dispute for custody, and it felt to Amanda like she'd been fighting to hang on ever since.

The walkers circled past the garage on another loop. Amanda stomped out her cigarette and headed inside.

"Seventeen hours," her mother said, greeting her.

Amanda sat down next to Libby on the couch, where Libby was watching daytime TV and scrolling through Facebook on her phone. Lately, Libby had been spending a few hours each day in a conversation group for addicts' mothers. It had more than 20,000 members, and Libby came to them for support, advice and most of all for a reminder that the addiction overtaking her house was also ongoing for

1.6 million other chronic heroin users and 8 million abusers of prescription drugs.

"I just got the call," read the first post of the day. "My son was alone in his hotel room. I can't breathe."

"OD #6 but he's alive," wrote another mother. "Hospital kept him a couple hours and put him back on the street barefoot in scrubs with a map."

Libby set down her phone. She looked up at the clock. Still almost 17 hours to go. "These days are like dog years," she said. She leaned her head against Amanda's shoulder and kept scrolling through her phone.

"My addict son and his girlfriend were just found passed out at home with their baby crying. When does this nightmare end?"

"Dead in a walmart parking lot . . ."

"On our way to view her remains . . ."

"My daughter was last seen around midnight . . ."

Libby stood up and walked into the kitchen. How many times had she reworked Amanda's obituary in her head: a sarcastic sense of humor, a sharp wit, a patient mother of young twins, a woman so disarming that once, when agents from the Drug Enforcement Administration came to confiscate her prescription pills, she wound up dating one of the agents.

"Do you want a Mountain Dew?" Libby called out to Amanda, but when Libby looked into the living room, Amanda was pacing and talking on her phone.

"What do you mean there's a problem with my appointment?" Amanda was saying now, and Libby started cursing under her breath.

"I really need this to happen tomorrow," Amanda was saying, and Libby balled her fists and knocked them against the kitchen counter.

Amanda hung up and told Libby there had been a miscommunication between her Medicaid insurance and the doctor's office. She said Medicaid needed more time to approve coverage of the shot, and without coverage it would cost more than $1,000. Instead of getting the shot in 16 hours, she would have to wait five more days.

"That's not possible. Call back," Libby said, because she wasn't sure if Amanda was telling the truth or inventing a reason to put it off. Amanda dialed again. Libby stood close so she could listen.

"I'm seriously worried I'm going to relapse," she heard Amanda say.

"Please, I'm trying to do good here," she said. "There's really nothing you can do?"

"Fine. See you next Tuesday," she said, and then she hung up.

Amanda walked out to the garage to light a cigarette and Libby followed. "If this is all a big lie, just tell me now," Libby said.

"Jesus. Can't you ever trust me?" Amanda said. "I want this shot way more than you."

"How are you going to make it five days?" Libby said, her tone softening. "You need a plan."

"You're the one freaking out," Amanda said. "What about you?"

Four days left to go, three days, two, and as the hours crawled by until the appointment Libby decided she needed to leave the house. She asked her husband to keep an eye on Amanda and went to have dinner with two of the women she'd met in the Facebook group for addicts' mothers.

For nearly a decade, Libby had avoided talking to anyone about her daughter's addiction, mostly because Amanda didn't want people to know. "How's Amanda doing?" friends and relatives would ask, at every graduation, wedding and baby shower, and what was Libby supposed to tell them? That while everyone else's life was marching along in neat succession, her daughter was still sleeping late in the basement? That she was giving Amanda an allowance for cigarettes and cleaning up her moldy cereal bowls? "She's just fine," was what Libby had always said, until eventually people stopped asking, which felt even worse. So Libby had started spending more time at home, and then more time on Facebook, where she had connected with a group of local addicts' mothers who had become her closest friends.

"How's Amanda?" asked one of them, Mary Carr, as they sat down at a restaurant and ordered drinks.

"Who knows?" Libby said. "Clean? Using? You'd think by now I could figure it out, but I honestly have no idea."

"They're masters of manipulation," said another mother, Dana.

"My rule at this point is don't believe anything," Mary said. "Otherwise you end up feeling naive. I'm done with that."

Mary said that she had bumped into her son a few nights earlier in their neighborhood. He was 27, and he had been homeless for parts of the last 12 years, but lately he had been living with a girlfriend. He looked good and it was nice to see him, Mary said, but later that night he had called her a dozen times, harassing her and begging for money.

"Do you know how many times he's done that?" Mary said. "So I'm finished. For the first time ever, I actually blocked him on my phone."

"See, that's the part I'm no good at," Libby said. "I can't let go. I always think I can save her."

Libby had only been a mother for three months the first time Amanda got sick. Doctors had told her it was just a stubborn cold, until one night Libby went to check on her infant daughter and found her wheezing in the crib. The baby was turning blue. She couldn't breathe. Libby picked her up, blew air into her mouth and rushed her to the emergency room. They stayed in the neonatal unit for the next two months as doctors ran tests to see what was wrong. Finally Amanda had been diagnosed with a severe kind of asthma, treated and sent home, and for the next year Libby had stood over her crib for a little while each night watching her breathe.

Now she had spent 11 more years trapped in that cycle— expecting her daughter to die, sacrificing her sanity to save her, and doing most of it alone. She rarely talked to her ex-husband about Amanda's addiction; her current husband was patient and supportive, but sometimes, as Amanda's mother, Libby felt that the responsibility was mostly hers. So Libby had gone by herself to heroin awareness rallies at the state capitol. She had forced Amanda to take monthly drug tests and locked her out of the house. She had gone through the medical records Amanda left lying around and cursed out the doctors, pill mills and pharmacists who continued filling her prescriptions. She had tried, most of all, to be loving and patient with her daughter and to remember what so many experts had told her, that addiction was not a choice but a disease, even as Amanda stole her checks and then her credit cards, running up more than $50,000 of debt.

And then, finally, nine years into her daughter's addiction, Libby had come up with a plan to be done with all of it. She had put on a bathing suit beneath her beautician uniform one morning and driven out of the city toward Kensington Lake. She had been a competitive swimmer as a teenager, but now she was out of shape. If she could swim out for a mile or so, she would be too exhausted to make it back. Nobody would see her. Nobody would hear her. She sat at a picnic table and stared out at the water. She watched a family shove their canoe into the lake. She watched two kids throwing rocks. She sat for hours until the sun descended over the water and then she got back in her car and drove home, resolved to seek help. She met with a therapist, confided in her husband, consulted with a bankruptcy lawyer and started talking regularly with the mothers she'd met online.

"If I cut the cord with Amanda, would she recover faster?" Libby asked them now. "Would it be easier on both of us?"

"There's no one right way," Mary said.

"I worry about enabling," Libby said. "But what if I kick her out and she dies in some abandoned house? How do I live with myself?"

Nobody answered. They sat in silence for a moment and Mary reached for Libby's hand. "You're doing everything you can," she said.

"I don't know where to draw the line," Libby said.

"I need your pee," Amanda was saying to her mother now, on the last day, just hours before her appointment for the shot. She had come upstairs with darkened eyes, a runny nose and a confession.

"Excuse me? You need what?" Libby said.

"I need your pee. For the drug test. Otherwise I'm not going to pass and I can't get the shot."

"What are you even saying?" Libby said, and so Amanda began unwinding the lies she had been telling her mother for the past week.

That day she jumped out of the car in Southwest Detroit and then disappeared for 12 minutes? She had been trying to find Sammy, but she had also been trying to buy heroin, and she hadn't been able to find any. The appointment five days earlier that had been postponed at the last minute because of insurance? She had actually canceled it and then made a series of fake phone calls to confuse her mother. That night earlier in the week when she said she was going to sleep over with her twins? She had stayed with them for a while, played with them and taken them to a movie, but then she had found a babysitter and gone to a motel with a friend, where she had gotten high on $50 worth of methadone, a long-acting opiate that was still running through her body now.

It would be at least two weeks before the methadone was out of her system and she could pass a drug test. In two weeks, Amanda said, "I'll probably be using and back out on the street."

Libby started to shake her head and bite her nails, cursing under her breath. "It's always the same with you, isn't it?" she said.

"I need the shot now or I'll never do it," Amanda said. "I can deal with the sudden withdrawal."

"I can't believe you're even asking me to do this," Libby said, but she had already decided that she would help Amanda, even if it required going to extremes. Withdrawal might send Amanda to the emergency room, but it was still safer than going back on heroin.

Libby went into the bathroom and came out carrying a small bottle, and they drove together to a clinic wedged between a liquor store and a pharmacy near the Detroit River. Amanda checked in at the main desk and then waited outside the front door, smoking a cigarette until a nurse came out to get her. "There are a few things we need to go over first," the nurse said, leading her back to a small exam room.

She explained that the shot was an opiate antagonist. She explained that if Amanda still had drugs in her body the shot would cause an immediate and severe reaction: muscle spasms, cold sweats, abdominal cramps, vomiting, diarrhea, fever, impaired breathing.

"When did you last have opiates in your system," the nurse asked.

"I'm not really sure," Amanda said, looking down, picking at her nail beds.

"Has it been over 14 days?"

"I think so."

"No heroin? No Suboxone or methadone?"

Amanda looked across the room at Libby, who stared back at her and nodded. Amanda sat for a minute and thought about telling the truth. Her appointment would be rescheduled. No shot. No muscle spasms or impaired breathing. She would be outside in a few minutes smoking a cigarette, and she could catch a ride to Southwest Detroit and be high within an hour.

"Yes. I'm clean," Amanda said finally. "It's probably been like 20 days."

"We'll need to do a drug test," the nurse said, handing her a small cup for a urine sample. She said the test was mostly for record keeping.

"Right now?" Amanda said. "I don't really have to go."

"That's fine. You can do it after the shot," the nurse said.

The nurse left and returned with a long needle. "I'm not ready. I'm not ready," Amanda said, and then she said to just do it and closed her eyes. The shot was over in 10 seconds. She thanked the nurse, went into the bathroom to leave Libby's urine sample and then hurried outside. She lit a cigarette. She took a deep breath and wiggled her toes and squeezed her arms and rolled her neck and decided she felt . . . fine. "I think I'm actually okay," she told Libby.

"You're great. You're clean," Libby said. She looked at Amanda with relief and then reached over to squeeze her shoulders. "Twenty-eight days without having to worry about this nightmare."

"I can't believe I actually did it," Amanda said.

"Pretty damn brave," Libby said, but now as she looked at her daughter she saw that her face was turning pale and there was sweat on her forehead. Amanda's right leg began to tremble. Her left leg jolted forward and she almost fell to the curb. She dropped her cigarette and crawled into the back seat of the car. "Take me to the emergency room," she said, and Libby started driving.

By the time they arrived at the hospital 10 minutes later, Amanda was in full withdrawal because of the methadone that had still been in her system. She couldn't stand, so Libby got her into a wheelchair. She couldn't steady her hand to fill out the intake forms, so Libby helped do them for her.

"Heroin?" the receptionist asked, because the hospital had already seen 11 of those cases in the last 24 hours.

"Yes," Libby said, and then added: "Recovering."

"Okay. Have a seat and wait to be called," the receptionist said. They sat in the waiting room for five minutes, then 10, then 30. "I need medicine," Amanda began to moan. "Put me to sleep. Give me something." She started to tremble and then convulse. Her arms swung wildly and collided hard against her legs. Her muscles cramped, and she slumped in the wheelchair and slid toward the floor. "Can I get some help over here?" Libby asked, but nobody answered. Amanda threw up in the bucket, in a trash can, and then all over the bathroom floor.

"How much longer until we get seen?" Libby asked, and finally after about half an hour a nurse came out to check on them.

"Sorry, ma'am," she said. "We'll get to you soon."

"But there's no one else here," Libby said, gesturing around the empty waiting room.

"We have to go by priority," the nurse said. "People who are having chest pain come before other things."

"And this isn't a priority?" Libby said, pointing to Amanda, who now was crying and saying that she needed a sedative, that she wanted to be knocked out. She had vomit caked in her hair and welts rising on her legs in the places where she'd been hitting herself.

"She'll make it," the nurse said, looking down at Amanda. "We see a lot of addicts in withdrawal."

"She needs help," Libby said, her voice rising. "It's too much. Can't you see that?"

The nurse walked away and then a few minutes later a doctor

came out into the waiting room. He grabbed Amanda's wheelchair and started rolling her back into triage. He told Amanda the hospital would take good care of her. He said she would be out of withdrawal and feeling better within three or four days. "Congratulations on Day One," he said, but Amanda didn't seem to hear him. Every nerve in her body was on fire. She was sick. She was clean. She was scared. She was feeling all of it now, so many sensations rushing in at once. "Please," she said, reaching up for the doctor's arm, tugging at it. "Make me feel nothing."

DRUG FIRMS POURED 780M PAINKILLERS INTO WV AMID RISE OF OVERDOSES

Eric Eyre

Charleston Gazette-Mail, December 17, 2016

Follow the pills and you'll find the overdose deaths.
The trail of painkillers leads to West Virginia's southern coalfields, to places like Kermit, population 392. There, out-of-state drug companies shipped nearly 9 million highly addictive—and potentially lethal—hydrocodone pills over two years to a single pharmacy in the Mingo County town.

Rural and poor, Mingo County has the fourth-highest prescription opioid death rate of any county in the United States.

The trail also weaves through Wyoming County, where shipments of OxyContin have doubled, and the county's overdose death rate leads the nation. One mom-and-pop pharmacy in Oceana received 600 times as many oxycodone pills as the Rite Aid drugstore just eight blocks away.

In six years, drug wholesalers showered the state with 780 million hydrocodone and oxycodone pills, while 1,728 West Virginians fatally overdosed on those two painkillers, a Sunday Gazette-Mail investigation found.

The unfettered shipments amount to 433 pain pills for every man, woman and child in West Virginia.

"These numbers will shake even the most cynical observer," said former Delegate Don Perdue, D-Wayne, a retired pharmacist who finished his term earlier this month. "Distributors have fed their greed on human frailties and to criminal effect. There is no excuse and should be no forgiveness."

The Gazette-Mail obtained previously confidential drug shipping sales records sent by the U.S. Drug Enforcement Administration to West Virginia Attorney General Patrick Morrisey's office. The records disclose the number of pills sold to every pharmacy in the state and the drug companies' shipments to all 55 counties in West Virginia between 2007 and 2012.

The wholesalers and their lawyers fought to keep the sales numbers secret in previous court actions brought by the newspaper.

The state's southern counties have been ravaged by a disproportionate number of pain pills and fatal drug overdoses, records show.

The region includes the top four counties—Wyoming, McDowell, Boone and Mingo—for fatal overdoses caused by pain pills in the U.S., according to CDC data analyzed by the Gazette-Mail.

Another two Southern West Virginia counties—Mercer and Raleigh—rank in the top 10. And Logan, Lincoln, Fayette and Monroe fall among the top 20 counties for fatal overdoses involving prescription opioids.

While the death toll climbed, drug wholesalers continued to ship massive quantities of pain pills.

Mingo, Logan and Boone counties received the most doses of hydrocodone—sold under brand names such as Lortab, Vicodin and Norco—on a per-person basis in West Virginia. Wyoming and Raleigh counties scooped up OxyContin pills by the tens of millions.

The nation's three largest prescription drug wholesalers— McKesson Corp., Cardinal Health and AmerisourceBergen Drug Co.—supplied more than half of all pain pills statewide.

For more than a decade, the same distributors disregarded rules to report suspicious orders for controlled substances in West Virginia to the state Board of Pharmacy, the Gazette-Mail found. And the board failed to enforce the same regulations that were on the books since 2001, while giving spotless inspection reviews to small-town pharmacies in the southern counties that ordered more pills than could possibly be taken by people who really needed medicine for pain.

As the fatalities mounted—hydrocodone and oxycodone overdose deaths increased 67 percent in West Virginia between 2007 and 2012—the drug shippers' CEOs collected salaries and bonuses in the tens of millions of dollars. Their companies made billions. McKesson has grown into the fifth-largest corporation in America. The drug distributor's CEO was the nation's highest-paid executive in 2012, according to Forbes.

In court cases, the companies have repeatedly denied they played any role in the nation's pain-pill epidemic.

Their rebuttal goes like this: The wholesalers ship painkillers from drug manufacturers to licensed pharmacies. The pharmacies fill prescriptions from licensed doctors. The pills would never get in the hands of addicts and dealers if not for unscrupulous doctors who write illegal prescriptions.

In other words, don't blame the middleman.

"The two roles that interface directly with the patient—the doctors who write the prescriptions and the pharmacists who fill them—are in a better position to identify and prevent the abuse and diversion of potentially addictive controlled substance," McKesson General Counsel John Saia wrote in a recent letter released by the company last week.

But the doctors and pharmacists weren't slowing the influx of pills.

Cardinal Health saw its hydrocodone shipments to Logan County increase six-fold over three years. AmerisourceBergen's oxycodone sales to Greenbrier County soared from 292,000 pills to 1.2 million pills a year. And McKesson saturated Mingo County with more hydrocodone pills in one year—3.3 million—than it supplied over five other consecutive years combined.

Year after year, the drug companies also shipped pain pills in increasingly stronger formulations, DEA data shows. Addicts crave stronger pills over time to maintain the same high.

"It starts with the doctor writing, the pharmacist filling and the wholesaler distributing. They're all three in bed together," said Sam Suppa, a retired Charleston pharmacist who spent 60 years working at retail pharmacies in West Virginia. "The distributors knew what was going on. They just didn't care."

Mary Kathryn Mullins' path of dependence took her to pain clinics that churned out illegal prescriptions by the hundreds, pharmacies that dispensed doses by the millions and, on many occasions, to a Raleigh County doctor who lectured her about the benefits of vitamins but handed her prescriptions for OxyContin.

"She'd get 90 or 120 pills and finish them off in a week," recalled Kay Mullins, Mary Kathryn's mother. "Every month, she'd go to Beckley, they'd take $200 cash, no insurance, and the pills, they'd be gone within a week."

Mary Kathryn Mullins' addiction, her mother said, started after a car crash near her home in Boone County. Her back was hurting. A doctor prescribed OxyContin.

"She got messed up," Kay Mullins said. "They wrote her the pain pills, and she just got hooked."

Kay Mullins has a hard time talking about the 10 years that followed, all the lies her daughter told to cover her addiction, stealing from her brother, the time she shot herself in the stomach in an attempt to end her life.

Mary Kathryn Mullins would go to dozens of doctors for prescriptions. She was a "doctor shopper."

Her mother can't recall most of the doctors by name. She said she believes the doctor who talked to her daughter about vitamins was recently in the news after being charged with prescription fraud. Many rogue pain clinics have been shut down in recent years.

"She'd go to his house in the woods for prescriptions," Kay Mullins said.

There also were stops at multiple pharmacies in Madison, Logan, Beckley and Williamson. Mary Kathryn Mullins always would find a way to get pills. She kept most for herself, but sometimes she sold them to others, her mother said.

"It tore my family up," said Kay Mullins, who works at a flower shop in Madison. "You don't sleep. One time she would be OK, and you think she would come out of it, but then something else happens."

Last December, Mary Kathryn Mullins' hunt for pain pills led her to South Charleston. A doctor prescribed her OxyContin and an anti-anxiety medication, her mother said. A pharmacy in Alum Creek filled it.

Two days later, she stopped breathing in her bed. Her brother, Nick Mullins, a Madison police officer, responded to the 911 call. He tried chest compressions, but he could not revive his sister.

At age 50, Mary Kathryn Mullins was dead.

After the funeral, her mother had one last thing to do. She found an appointment reminder card for Mary Kathryn Mullins' next scheduled visit to the doctor who wrote her final prescription. She dialed the phone number of the doctor's office and spoke to the receptionist.

"I told her my daughter was there Dec. 20," Kay Mullins recalled. "I said, 'Y'all wrote these prescriptions, and she's gone Dec. 23. I just wanted to let you know she won't be back.'"

In the drug distribution industry, they're called the "Big Three"—McKesson, Cardinal Health, AmerisourceBergen—and they bear no resemblance to the mom-and-pop pharmacies that ordered massive quantities of the drugs the wholesalers delivered in West Virginia.

The Big Three wholesalers together are nearly as large as Wal-Mart, with total revenues of more than $400 billion. Their revenues account for about 85 percent of the drug distribution market in the U.S.

Between 2007 and 2012—when McKesson, Cardinal Health and AmerisourceBergen collectively shipped 423 million pain pills to West Virginia, according to DEA data analyzed by the Gazette-Mail—the companies earned a combined $17 billion in net income.

Over the past four years, the CEOs of McKesson, Cardinal Health and AmerisourceBergen collectively received salaries and other compensation of more than $450 million.

In 2015, McKesson's CEO collected compensation worth $89 million—more money than what 2,000 West Virginia families combined earned on average.

"What's most remarkable is that the boards of the companies are paying the CEOs as if they were innovators and irreplaceable entrepreneurs, when in fact they are just highly paid middlemen, betting on market consolidation and ever-rising drug prices," said Ken Hall, international secretary-treasurer of the Teamsters union.

Last month, the Teamsters sent a letter to McKesson board members urging them to investigate allegations raised by Morrisey in a lawsuit he filed against the company earlier this year. The complaint alleges McKesson "flooded" West Virginia with pain pills and gave bonuses and commissions to employees based on sales of highly addictive prescription drugs. The Teamsters' pension funds hold a stake in McKesson.

In a letter to the Teamsters released by McKesson last week, the company denied it gave incentives to executives and other personnel for sales of controlled substances.

McKesson added Morrisey's lawsuit assigns blame to drug wholesalers for West Virginia's opioid crisis "without acknowledging the role played by doctors, pharmacists and the regulatory agencies that oversee doctors and pharmacists."

"McKesson's shipments were in response to orders placed by these registered entities," the company's chief lawyer wrote. "Thus, McKesson lawfully shipped controlled substances to registered pharmacies."

A spokesman for AmerisourceBergen suggested health experts and law enforcement authorities would be better able to comment on whether there's a link between pain-pill volumes and overdose deaths.

Cardinal Health said it shipped 3.4 billion doses of medication in West Virginia between 2007 and 2012. So hydrocodone and oxycodone sales made up about 17 percent of the company's shipments.

"All parties including pharmacies, doctors, hospitals, manufacturers, patients and state officials share the responsibility to fight opioid abuse," said Ellen Barry, a spokeswoman for Cardinal Health.

In Southern West Virginia, many of the pharmacies that received the largest shipments of prescription opioids were small, independent drugstores like ones in Raleigh and Wyoming counties that ordered 600,000 to 1.1 million oxycodone pills a year. Or they were locally owned pharmacies in Mingo and Logan counties, where wholesalers distributed 1.4 million to 4.7 million hydrocodone pills annually.

By contrast, the Wal-Mart at Charleston's Southridge Centre, one of the retail giant's busiest stores in West Virginia, was shipped about 5,000 oxycodone and 9,500 hydrocodone pills each year.

At the height of pill shipments to West Virginia, there were other warning signs the prescription opioid epidemic was growing.

Drug wholesalers were shipping a declining number of oxycodone pills in 5 milligram doses—the drug's lowest and most common strength—and more of the painkillers in stronger formulations.

A DEA agent warned Morrisey's aides about the disturbing trend in January 2015, according to an email released by the attorney general in response to a Freedom of Information Act request from the Gazette-Mail.

Between 2007 and 2012, the number of 30-milligram Oxy-Contin tablets increased six-fold, the supply of 15-milligram pills tripled and 10-milligram oxycodone nearly doubled, the DEA records sent to Morrisey's office show.

In the email to Morrisey, DEA agent Kyle Wright said the higher-strength oxycodone pills were commonly abused.

The DEA agent sent Morrisey's office a separate email about hydrocodone shipments to the state. West Virginia pharmacies were mostly buying 10-milligram hydrocodone tablets—the most potent dosage at the time.

Once hooked on painkillers, addicts typically demand higher and higher doses.

Chelsea Carter, a recovering 30-year-old addict who now works as a therapist at a drug treatment center in Logan County, remembers crushing, snorting and injecting OxyContin—always wanting the strongest pills she could get her hands on. She once shot up with eight to 10 doses of oxycodone, passed out and woke up with the needle still stuck in her arm.

"You're turned on to this potent substance, and your tolerance grows," said Carter, who quit using pills in 2008, the day she went to jail after taking part in a theft ring that sold stolen goods for painkillers.

"When they handcuff you, and you walk through the doors, and you're in an orange jumpsuit and they slam the doors behind you, that's when you wonder, 'is two to 20 years worth it for one Oxy-Contin?'" Carter said. "That's when I hit my knees and prayed, 'Lord, if you ever bring me out of this, I'll never touch another drug again.'"

The addicted come to see Carter at the clinic just off Main Street in downtown Logan. They want to get off pain pills or heroin—a street drug causing more and more overdose deaths in West Virginia every year.

They talk to Carter, eight to 10 of them a day. They've lost children, parents, grandparents. They've lost homes. They're tired of living that way.

Carter listens and tells them her story, how every day she wakes up and makes a decision not to use pills.

"I've buried a lot of friends from drug addiction," Carter said. "I don't want to bury another one."

Her trail follows the direction of hope.

WHEN A DRUG EPIDEMIC'S VICTIMS ARE WHITE: HOW RACIAL BIAS AND SEGREGATION MOLDED A GENTLER RESPONSE TO THE OPIOID CRISIS

German Lopez

Vox, April 4, 2017

When New Jersey Gov. Chris Christie discusses his compassionate approach to the ongoing opioid epidemic, he frequently brings up a close friend from law school. He describes this friend as perfect—incredibly smart, with a successful law practice, with a beautiful and brilliant wife and kids, and both good looking *and* athletic. "So we loved him, but we hated him," Christie joked at a 2015 town hall. "Because the guy had everything, right?"

This friend, however, had a drug problem. Starting with a back injury from running, he was prescribed opioid painkillers. That initial prescription eventually grew into a full-blown addiction. And despite Christie's and others' attempts to help, the addiction consumed his friend, whom Christie has kept anonymous to protect the family from media attention. Over the next 10 years, despite some stints in rehab, his friend lost his wife, his home, his money, the ability to see his girls, his law practice, and even his driver's license. Then, he overdosed and died at 52 years old.

"By every measure that we define success in this country, this guy had it," Christie said. "He's a drug addict. And he couldn't get help. And he's dead." He added, "When I sat there as the governor of New Jersey at his funeral, and looked across the pew at his three daughters sobbing 'cause their dad is gone, there but for the grace of God go I. It can happen to anyone. And so we need to start treating people in this country, not jailing them. We need to give them the tools they need to recover, because every life is precious."

This is the kind of story that not just Christie but countless lawmakers across the US have told in reaction to the opioid epidemic: how a close experience with a personal friend or family member drove them to understand drug addiction and the opioid crisis in a much more compassionate way—one that emphasizes treating drug misuse as a public health issue.

Similarly, President Donald Trump, who appointed Christie to a commission studying the opioid epidemic, often brings up the alcohol addiction that consumed and killed his brother. Businesswoman Carly Fiorina, who briefly ran for president in 2016, also mentioned her daughter's death due to drugs on the campaign trail. Former Florida Gov. Jeb Bush wrote an article on his daughter's drug struggles on Medium. And that doesn't even begin to get into the many, many state lawmakers who have shared similar stories about husbands, wives, sons, daughters, friends, and coworkers who struggled with addiction.

This, they all say, has led them to believe in the need for better, comprehensive drug treatment.

These stories show how lived experiences and personal relationships can influence serious policy discussions. After all, politicians bring up the people in their lives who they saw needlessly suffer and die due to drugs for a specific purpose: to call for an approach to addiction focused on public health over criminal justice.

But in this way, these stories also expose the impact of another issue that may not seem related at first: race.

Even after decades of progress on racial issues, America remains a very segregated country. On a day to day basis, most Americans closely interact only with people of the same race. And that impacts our politics and policies.

Consider the opioid epidemic, which contributed to the record 52,000 drug overdose deaths reported in 2015. Because the crisis has disproportionately affected white Americans, white lawmakers—who make up a disproportionate amount of all levels of government—are more likely to come into contact with people afflicted by the opioid epidemic than, say, the disproportionately black drug users who suffered during the crack cocaine epidemic of the 1980s and '90s. And that means a lawmaker is perhaps more likely to have the kind of interaction that Christie, Trump, Bush, and Fiorina described—one that might lead them to support more compassionate drug policies—in the current crisis than the ones of old.

Is it any wonder, then, that the crack epidemic led to an incredibly punitive "tough on crime" crackdown focused on harsher prison sentences and police tactics, while the current opioid crisis has led to more compassionate rhetoric and calls for legislation, including a measure Congress passed last year, to focus on treatment instead of incarceration? (Although some states have passed "tough on crime" laws in response to the opioid epidemic.)

Ithaca, New York, Mayor Svante Myrick, who's black, told me this has led to resentment in much of the black community in his predominantly white town. "It's very real," he acknowledged. The typical response from his black constituents, he said, goes something like this: "Oh, when it was happening in my neighborhood it was 'lock 'em up.' Now that it's happening in the [largely white, wealthy] Heights, the answer is to use my tax dollars to fund treatment centers. Well, my son could have used a treatment center in 1989, and he didn't get one."

Still, Myrick added, "I'm as angry about this as anybody. But just because these are now white kids dying doesn't mean we shouldn't care, because these are still kids dying."

Stories like Christie's, Trump's, Fiorina's, and Bush's show one of the many ways we got to this point, where a political response can vary largely based on a victim's race. They demonstrate that it's not just personal racism that can lead to racially disparate politics and even policies, but structural factors like segregation as well.

Segregation Blinds Us to Others' Experiences, Robbing Us of Empathy

Rachel Godsil, co-founder and director of research at the Perception Institute, said that the empirical literature shows this to be the case: People are more likely to associate with and relate to people in their own racial group. And they're more likely to run into people in their own racial group in their day-to-day lives, over time building a personal connection with them. As a result, they're more likely to feel compassion and empathy for people in their own group and community who stumble and suffer—and demand policy solutions to ease that suffering.

"Not seeing people in casual contexts—like in your neighborhood and your place of worship and your school—it just completely changes the nature of the dynamic that you experience," Godsil said. "And people [of other races] seem very othered."

Godsil pointed to a 2007 study, which she did not take part in, that looked at the aftermath of Hurricane Katrina in 2005. In that study, researchers found that people tended to believe that victims in racial outgroups suffered fewer "uniquely human" emotions like anguish, mourning, and remorse than victims in racial ingroups. And, in the aftermath of a natural disaster, that perception of fewer "uniquely human" emotions led participants to be less willing to help victims in racial outgroups.

In short, people showed more empathy to victims of the same race than they did to victims of a different race—in a way that affected people's willingness to help after Katrina.

The Katrina research is just one example. A 2009 study found that, when looking at images of others in pain, the parts of people's brains that respond to pain tended to show more activity if the person in the image was of the same race as the participant. Those researchers concluded that their findings "support the view that shared common membership enhances a perceiver's empathic concerns for others." Other studies reached similar conclusions.

Another analogue: same-sex marriage. Before marriage equality became law of the land, surveys showed that Americans who had personal relationships with gay people were more likely to support same-sex marriage rights. Just ask Sen. Rob Portman, a Republican from Ohio, who announced his support for marriage equality in 2013, two years after his son came out as gay.

Really, it seems like common sense: Once someone can relate to the person who's suffering, it becomes much easier to empathize. And, when it comes to politicians, empathy can then translate to more sympathetic policy preferences and outcomes.

With this in mind, let's go back to the opioid epidemic. The data shows that the crisis has hit white communities harder than minority communities, leading to many more overdose deaths among white Americans than their black or Latino peers—making it largely unique in the history of drug epidemics in America.

We also know that the US is very racially segregated. Population data from the University of Virginia Weldon Cooper Center for Public Service, for instance, shows that Washington, DC, can be almost cleanly divided from east to west based on race, with only a bit of overlap in between.

Godsil said she drives this home to people through a personal thought experiment: "Think about who your neighbors are. Think about who you see walking down the street in your neighborhood. Think about who you see when you go to the grocery store—not when you're checking out, but who's buying vegetables next to you. If you're in a religious organization, who you see in your places of worship. Who you see when you take your kids to school. Who you talk to when you're in the playground."

This means that people in white communities are much more likely to encounter a friend or family member struggling with opioid addiction, since the crisis has hit white Americans harder. Since that person struggling with addiction will be of the same race and social network, these communities are going to approach that person with a much more empathetic perspective. And that empathetic perspective can lead to softer policies that emphasize treatment for addiction.

As Michael Botticelli, President Barack Obama's drug czar, put it to the New York Times in 2015, "Because the demographic of people affected are more white, more middle class, these are parents who are empowered. They know how to call a legislator, they know how to get angry with their insurance company, they know how to advocate. They have been so instrumental in changing the conversation."

In contrast, the crack epidemic, because it largely hit black, urban communities, was often framed as a drug problem of "other" people. The problem in much of the public eye, in fact, wasn't that people were suffering from crack addiction, but that people's crack addiction and the black market for crack led to crime and murders that could, in turn, damage white communities. So the focus fell on controlling crime—and that led to more punitive "tough on crime" policies, largely affecting communities of color.

This applies not just to lawmakers, but the media, which is also disproportionately white, and the public, which is majority white, as well. Consider the media coverage of the crack versus opioid epidemics: While the crack epidemic gave rise to headlines like "New Violence Seen in Users of Cocaine" in the New York Times, the opioid epidemic has led to sympathetic headlines like "In Heroin Crisis, White Families Seek Gentler War on Drugs" in the same newspaper 28 years later.

"The media portrayals during the crack epidemic were exceedingly hostile," Godsil said. "When they talked about mothers who were crack addicted, there wasn't 'what kind of treatment can we provide for them?' but 'what kind of criminalization can we impose upon them?' "

The result: different policy discussions for similar kinds of problems.

Race Has Permeated the Opioid Epidemic

Of course, the effect of racial segregation isn't the only way that race has impacted the opioid epidemic.

For one, the reason that white Americans have been dispropor-tionately harmed by the epidemic is, in part, racism.

The epidemic began with doctors prescribing far too many opi-oids, leading the drugs to proliferate not just among patients, but children rummaging through their parents' cabinets, family mem-bers and friends getting the drugs as gifts, and the black market, where patients sold excess pills.

Yet studies show that doctors have generally been more reluctant to prescribe painkillers to minorities, because doctors mistakenly be-lieve that minority patients feel less pain or are more likely to misuse and sell the drugs. In a perverse way, this shielded minority patients from the tsunami of opioid painkiller prescriptions that got white Americans addicted to opioids, including heroin, and led to a wave of deadly overdoses.

More explicit kinds of racism probably affected the policy re-sponse as well. Studies show, for example, that Americans in general are more likely to associate black people with violence and criminal-ity. There is really no end to this kind of research—from a 2014 study that found people were more likely to view black children as less in-nocent to a 2017 series of studies that found white people are more likely to view their black peers as larger and more threatening.

Considering this research, it's sadly not surprising that when Americans saw a drug crisis that disproportionately affected black folks in the crack epidemic, they were more likely to demand "tough on crime" policies—especially given the higher crime rates of the era. And it's sadly not surprising that the more white drug crisis of the opioid epidemic has led to more of the opposite response.

As Anna Lembke, a Stanford psychiatrist and author of *Drug Dealer, MD*, recently put it to me, "This opioid epidemic in particu-lar has penetrated the white middle class, and because of that it's now being conceptualized as a disease instead of a moral failing."

But even beyond personal biases, there are political and socioeco-nomic structures in place that are simply more likely to punish black people. Police, for example, are more likely to be deployed in minor-ity neighborhoods (in part because they have higher crime rates) and resort to dragnet tactics like "stop and frisk" that focus on stopping, interrogating, and locking up as many people as possible. This is just one example, but it shows the kind of mechanisms that are in place to punish, as opposed to help, black people when problems arise in their communities.

Of course, race isn't the only factor in the response to the opioid epidemic. Since the Great Recession, the opioid epidemic coincided with a criminal justice reform effort that largely began before the current drug crisis was well-known in the mainstream—with dozens of states passing laws loosening their prison sentences, particularly for nonviolent drug offenses, to save money on prison spending. So before the public and lawmakers knew much about the opioid epidemic, they were already preparing to draw down the harsh anti-drug policies of the past.

But since the opioid epidemic was the first major drug crisis to hit since those reforms, the disproportionately affected white drug users have been the first to really benefit.

Class likely plays a role as well. The meth epidemic was predominantly linked to white Americans, yet it invited a punitive "tough on crime" response. That may be because it was also linked to *poor* white Americans, while the opioid epidemic is associated more with *middle-class* white Americans. And economic segregation is an issue in the US too, so it likely played a role in the public reaction to the opioid epidemic versus the meth epidemic.

Another issue is that the opioid epidemic is fundamentally rooted in the health care system, giving it a natural starting point to becoming a public health issue. After all, the epidemic began with doctors prescribing too many drugs. That over time led to opioid addiction that evolved from painkillers to other opioids like heroin and fentanyl—and tens of thousands of deadly overdoses annually for the past several years.

"Doctors can no longer ignore addiction," Lembke argued, "when they themselves are complicit in the process."

All of this, along with advocacy and advances in the public understanding of addiction, helped push the country in a direction where addiction, particularly in the frame of the opioid crisis, is viewed more as a disease that needs to be treated than a moral failure that needs to be punished.

But when you put all the evidence together, it's clear that, despite some of the other factors in play, race played a big role in why the crack epidemic produced a crackdown focused almost entirely on "tough on crime" strategies while the current crisis has not to the same extent.

People Need to Get Out of Their Own Bubbles

If there's a lesson in any of this, it's that people, particularly white Americans, need to do more to get out of their racial bubbles and confront their racial biases—or else they'll risk succumbing to more policy demands and solutions that don't account for the suffering of other communities.

There is evidence this can be done. In *The Science of Equality*, Godsil and her co-authors proposed several tactics that seem, based on the research, promising: presenting people with examples that break stereotypes, asking them to think about people of color as individuals rather than as a group, tasking them with taking on first-person perspectives of people of color, and increasing contact between people of different races. All of these interventions appear to reduce racial biases, while interracial contact appears most promising for reducing racial anxiety more broadly.

The key, then, seems to be personal contact that helps build empathy.

"What individuals can do immediately is really begin to be mindful of how they're interacting with people who are in their orbit," Godsil said. "If we're not cognizant of the way we may be seeing people with a kind of filter bias, we might not be treating them with the dignity or respect that we would be if they were in our group—and we might not even know it."

In some cases, activists interested in tearing down discriminatory barriers may be able to take on the work themselves. A 2016 study, for example, found that canvassing people's homes and having a 10-minute, nonconfrontational conversation about transgender rights—in which people's lived experiences were relayed so they could understand how prejudice feels personally—managed to reduce voters' anti-trans attitudes for at least three months. Perhaps a similar model could be adapted to reach people with other kinds of prejudiced views, although this idea needs more study.

At a more systemic level, it also means better integrating communities—encouraging policies that better diversify neighborhoods, schools, and other places where people come together.

Whatever approach is taken, Godsil argues it's necessary—to make lawmakers more sympathetic to constituents outside their social networks, to make the media more likely to cover people of all racial groups in an equally empathetic way, and to make the public more understanding in approaching problems that happen in neighborhoods outside of their own.

Looking back at Christie's comments, there's a clear criticism of the drug policies of old. Christie has explicitly suggested that the old war on drugs has been a failure, previously saying that "what we've seen over the last 30 years is it just hasn't worked." At this point, this isn't a new argument from politicians; it's almost a cliché for them to say that the old drug war has obviously failed—with people from Christie to Botticelli, Obama's former drug czar, to Vermont Sen. Bernie Sanders now making the claim.

Yet based on the evidence on race and policy, these policies may very well have been prevented if people had social networks that crossed racial barriers. That would have let them see the real pain that previous drug crises were inflicting on black Americans, just like the current drug crisis is inflicting so much pain on white Americans. And that may have led them to demand drug treatment instead of prison time, just like Christie, Botticelli, and Sanders do today.

To put it another way: It is good that politicians are taking a more compassionate view toward the opioid crisis. But if we want to avoid the crueler policies from popping up again during future crises, the research suggests that tearing down racial boundaries will need to be a part of the solution. Otherwise, history may just repeat itself when a problem inevitably hits a neighborhood that we consider different from our own.

AMERICAN CARNAGE

Christopher Caldwell

First Things, April 2017

"We should all be dead," said Jonathan Goyer one bright morning in January as he looked across a room filled with dozens of his coworkers and clients. The Anchor Recovery Community Center, which Goyer helps run, occupies the shell of an office building in Pawtucket, Rhode Island. Founded seven years ago, Anchor specializes in "peer-to-peer" counseling for drug addicts. With state help and private grants, Anchor throws everything but the kitchen sink at addiction. It hosts Narcotics Anonymous meetings, cognitive behavioral therapy sessions, art workshops, and personal counseling. It runs a telephone hotline and a hospital outreach program. It has an employment center for connecting newly drug-free people to sympathetic hirers, and banks of computers for those who lack them. And all the people who work here have been in the very pit of addiction—shoplifting to pay for a morning dose, selling their bodies, or dragging out their adult lives in prison. Some have been taken to emergency rooms and "hit" with powerful anti-overdose drugs to bring them back from respiratory failure.

That is how it was with Goyer. His father died of an overdose at forty-one, in 2004. His twenty-nine-year-old brother OD'd and died in 2009. When he was shooting heroin he slept on the floor of a public garage. He would pick up used hypodermic needles if they were new enough that the volume gauges inked on the outside hadn't been rubbed off with use. He OD'd several times before getting clean in

2013. Now he visits people after overdoses and tells them, "I was right where you're at."

There have always been drug addicts in need of help, but the scale of the present wave of heroin and opioid abuse is unprecedented. Fifty-two thousand Americans died of overdoses in 2015—about four times as many as died from gun homicides and half again as many as died in car accidents. Pawtucket is a small place, and yet 5,400 addicts are members at Anchor. Six hundred visit every day. Rhode Island is a small place, too. It has just over a million people. One Brown University epidemiologist estimates that 20,000 of them are opioid addicts—2 percent of the population.

Salisbury, Massachusetts (pop. 8,000), was founded in 1638, and the opium crisis is the worst thing that has ever happened to it. The town lost one young person in the decade-long Vietnam War. It has lost fifteen to heroin in the last two years. Last summer, Huntington, West Virginia (pop. 49,000), saw twenty-eight overdoses in four hours. Episodes like these played a role in the *decline* in U.S. life expectancy in 2015. The death toll far eclipses those of all previous drug crises.

And yet, after five decades of alarm over threats that were small by comparison, politicians and the media have offered only a muted response. A willingness at least to talk about opioid deaths (among other taboo subjects) surely helped Donald Trump win last November's election. In his inaugural address, President Trump referred to the drug epidemic (among other problems) as "carnage." Those who call the word an irresponsible exaggeration are wrong.

Jazz musicians knew what heroin was in the 1950s. Other Americans needed to have it explained to them. Even in the 1960s and 1970s, with bourgeois norms and drug enforcement weakening, heroin lost none of its terrifying underworld associations. People weren't shooting it at Woodstock. Today, with much of the discourse on drug addiction controlled by medical bureaucrats, it is common to speak of addiction as an "equal-opportunity disease" that can "strike anyone." While this may be true on the pharmacological level, it was until quite recently a sociological falsehood. In fact, most of the country had powerful moral, social, cultural, and legal immunities against heroin and opiate addiction. For 99 percent of the population, it was an adventure that had to be sought out. That has now changed.

America had built up these immunities through hard experience. At the turn of the nineteenth century, scientists isolated morphine, the active ingredient in opium, and in the 1850s the hypodermic needle was invented. They seemed a godsend in Civil War field hospitals, but many soldiers came home addicted. Zealous doctors prescribed opiates to upper-middle-class women for everything from menstrual cramps to "hysteria." The "acetylization" of morphine led to the development of heroin. Bayer began marketing it as a cough suppressant in 1898, which made matters worse. The tally of wrecked middle-class families and lives was already high by the time Congress passed the Harrison Narcotics Tax Act in 1914, threatening jail for doctors who prescribed opiates to addicts. Americans had had it with heroin. It took almost a century before drug companies could talk them back into using drugs like it.

If you take too much heroin, your breathing slows until you die. Unfortunately, the drug sets an addictive trap that is sinister and subtle. It provides a euphoria—a feeling of contentment, simplification, and release—which users swear has no equal. Users quickly develop a tolerance, requiring higher and higher amounts to get the same effect. The dosage required to attain the feeling the user originally experienced rises until it is *higher* than the dosage that will kill him. An addict can get more or less "straight," but approaching the euphoria he longs for requires walking up to the gates of death. If a heroin addict sees on the news that a user or two has died from an overly strong batch of heroin in some housing project somewhere, his first thought is, "Where *is* that? That's the stuff I want."

Tolerance ebbs as fast as it rises. The most dangerous day for a junkie is not the day he gets arrested, although the withdrawal symptoms—should he not receive medical treatment—are painful and embarrassing, and no picnic for his cellmate, either. But withdrawals are not generally life-threatening, as they are for a hardened alcoholic. The dangerous day comes when the addict is released, for the dosage he had taken comfortably until his arrest two weeks ago may now be enough to kill him.

The best way for a society to avoid the dangers of addictive and dangerous drugs is to severely restrict access to them. That is why, in the twentieth century, powerful opiates and opioids (an opioid is a synthetic drug that mimics opium) were largely taboo—confined to patients with serious cancers, and often to end-of-life care. But two decades ago, a combination of libertarian attitudes about drugs and a massive corporate marketing effort combined to instruct millions of vulnerable people about the blessed relief opioids could bring, if only mulish oldsters in the medical profession could get over their hangups and be convinced to prescribe them. One of the rhetorical tactics is now familiar from debates about Islam and terrorism: Industry advocates accused doctors reluctant to prescribe addictive medicines of suffering from "opiophobia."

In 1996, Purdue Pharmaceuticals brought to market OxyContin, an "extended release" version of the opioid oxycodone. (The "-contin" suffix comes from "continuous.") The time-release formula meant companies could pack lots of oxycodone into one pill, with less risk of abuse, or so scientists claimed. Purdue did not reckon with the ingenuity of addicts, who by smashing or chewing or dissolving the pills could release the whole narcotic load at once. That is the charitable account of what happened. In 2007, three of Purdue's executives pled guilty to felony misbranding at the time of the release of OxyContin, and the company paid $600 million in fines. In 2010, Purdue brought out a reformulated OxyContin that was harder to tamper with. Most of Purdue's revenues still come from OxyContin. In 2015, the Sackler family, the company's sole owners, suddenly appeared at number sixteen on *Forbes* magazine's list of America's richest families.

Today's opioid epidemic is, in part, an unintended consequence of the Reagan era. America in the 1980s and 1990s was guided by a coalition of profit-seeking corporations and concerned traditional communities, both of which had felt oppressed by a high-handed government. But whereas Reaganism gave real power to corporations, it gave only rhetorical power to communities. Eventually, when the interests of corporations and communities clashed, the former were in a position to wipe the latter out. The politics of the 1980s wound up enlisting the American middle class in the project of its own dispossession.

OxyContin was only the most commercially successful of many new opioids. At the time, the whole pharmaceutical industry was engaged in a lobbying and public relations effort to restore opioids to the average middle-class family's pharmacopeia, where they had not been found since before World War I. The American Pain Foundation, which presented itself as an advocate for patients suffering chronic conditions, was revealed by the *Washington Post* in 2011 to have received 90 percent of its funding from medical companies.

"Pain centers" were endowed. "Chronic pain" became a condition, not just a symptom. The American Pain Society led an advertising campaign calling pain the "fifth vital sign" (after pulse, respiration, blood pressure, and temperature). Certain doctors, notoriously the anesthesiologist Russell Portenoy of the Beth Israel Medical Center, called for more aggressive pain treatment. "We had to destigmatize these drugs," he later told the *Wall Street Journal*. A whole generation of doctors was schooled in the new understanding of pain. Patients threatened malpractice suits against doctors who did *not* prescribe pain medications liberally, and gave them bad marks on the "patient satisfaction" surveys that, in some insurance programs, determine doctor compensation. Today, more than a third of Americans are prescribed painkillers every year.

Very few of them go on to a full-blown addiction. The calamity of the 1990s opioid revolution is not so much that it turned real pain patients into junkies—although that did happen. The calamity is that a broad regulatory and cultural shift released a massive quantity of addictive drugs into the public at large. Once widely available, the supply "found" people susceptible to addiction. A suburban teenager with a lot of curiosity might discover that Grandpa, who just had his knee replaced, kept a bottle of hydrocodone on the bedside table. A construction boss might hand out Vicodin at the beginning of the workday, whether as a remedy for back pain or a perquisite of the job. Pills are dosable—and they don't require you to use needles and run the risk of getting AIDS. So a person who would never have become a heroin addict in the old days of the opioid taboo could now become the equivalent of one, in a more antiseptic way.

But a shocking number of people wound up with a classic heroin problem anyway. Relaxed taboos and ready supply created a much wider appetite for opioids. Once that happened, heroin turned out to be very competitively priced. Not only that, it is harder to crack down on heavily armed drug gangs that sell it than on the unscrupulous doctors who turned their practices into "pill mills." Addicts in Maine complain about the rising price of black-market pharmaceutical pills: They have risen far above the dollar-a-milligram that used to constitute a kind of "par" in the drug market. An Oxy 30 will now run you forty-five bucks. But you can shoot heroin when the pills run out, and it will save you money. A lot of money. Heroin started pouring into the eastern United States a decade ago, even before the price of pills began to climb. Since then, its price has fallen further, its purity has risen—and, lately, the number of heroin deaths is rising sharply everywhere. That is because, when we say heroin, we increasingly mean fentanyl.

Fentanyl is an opioid invented in 1959. Its primary use is in transdermal patches given to people for end-of-life care. If you steal a bunch of these, you can make good money with them on the street. Addicts like to suck on them—an extremely dangerous way to get a high. Fentanyl in its usual form is about fifty times as strong as street heroin. But there are many different kinds of fentanyl, so the wallop it packs is not just strong but unpredictable. There is butyrfentanyl, which is about a quarter the strength of ordinary fentanyl. There is acetylfentanyl, which is also somewhat weaker. There is carfentanil, which is 10,000 times as strong as morphine. It is usually used as an animal tranquilizer, although Russian soldiers used an aerosol version to knock out Chechen hostage-takers before their raid on a Moscow theater in 2002. A Chinese laboratory makes its own fentanyl-based animal tranquilizer, W-18, which finds its way into Maine through Canada.

China manufactures a good deal of the fentanyl that comes to the U.S., one of those unanticipated consequences of globalization. The dealers responsible for cutting it by a factor of fifty are unlikely to be trained pharmacists. The cutting lab may consist of one teenager flown up from the Dominican Republic alone in a room with a Cuisinart and a box of starch or paracetamol. It takes considerable skill to distribute the chemicals evenly throughout a package of drugs. Since a shot of heroin involves only the tiniest little pinch of the substance, you might tap into a part of the baggie that is all cutting agent, no drug—in which case you won't get high. On the other hand, you could get a fentanyl-intensive pinch—in which case you will be found dead soon thereafter with the needle still sticking out of your arm. This is why fentanyl-linked deaths are, in some states, *multiplying* year on year. The federal CDC has lagged in reporting in recent years, but we can get a hint of the nationwide toll by looking at fentanyl deaths state by state. In Maryland, the first six months of 2015 saw 121 fentanyl deaths. In the first six months of 2016, the figure rose to 446.

Sometimes arrested or hospitalized users are surprised to find that what they thought was heroin was actually fentanyl. But there are addicts who swear they can tell what's in the barrel of their needles. One in Rhode Island, whom we'll call Gilberto, says heroin has a pleasant caramel brown tint, like the last sip of Coca-Cola in a glass. Fentanyl is clear. And many addicts claim they can recognize the high. "Fentanyl just hits you. Hard," Gilberto says. "But it's got no legs on it. It lasts about two hours. Heroin will hold you." This makes fentanyl a distinctly inconvenient drug, but many addicts prefer it. All dealers, at least around Rhode Island, describe their heroin as "the fire," in the same way all chefs describe their ribs as so tender they just fall off the bone.

"I knew we were screwed, as a state and as a country," Jonathan

Goyer says, "when I had a conversation with a kid who was going through withdrawals." Although he had enough money to get safer drugs, the kid was going to wait through the sweats and the diarrhea and the nausea until his dealer came in at 5 p.m. That would allow him to risk his life on fentanyl.

Those in heroin's grip often say: "There are only two kinds of people—the ones I get money from and the ones I give money to." A man who is dead to his wife and his children may be desperate to make a connection with his dealer. They don't buy much besides heroin—perhaps a plastic cup of someone else's drug-free urine on a day when they need to take a drug test for a hospital or employer. This will set them back twenty or thirty dollars. In addiction, as in more mainstream endeavors, the lords of hedonism are the slaves of money. Gilberto in Rhode Island claims to have put a million dollars into each of his needle-pocked arms, at the rate of three fifty-bag "bricks" of heroin a day.

Dealers are businessmen and behave like businessmen, albeit heavily armed ones. They may "throw something" to a particularly reliable customer—that is, give him enough heroin from time to time to allow him to deal a bit on his own account and stay solvent. An addict who discovers that the 10mg pills he is paying $18 each for in Maine are available for $10 in Boston, a three-hour drive away, may be tempted to sell them to support his own habit. The line between users and pushers blurs, rendering impractical the policy that most people prefer—be merciful to drug users, but come down hard on dealers.

Addicts wake up "sick," which is the word they use for the tremulous, damp, and terrifying experience of withdrawal. They need to "make money," which is their expression for doing something illegal. Some neighborhood bodegas—the addicts know which ones—will pay 50 cents on the dollar for anything stolen from CVS. That is why razor blades, printer cartridges, and other expensive portable items are now kept under lock and key where you shop. Addicts shoplift from Home Depot and drag things from the loading docks. They pull off scams. They will scavenge for thrown-out receipts in trash cans outside an appliance store, enter the store, find the receipted item, and try to return it for cash. On the edge of the White Mountains in Maine, word spread that the policy at Hannaford, the dominant supermarket chain, was not to dispute returns of under $25. For a while, there was a run on the big cans of extra virgin olive oil that sold for $24.99, which were brought to the cash registers every day by a succession of men and women who did not, at first sight, look like connoisseurs of Mediterranean cuisine. Women prostitute themselves on Internet sites. Others go into hospital emergency rooms, claiming a desperately painful toothache that can be fixed only with some opioid. (Because if pain is a "fifth vital sign," it is the only one that requires a patient's own testimony to measure.) This is generally repeated until the pain-sufferer grows familiar enough to the triage nurses to get "red-flagged."

The population of addicts is like the population of deer. It is highest in rustic places with access to urban supplies. Missouri's heroin problem is worst in the rural counties near St. Louis. New Hampshire's is worst in the small cities and towns an hour or so away from the drug markets of Massachusetts: Lawrence, Lowell, and Boston. But the opioid epidemic of the past decade is unusually diverse. Anchor's emergency room clients are 82 percent white, 9 percent Hispanic, and 6 percent black. The state of Rhode Island is 85 percent white, 9 percent Hispanic, and 5 percent black. "I try to target outreach," Goyer says, "but the demographics are too random for that."

Drug addiction used to be a ghetto thing. Now oxycodone has joined shuttered factories and Donald Trump as a symbol of white working-class desperation and fecklessness. The reaction has been unsympathetic. Writes Nadja Popovich in *The Guardian*: "Some point to this change in racial and economic demographics as one reason many politicians have re-evaluated the tough 'war on drugs' rhetoric of the past 30 years."

The implicit accusation is that only now that whites are involved have racist authorities been roused to act. This is false in two ways. First, authorities have *not* been roused to act. Second, when they do, they will have epidemiological, and not just tribal, grounds for doing so. A plague afflicting an entire country, across ethnic groups, is by definition more devastating than a plague afflicting only part of it. A heroin scourge in America's housing projects coincided with a wave of heroin-addicted soldiers brought back from Vietnam, with a cost peaking between 1973 and 1975 at 1.5 overdose deaths per 100,000. The Nixon White House panicked. Curtis Mayfield wrote his soul ballad "Freddie's Dead." The crack epidemic of the mid- to late 1980s was worse, with a death rate reaching almost two per 100,000. George H. W. Bush declared war on drugs. The present opioid epidemic is killing 10.3 people per 100,000, and that is without the fentanyl-impacted statistics from 2016. In some states it is far worse: over thirty per 100,000 in New Hampshire and over forty in West Virginia.

In 2015, the Princeton economists Angus Deaton and Anne Case released a paper showing that the life expectancy of middle-aged white people was falling. Prominent among the causes cited were "the increased availability of opioid prescriptions for pain" and the falling price and rising potency of heroin. Census figures show that Case and Deaton had put the case mildly: Life expectancy was falling for *all* whites. Although they are the only racial group to have experienced a decline in longevity—other races enjoyed steep increases—there are still enough whites in the United States that this meant longevity fell for the country as a whole.

Bill Clinton alluded to the Case-Deaton study often during his wife's presidential campaign. He would say that poor white people are "dying of a broken heart." Heroin has become a symbol of both working-class depravity and ruling-class neglect—an explosive combination in today's political climate.

Maine's politicians have taken the opioid epidemic as seriously as any in the country. Various new laws have capped the maximum daily strength of prescribed opioids and limited prescriptions to seven days. The levels are so low that they have led some doctors to warn that patients will go onto the street to get their dosages topped off. "We were sad," State Representative Phyllis Ginzler said in January, "to have to come between doctor and patient." She felt the deadly stakes of Maine's problem gave her little alternative.

Paul LePage, the state's garrulous governor, has been even more direct. Speaking of drug dealers at a town hall in rural Bridgton in early 2016, he said: "These are guys with the name D-Money, Smoothie, Shifty, these types of guys. They come from Connecticut and New York, they come up here, they sell their heroin, they go back home. Incidentally, half the time they impregnate a young white girl before they leave." This is what the politics of heroin threatens to become nationwide: To break the bureaucratic inertia, one side will go to any rhetorical length, even invoking race. To protect governing norms, the other side will invoke decency, even as the damage mounts. It is what the politics of *everything* is becoming nationwide. From town to town across the country, the correlation of drug overdoses and the Trump vote is high.

The drug problem is already political. It is being reframed by establishment voices as a problem of minority rights and stigmatization. A documentary called *The Anonymous People* casts the country's 20 million addicts as a subculture or "community" who have been denied resources and self-respect. In it, Patrick Kennedy, who was Rhode Island's congressman until 2011 and who was treated for OxyContin addiction in 2006, says: "If we can ever tap those 20 million people in long-term recovery, you've changed this overnight." What's needed is empowerment. Another interviewee says, "I refuse to be ashamed of what I am."

This marks a big change in attitudes. Difficult though recovery from addiction has always been, it has always had this on its side: It is a rigorously truth-focused and euphemism-free endeavor, something increasingly rare in our era of weasel words. The face of addiction a generation ago was that of the working-class or upper-middle-class man, probably long and intimately known to his neighbors, who stood up at an AA meeting in a church basement and bluntly said, "Hi, I'm X, *and I'm an alcoholic.*"

The culture of addiction treatment that prevails today is losing touch with such candor. It is marked by an extraordinary level of political correctness. Several of the addiction professionals inter-viewed for this article sent lists of the proper terminology to use when writing about opioid addiction, and instructions on how to write about it in a caring way. These people are mostly generous, hard-working, and devoted. But their codes are neither scientific nor explanatory; they are political.

The director of a Midwestern state's mental health programs emailed a chart called " 'Watch What You Call Me': The Changing Language of Addiction and Mental Illness," compiled by the Boston University doctor Richard Saltz. It is a document so Orwellian that one's first reaction is to suspect it is a parody, or some kind of "fake news" dreamed up on a cynical website. We are not supposed to say "drug abuse"; use "substance use disorder" instead. To say that an ad-dict's urine sample is "clean" is to use "words that wound"; better to say he had a "negative drug test." "Binge drinking" is out—"heavy alcohol use" is what you should say. Bizarrely, "attempted suicide" is deemed unacceptable; we need to call it an "unsuccessful suicide." These terms are periphrastic and antiscientific. Imprecision is their goal. Some of them (like the concept of a "successful suicide") are downright insane. This habit of euphemism and propaganda is not merely widespread. It is official. In January 2017, less than two weeks before the end of the last presidential administration, drug office head Michael Botticelli issued a memo called "Changing the Language of Addiction," a similarly fussy list of officially approved euphemisms.

Residents of the upper-middle-class town of Marblehead, Mas-sachusetts, were shocked in January when a beautiful twenty-four-year-old woman who had excelled at the local high school gave an interview to the *New York Times* in which she described her heroin addiction. They were perhaps more shocked by her description of the things she had done to get drugs. A week later, the police chief an-nounced that the town had had twenty-six overdoses and four deaths in the past year. One of these, the son of a fireman, died over La-bor Day. At the burial, a friend of the dead man overdosed and was rushed to the hospital. One fireman there said to a mourner that this was not uncommon: Sometimes, at the scene of an overdose, they will find a healthy- and alert-looking companion and bring him along to the hospital too, assuming he might be standing up only because the drug hasn't hit him yet. In communities like this, concerns about "hurtful" words and stigma can seem beside the point.

Former Bush administration drug czar John Walters and two other scholars wrote last fall, "There is another type of 'stigma' afflicting drug users—that their crisis is somehow undeserving of the full resources necessary for their rescue." Walters is talking largely about law enforcement. As he said more recently: "If someone were getting food poisoning from cans of tuna, the whole way we're doing this would be more aggressive."

Which is not the direction we're going. In state after state, voters have chosen to liberalize drug laws regarding marijuana. If you want an example of mass media–induced groupthink, Google the phrase "We cannot arrest our way out of the drug problem" and count the number of politicians who parrot it. It is true that we cannot arrest our way out of a drug problem. But we cannot medicate and counsel our way out of it, either, and that is what we have been trying to do for almost a decade.

Calling addiction a disease usefully describes certain measurable aspects of the problem—particularly tolerance and withdrawal. It fails to capture what is special and dangerous about the way drugs bind with people's minds. Almost every known disease is something people wish to be rid of. Addiction is different. Addicts resist known cures—even to the point of death. If you do not reckon with why addicts go to such lengths to continue suffering, you are unlikely to figure out how to treat them. This turns out to be an intensely personal matter.

Medical treatment plays an obvious role in addressing the heroin epidemic, especially in the efforts to save those who have overdosed or helping addicts manage their addictions. But as an overall approach, it partakes of some of the same fallacies as its supposed opposite, "heartless" incarceration. Both leave out the addict and his drama. Medicalizing the heroin crisis may not stigmatize him, but it belittles him. Moral condemnation is an incomplete response to the addict. But it has its place, because it does the addict the compliment of assuming he has a conscience, a set of thought processes. Those thought processes are what led him into his artificial hell. They are his best shot at finding a way out.

In 1993, Francis F. Seeburger, a professor of philosophy at the University of Denver, wrote a profound book on the thought processes of addicts called *Addiction and Responsibility*. We tend to focus on the damage addiction does. A cliché among empathetic therapists, eager to describe addiction as a standard-issue disease, is that "no one ever decides to become an addict." But that is not exactly true, Seeburger shows. "Something like an addiction to addiction plays a role in *all* addiction," he writes. "Addiction itself . . . is tempting; it has many attractive features." In an empty world, people have a need to need. Addiction supplies it. "Addiction *involves* the addict. It does not present itself as some externally imposed condition. Instead, it comes toward the addict as the addict's very self." Addiction plays on our strengths, not just our failings. It simplifies things. It relieves us of certain responsibilities. It gives life a meaning. It is a "perversely clever copy of that transcendent peace of God."

The founders of Alcoholics Anonymous thought there was something satanic about addiction. The mightiest sentence in the book of *Alcoholics Anonymous* is this: "Remember that we deal with alcohol—cunning, baffling, powerful!" The addict is, in his own, life-damaged way, rational. He's *too* rational. He is a *dedicated* person—an oblate of sorts, as Seeburger puts it. He has commitments in another, nether world.

That makes addiction a special problem. The addict is unlikely ever to take seriously the counsel of someone who has not heard the call of that netherworld. Why should he? The counsel of such a person will be, measured against what the addict knows about pleasure and pain, uninformed. That is why Twelve Step programs and peer-to-peer counseling, of the sort offered by Goyer and his colleagues, have been an indispensable element in dragging people out of addiction. They have authority. They are, to use the street expression, legit.

The deeper problem, however, is at once metaphysical and practical, and we're going to have a very hard time confronting it. We in the sober world have, for about half a century, been renouncing our allegiance to anything that forbids or commands. Perhaps this is why, as this drug epidemic has spread, our efforts have been so unavailing and we have struggled even to describe it. Addicts, in their own short-circuited, reductive, and destructive way, are armed with a sense of purpose. We aren't. It is not a coincidence that the claims of political correctness have found their way into the culture of addiction treatment just now. This sometimes appears to be the only grounds for compulsion that the non-addicted part of our culture has left.

THE ADDICTS NEXT DOOR

Margaret Talbot

The New Yorker, June 5, 2017

Michael Barrett and Jenna Mulligan, who work as emergency paramedics in Berkeley County, West Virginia, recently got a call that sent them to the youth softball field in a tiny town called Hedgesville. It was the first practice of the season for the girls' Little League team, and dusk was descending. Barrett and Mulligan drove past a clubhouse with a blue-and-yellow sign that read "Home of the Lady Eagles," and stopped near a scrubby set of bleachers, where parents had gathered to watch their daughters bat and field.

Two of the parents were lying on the ground, unconscious, several yards apart. As Barrett later recalled, the couple's thirteen-year-old daughter was sitting behind a chain-link backstop with her teammates, who were hugging and comforting her. The couple's younger children, aged ten and seven, were running back and forth between their parents, screaming, "Wake up! Wake up!" When Barrett and Mulligan knelt down to administer Narcan, a drug that reverses heroin overdoses, some of the other parents got angry. "You know, saying, 'This is bullcrap,'" Barrett told me. "'Why's my kid gotta see this? Just let 'em lay there.'" After a few minutes, the man and woman began to groan as they revived. Adults ushered the younger children away. From the other side of the backstop, the older kids asked Barrett if the parents had overdosed. "I was, like, 'I'm not gonna say.' But the kids aren't stupid. They know people don't just pass out for no reason." During the chaos, someone made a call to Child Protective Services.

At this stage of the American opioid epidemic, many addicts are collapsing in public—in gas stations, in restaurant bathrooms, in the aisles of big-box stores. Brian Costello, a former Army medic who is the director of the Berkeley County Emergency Medical Services, believes that more overdoses are occurring in this way because users figure that somebody will find them before they die. "To people who don't have that addiction, that sounds crazy," he said. "But, from a health-care provider's standpoint, you say to yourself, 'No, this is survival to them.' They're struggling with using but not wanting to die."

A month after the incident, the couple from the softball field, Angel Dawn Holt, who is thirty-five, and her boyfriend, Christopher Schildt, who is thirty-three, were arraigned on felony charges of child neglect. A local newspaper, the Martinsburg *Journal*, ran an article about the charges, noting that the couple's children, who had been "crying when law enforcement arrived," had been "turned over to their grandfather."

West Virginia has the highest overdose death rate in the country, and heroin has flooded into the state's Eastern Panhandle, which includes Hedgesville and the larger town of Martinsburg. Like the vast majority of residents there, nearly all the addicts are white, were born in the area, and have modest incomes. Some locals view them with empathy; others as community embarrassments. Many people in the Panhandle have embraced the idea of addiction as a disease, but a vocal cohort dismisses that view as sentimental claptrap disseminated by urban liberals.

These tensions were evident in the online comments that soon amassed beneath the *Journal* article. A waitress named Sandy wrote, "Omgsh, How sad!! Shouldnt be able to have there kids back! Seems the heroin was more important to them, than watchn there kids have fun play ball, and have there parents proud of them!!" A poster named Valerie wrote, "Stop giving them Narcan! At the tax payers expense." Such dismissals were countered by a reader named Diana: "I'm sure the parents didn't get up that morning and say hey let's scar the kids for life. I'm sure they wished they could sit through the kids practice without having to get high. The only way to understand it is to have lived it. The children need to be in a safe home and the adults need help. They are sick, i know from the outside it looks like a choice but its not. Shaming and judging will not help anyone."

One day, Angel Holt started posting her own comments. "I don't neglect," she wrote. "Had a bad judgment I love my kids and my kids love me there honor roll students my oldest son is about to graduate they play sports and have a ruff over there head that I own and food, and things they just want I messed up give me a chance to prove my self I don't have to prove shit to none of u just my children n they know who I am and who I'm not."

A few weeks later, I spoke to Holt on the phone. "Where it happened was really horrible," she said. "I can't sit here and say different." But, she said, it had been almost impossible to find help for her addiction. On the day of the softball practice, she had ingested a small portion of a package of heroin that she and Schildt had just bought, figuring it wasn't enough to lay her out flat. She had promised her daughter that she'd be at practice and she really wanted to come through. But the heroin had a strange purple tint—it must have been cut with something nasty, she wasn't sure what. She started feeling weird, and passed out. She knew that she shouldn't have touched heroin that was so obviously adulterated. But, she added, "if you're an addict, and if you have the stuff, you do it."

In Berkeley County, which has a population of a hundred and fourteen thousand, when someone under sixty dies, and the cause of death isn't mentioned in the paper, people just assume that it was an overdose. It's becoming the default explanation when an ambulance stops outside a neighbor's house, and the best guess for why someone is sitting in his car on the side of the road in the middle of a sunny afternoon. On January 18th, county officials started using a new app to record overdoses. According to this data, during the next two and a half months emergency medical personnel responded to a hundred and forty-five overdoses, eighteen of which were fatal. This is almost certainly an underestimate, since not all overdoses prompt 911 calls. Last year, the county's annual budget for emergency medication was twenty-seven thousand dollars. Narcan, which costs fifty dollars a dose, consumed two-thirds of that allotment. The medication was administered two hundred and twenty-three times in 2014, and four hundred and three times in 2016.

One Thursday in March, a few weeks before Michael Barrett responded to Angel Holt's overdose, I rode with him in his paramedic vehicle, a specially equipped S.U.V. He had started his day as he often does, with bacon and eggs at the Olde Country Diner, in Martinsburg. Barrett, who is thirty-three, with a russet-colored beard and mustache, works two twenty-four-hour shifts a week, starting at 7 A.M. The diner shares a strip mall with the E.M.T. station, and, if he has to leave on a call before he can finish eating, the servers know to box up his food in a hurry. Barrett's father and his uncles were volunteer firemen in the area, and, growing up, he often accompanied them in the fire truck. As they'd pull people from crumpled cars or burning buildings, he'd say to himself, "Man, they *doing* stuff— they're awesome." When Barrett became a paramedic, in his twenties, he knew that he could make a lot more money "going down the road," as people around here say, referring to Baltimore or Washington, D.C. But he liked it when older colleagues told him, "I used to hold you at the fire department when you were a baby."

Barrett's first overdose call of the day came at 8 A.M., for a twenty-year-old woman. Several family members were present at the home, and while Barrett and his colleagues worked on the young woman, the family members cried and blamed one another, and themselves, for not watching her more closely. The woman was given Narcan, but she was too far gone; she died after arriving at the hospital.

We stopped by a local fire station, where the men and women on duty talked about all the O.D. calls they took each week. Sometimes they knew the person from high school or were related to the person. Barrett said that in such cases you tended "to get more angry at them—you're, like, 'Man, you got a *kid*, what the hell's wrong with you?'"

Barrett sometimes had to return several times in one day to the same house—once, a father, a mother, and a teen-age daughter overdosed on heroin in succession. Such stories seemed like a dark twist on the small-town generational solidarity he so appreciated; as Barrett put it, even if one family member wanted to get clean, it would be next to impossible unless the others did, too. He was used to O.D. calls by now, except for the ones in which kids were present. He once arrived at a home to find a seven-year-old and a five-year-old following the instructions of a 911 operator and performing C.P.R. on their parents. (The parents survived.)

Around three o'clock, the dispatcher reported that a man in Hedgesville was slumped over the steering wheel of a jeep. By the time we got there, the man, who appeared to be in his early thirties, had been helped out of his vehicle and into an ambulance. A skinny young sheriff's deputy on the scene showed us a half-filled syringe: the contents resembled clean sand, which suggested pure heroin. That was a good thing—these days, the narcotic is often cut with synthetic opioids such as fentanyl, which is fifty times as powerful as heroin.

The man had floppy brown hair and a handsome face; he was wearing jeans, work boots, and a black windbreaker. He'd been revived with oxygen—he hadn't needed Narcan—but as he sat in the ambulance his eyes were only partly opened, the pupils constricted to pinpoints. Barrett asked him, "Did you take a half syringe? 'Cause there's half a syringe left." The man looked up briefly and said, "Yeah? I was trying to take it all." He said that he was sorry—he'd been clean for a month. Then he mumbled something about having a headache. "Well, sure you do," another paramedic said. "You weren't breathing there for a while. Your brain didn't have any oxygen."

I looked over and noticed that the man's jeep was still sitting in the middle of a sloping street, doors flung open, as though it had been dropped by a cyclone. A woman surveying the scene, with her arms folded across her chest, introduced herself to me as Ethel. She had been driving behind the man when he lost consciousness. "I just rolled up, saw he was slumped over the wheel," she said. "I knew what it was right away." She beeped her horn, but he didn't move. She called 911 and stayed until the first responders showed up, "in case he started to roll forward, and maybe I could stop traffic—and to make sure he was O.K." I asked if the man's jeep had been running during this time. "Oh, yeah," said Ethel, looking over to check on a young kid in the backseat of her own car. "He just happened to stop with his foot on the brake." Barrett shared some protocol: whenever he came across people passed out in a car, he put the transmission in park and took their keys, in case they abruptly revived. He'd heard of people driving off with E.M.T. personnel halfway inside.

The sky was a dazzling blue; fluffy white clouds scudded overhead. The man took a sobriety test, wobbling across the tidy lawn of a Methodist church. "That guy's still high as a kite," somebody said.

We were driving away from Hedgesville when the third overdose call of the day came, for a twenty-nine-year-old male. Inside a nicely kept house in a modern subdivision, the man was lying unconscious on the bathroom floor, taking intermittent gasps. He was pale, though not yet the blue-tinged gray that people turn when they've been breathing poorly for a while. Opioid overdoses usually kill people by inhibiting respiration: breathing slows and starts to sound labored, then stops altogether. Barrett began preparing a Narcan dose. Generally, the goal was to get people breathing well again, not necessarily to wake them completely. A full dose of Narcan is two milligrams, and in Berkeley County the medics administer 0.4 milligrams at a time, so as not to snatch patients' high away too abruptly: you didn't want them to go into instant withdrawal, feel terribly sick, and become belligerent. Barrett crouched next to the man and started an I.V. A minute later, the man sat up, looking bewildered and resentful. He vomited. Barrett said, "Couple more minutes and you would have died, buddy."

"Thank you," the man said.

"You're welcome—but now you need to go to the hospital."

The man's girlfriend was standing nearby, her hair in a loose bun. She responded calmly to questions: "Yeah, he does heroin"; "Yeah, he just ate." The family dog was snuffling at the front door, and one of the sheriff's deputies asked if he could let it outside. The girlfriend said, "Sure." Brian Costello had told me that family members sometimes seemed unfazed by these E.M.T. visits: "That's the scary part—that it's becoming the norm." The man stood up, and then, swaying in the doorway, vomited a second time.

"We're gonna take him to the hospital," Barrett told the girlfriend. "He could stop breathing again."

As we drove away, Barrett predicted that the man would check himself out of the hospital as soon as he could; most of the O.D. patients he saw refused further treatment. "It's kind of hard to feel good about it," Barrett said of the intervention. "Though he did say, 'Thanks for waking me up.' Well, that's our job. But do you feel like you're really making a difference? Ninety-nine per cent of the time, no." The next week, Barrett's crew was called back to the same house repeatedly. The man overdosed three times; his girlfriend, once.

It was getting dark, and Barrett stopped at a convenience store for a snack—chocolate milk and a beef stick. That evening, he dealt with one more O.D. A young woman had passed out in her car in the parking lot of a 7-Eleven, with her little girl squirming in a car seat. An older woman who happened on the scene had taken the girl, a four-year-old, into the store and bought her some hot chocolate and Skittles. After the young woman received Narcan, Barrett told her that she could have killed her daughter, and she started sobbing. Meanwhile, several guys in the parking lot were becoming agitated. They had given the woman C.P.R., but someone had called 911 and suggested that they had supplied her with the heroin. The men were black and everybody else—the overdosing woman, the older woman, the cops, the ambulance crew—was white. The men were told to remain at the scene while the cops did background checks. Barrett attempted to defuse the tension by saying, "Hey, you guys gave her C.P.R.? Thanks. We really appreciate that." The criminal checks turned up nothing; there was no reason to suspect that the men were anything but Good Samaritans. The cops let the men go, the young woman went to the E.R., and the little girl was retrieved by her father.

Heroin is an alluringly cheap alternative to prescription pain medication. In 1996, Purdue Pharma introduced OxyContin, marketing it as a safer form of opiate—the class of painkillers derived from the poppy plant. (The term "opioids" encompasses synthetic versions of opiates as well.) Opiates such as morphine block pain but also produce a dreamy euphoria, and over time they cause physical cravings. OxyContin was sold in time-release capsules that levelled out the high and, supposedly, diminished the risk of addiction, but people soon discovered that the capsules could be crushed into powder and then injected or snorted. Between 2000 and 2014, the number of overdose deaths in the United States jumped by a hundred and thirty-seven per cent.

Some parts of the country were inundated with opiates. According to the Charleston *Gazette-Mail*, between 2007 and 2012 drug wholesalers shipped to West Virginia seven hundred and eighty million pills of hydrocodone (the generic name for Vicodin) and oxycodone (the generic name for OxyContin). That was enough to give each resident four hundred and thirty-three pills. The state has a disproportionate number of people whose jobs—coal mining, for instance—can result in chronic physical pain. It also has high levels of poverty and joblessness—sources of psychic pain. Mental-health services, meanwhile, are scant, as they are in many rural areas of the country. Chess Yellott, a retired family practitioner in Martinsburg, told me he often saw people self-medicate to mute depression, anxiety, and post-traumatic stress from sexual assault or childhood abuse. "Those things are treatable, and upper-middle-class parents generally get their kids treated," he said. "But, in families with a lot of chaos and money problems, kids don't get help."

In 2010, Purdue introduced a reformulated capsule that is harder to crush or dissolve. The Centers for Disease Control subsequently issued new guidelines stipulating that doctors should not routinely treat chronic pain with opioids, and instead should try approaches such as exercise and behavioral therapy. The number of prescriptions for opioids began to drop.

But when prescription opioids became scarcer their street price went up. Drug cartels sensed an opportunity, and began pouring heroin into rural America. Daniel Ciccarone, a professor at the

U.C.-San Francisco School of Medicine, studies the heroin market. He said of the cartels, "They're multinational, savvy, borderless entities. They worked very hard to move high-quality heroin into places like rural Vermont." They also kept the price low. In West Virginia, many addicts told me, an oxycodone pill now sells for about eighty dollars; a dose of heroin can be bought for about ten.

A recent paper from the National Bureau of Economic Research concludes, "Following the OxyContin reformulation in 2010, abuse of prescription opioid medications and overdose deaths decreased for the first time since 1990. However, this drop coincided with an unprecedented rise in heroin overdoses." According to the Centers for Disease Control, three out of four new heroin users report having first abused opioid pills.

"The Changing Face of Heroin Use in the United States," a 2014 study led by Theodore Cicero, of Washington University in St. Louis, looked at some three thousand heroin addicts in substance-abuse programs. Half of those who began using heroin before 1980 were white; nearly ninety per cent of those who began using in the past decade were white. This demographic shift may be connected to racially-charged prescribing patterns. A 2012 study by a University of Pennsylvania researcher found that black patients were thirty-four per cent less likely than white patients to be prescribed opioids for such chronic conditions as back pain and migraines, and fourteen per cent less likely to receive such prescriptions after surgery or traumatic injury.

But a larger factor, it seems, was the despair of white people in struggling small towns. Judith Feinberg, a professor at West Virginia University who studies drug addiction, described opioids as "the ultimate escape drugs." She told me, "Boredom and a sense of uselessness and inadequacy—these are human failings that lead you to just want to withdraw. On heroin, you curl up in a corner and blank out the world. It's an extremely seductive drug for dead-end towns, because it makes the world's problems go away. Much more so than coke or meth, where you want to run around and *do* things, you get aggressive, razzed and jazzed."

Peter Callahan, a psychotherapist in Martinsburg, said that heroin "is a very tough drug to get off of, because, while it was meant to numb *physical* pain, it numbs emotional pain as well—quickly and intensely." In tight-knit Appalachian towns, heroin has become a social contagion. Nearly everyone I met in Martinsburg had ties to someone—a child, a sibling, a girlfriend, an in-law, an old high-school coach—who has struggled with opioids. As Callahan put it, "If the lady next door is using, and so are other neighbors, and people in your family are, too, the odds are good that you're going to join in."

In 2015, Berkeley County created a new position, recovery-services coördinator, to connect residents with rehab. But there is a chronic shortage of beds in the state for addicts who want help. Kevin Knowles, who was appointed to the job, told me, "If they have private insurance, I can hook them right up. If they're on Medicaid—and ninety-five per cent of the people I work with are—it's going to be a long wait for them. Weeks, months." He said, "The number of beds would have to increase by a factor of three or four to make any impact."

West Virginia has an overdose death rate of 41.5 per hundred thousand people. (New Hampshire has the second-highest rate: 34.3 per hundred thousand.) This year, for the sixth straight year, West Virginia's indigent burial fund, which helps families who can't afford a funeral pay for one, ran out of money. Fred Kitchen, the president of the West Virginia Funeral Directors Association, told me that, in the funeral business, "we know the reason for that was the increase in overdose deaths." He added, "Families take out second mortgages, cash in 401(k)s, and go broke to try and save a son or daughter, who then overdoses and dies." Without the help of the burial fund, funeral directors must either give away caskets, plots, and cremation services—and risk going out of business—or, Kitchen said, look "mothers, fathers, husbands, wives, and children in the eye while they're saying, 'You have nothing to help us?'"

Martinsburg, which has a population of seventeen thousand, is a hilly town filled with brick and clapboard row houses. It was founded in 1778, by Adam Stephen, a Revolutionary War general. The town became a depot for the B. & O. Railroad and grew into an industrial center dominated by woolen mills. Interwoven, established in the eighteen-nineties, was the first electric-powered textile plant in the U.S. The company became the largest men's-sock manufacturer in the world. At its height, it employed three thousand people in Martinsburg, and commissioned sumptuous advertising illustrations of handsome men in snappy socks by the likes of Norman Rockwell. The Interwoven factory whistle could be heard all over town, summoning workers every morning at a quarter to seven. In 1971, when the mill closed, an editorial in the Martinsburg *Journal* mourned the passing of "what was once this community's greatest pride." In 2004, the last woolen mill in town, Royce Hosiery, ceased operations.

It would be simplistic to trace the town's opioid epidemic directly to the erosion of industrial jobs. Nevertheless, many residents I met brought up this history, as part of a larger story of lost purpose that has made the town vulnerable to the opioid onslaught. In 2012, Macy's opened a distribution center in the Martinsburg area, but, Knowles said, the company has found it difficult to hire long-time residents, because so many fail the required drug test. (The void has been filled, only partially, by people from neighboring states.) Knowles wonders if Procter & Gamble, which is opening a manufacturing plant in the area this fall, will have a similar problem.

The Eastern Panhandle is one of the wealthier parts of a poor state. (The most destitute counties depend on coal mining.) Berkeley County is close enough to D.C. and Baltimore that many residents commute for work. Nevertheless, Martinsburg feels isolated. Several people I met there expressed surprise, or sympathy, when I told them that I live in D.C., or politely said that they'd like to visit the capital one of these days. Like every other county in West Virginia, Berkeley County voted for Donald Trump.

Michael Chalmers is the publisher of an Eastern Panhandle newspaper, the *Observer*, which is based in Shepherdstown, a picturesque college town near the Maryland border. Chalmers, who is forty-two, grew up in Martinsburg, and in 2014 he lost his younger brother,

Jason, to an overdose. I asked him why he thought that Martinsburg was struggling so much with drugs. "In my opinion, the desperation in the Panhandle, and places like it, is a *social* vacancy," he said. "People don't feel they have a purpose." There was a "shame element in small-town culture." Many drug addicts, he explained, are "trying to escape the reality that this place doesn't give them anything." He added, "That's really hard to live with—when you look around and you see that seven out of ten of your friends from high school are still here, and nobody makes more than thirty-six thousand a year, and everybody's just bitching about bills and watching these crazy shows on reality TV and not *doing anything.*"

Queen Street, Martinsburg's main thoroughfare, has a bunch of thrift and antique shops, some of them no longer in business, their big, dusty display windows scattered with random items—a gumball machine and a gramophone, a couple of naked mannequins. It's not as if nobody's trying. The Chamber of Commerce hosts events to attract people downtown, and at Christmas there were snowmen painted by school kids. People always seemed to be eating burgers at the Blue White Grill. But as I walked along Queen Street one February afternoon, an older man in a cardigan stopped and asked me, "What in the world are they going to do with all these empty buildings?"

The Interwoven mill, derelict and grand, still dominates the center of town. One corner of it has been turned into a restaurant, but the rest sits empty. Lately, there's been talk of an ambitious renovation. A police officer named Andrew Garcia has a plan, called Martinsburg Renew, which would turn most of the mill into a rehab facility. One chilly, gray day, Todd Funkhouser, who runs the Berkeley County Historical Society, showed me around. "Martinsburg is an industrial town," he said. "That's its identity. But what's the industry now? Maybe it will be drug rehab."

In the past several months, I have returned to Martinsburg many times, and spoken to a number of people struggling with addiction. But in some ways I learned the most about the crisis from residents

who were not themselves drug users, but whose lives had been irrevo-
cably altered by others' addiction. Looking through the microcosm
of one town at a nationwide epidemic, I wanted to know how it had
blown people off course, and how they were responding.

Lori Swadley is a portrait and wedding photographer in Martinsburg. When I came across her website while researching local businesses, I could see she seemed to be in demand all over the area, and
her photographs were lovely: her brides glowed in golden hour light,
her high-school seniors looked polished and confident. But what
caught my attention was a side project she had been pursuing, called
52 Addicts—a series of portraits that called attention to the drug
epidemic in and around Martinsburg. It was clear that Swadley had a
full life: her husband, Jon, worked with her in the photography business, and they had three small children, Juniper, Bastian, and Bodhi.
Her Web site noted that she loved fashion and gardening, and included this message: "I'm happy that you've stumbled upon our little
slice of heaven!" The 52 Addicts series seemed like a surprising project for someone so busy and cheerful to have embarked upon.

We met one day at Mugs & Muffins, a cozy coffee shop on Queen
Street. Swadley is thirty-nine, tall and slender, and she looked elegant
in jeans, a charcoal-colored turtleneck, and knee-high boots. She and
her husband had moved to Martinsburg in 2010, she told me, looking for an affordable place to raise children close to where she had
grown up, in the Shenandoah Valley. Soon after they arrived, they
settled into a subdivision outside town, and Swadley started reading
the Martinsburg *Journal* online. She told me, "I'd see these stories
about addiction—whether it was somebody who'd passed away, and
the family wanted to tell their story, or it was the overdose statistics,
or whatever." Many of the stories were written by the same reporter,
Jenni Vincent. "She was very persistent, and—I don't know what
the word for it is—very *in your face*," Swadley said. "You could tell
she wanted the problem to be known. Because at that time it seemed
like everybody else wanted to hide it. And, to me, that seemed like
the worst thing you could do."

Swadley told me she had thirteen friends who had died of opioid overdoses. I said that seemed like an extraordinarily high number, especially for someone who was not herself a drug user. She agreed, but there it was. All thirteen were young men—Swadley had met most of them when she was in her early twenties, and she had been kind of an overgrown tomboy then, at ease with guys who treated her like a fun sister. She had been photographing a wedding for some mutual friends the first time she heard about one of the guys dying. A group of Swadley's buddies were sitting around a bonfire at the end of the day, when she happened to mention, laughing at the memory, the wacky horror film she and a guy named Jeremy had made together in high school. Somebody said Jeremy had died not long before, from a heroin overdose. Swadley felt like she'd been punched in the gut. She stood up and vomited, and then, driving home, ended up wrecking her car.

At the time, Swadley was hanging out with her old crowd in bars and restaurants every weekend. One by one, the group dwindled. Many of them—"the preppy boys, the hippie boys"—got into heroin eventually, she said. They tried to help one another, but "we were in our twenties—we had no clue." She'd call rehab places on friends' behalf and have to tell them that the price was staggering, and that in any case it might be six months before they could be admitted. As the overdoses piled up, she was appalled to realize that sometimes she had trouble keeping track of which of her friends were dead.

The funerals had a peculiar aspect. "The parents didn't want anyone to know how it had happened, and they tried to keep the friends out," she said. At the services for one of them—a sweet, goofy guy with shaggy blond hair—Swadley and her friends got close enough to the casket to see that his hair had been shorn, so that "he looked clean-cut." She went on, "It was clear that his mother didn't want us there. It was understandable—she didn't know if any of us had been supplying him."

One day Swadley decided that she needed to write down all thirteen names, before she forgot one. And in January, 2016, she started on another quest to see and remember: she would photograph addicts in recovery. In her introduction to the series, on Instagram, she wrote about her friends who had died and about the lack of drug treatment. She found the culture of denial enraging.

For the first few portraits, Swadley reached out to her subjects, but soon people started coming to her. She took their pictures, asked them about their lives, and told their stories in a paragraph or so. There are now two dozen images in the series.

In one of the portraits, an E.R. nurse hugs her daughter, Hope, from whom she'd been estranged. They had reconnected at the hospital, when the nurse saw Hope's name listed as an overdose patient in the emergency room. Swadley photographed a Martinsburg woman named Crystal, who'd been hit by a car one night when she was walking to her dealer's house; Crystal was now off drugs, but she was confined to a wheelchair. A woman named Tiffany posed holding a snapshot of her younger sister, Tabby. Both women had started on pills—Tabby had developed a problem after a gallbladder operation left her with a thirty-day supply of meds—and then got addicted to heroin. Tiffany had received treatment, but Tabby had fatally overdosed while she was waiting for a rehab bed. Swadley took the portrait in a park where Tiffany had once begged Tabby to stop using. When I called Tiffany, she told me that she had recently lost a second sister to heroin.

Swadley hopes that her photographs will someday be displayed all around town—in coffee shops, restaurants, the library. She wants a public reckoning with the stories she's collected. "The whole point of this project is to show naysayers out there that people do recover," she said. "They are good people. I want to show people they deserve a chance. I want it in people's faces, so they see that it could be their neighbor, or their best friend."

During one of our conversations, Swadley told me about a local effort against heroin addiction, called the Hope Dealer Project. It was run by three women: Tina Stride, who had a twenty-six-year-old son in recovery; Tara Mayson, whose close friend had gone through periods of addiction; and Lisa Melcher, whose son-in-law had died of an overdose, and whose thirty-two-year-old daughter, Christina, was struggling to overcome heroin addiction. All three had known addicts who wanted to get clean but had no place to go. Last fall, like car-pool moms with a harrowing new mission, they had begun driving people to detox facilities all over the state—any place that could take them, sometimes as far as five hours away. The few with private insurance could get rehab anywhere in the country, and the Hope Dealer women were prepared to suggest options. But most people in town had Medicaid or no insurance at all, and such addicts had to receive treatment somewhere in the state. Currently, the detox facility closest to Martinsburg is about two hours away.

Stride works full time at the General Services Administration, in Washington, but spends up to twenty-four hours a week giving rides to drug users. The other two focus on reaching out to people in addiction and families. Stride noted, "I have to talk to the addict, or the client—that's what we try to call them—all the way to that detox center. Because they're sick. And we pass hospitals all the way, and they're begging, 'Just take me there—they can help me!' But they really can't, the hospitals."

When Stride and her client arrive at a detox facility, nurses are waiting at the door. At that point, Stride said, "they're, like, 'What do you mean, you're *leaving* me?'" She went on, "They're scared, because now it's reality. They know they're not going to get their dope or their pills. For them to walk in those doors, that takes a lot. They're heroes to me."

After five to ten days in detox, patients are released. "When our clients get clean and the drugs are out of their system, they believe they're O.K.," Stride said. "And they're not. That's just getting the poison out of their bodies. So we try to explain to them, 'No, you need to go through rehab, and learn *why* you are using, and learn how to fight it.' Some will do it. Some won't. And then our issue becomes how we're going to find them a bed in rehab. If beds are all full, a lot of times they come back here to Martinsburg, because they have nowhere else to go." Stride tries to keep those clients under constant watch. "That addict brain is telling them, 'You know what you need, and it's right here—go get it.'"

Stride usually drives clients to a detox center immediately after picking them up. But there was one time when she had to put a stranger up overnight at her home, because a bed wasn't available for the woman until the morning. "All I said was 'Please, don't rob me," Stride recalled. "I'm here to help you. But I guess if you *are* gonna rob me there's not a whole lot I can do about it.' This young lady had to go through the night—she was so sick, she didn't sleep. I tried to stay up, but I knew I had to drive four hours to the detox place, and four hours back. So I slept some. We were up at 4 A.M., and at the detox place at eight. And she's doing good now—she calls me to touch base sometimes."

The Hope Dealer women and I met near an apartment complex that Melcher manages, and drank McDonald's mochas that she had brought for all of us. Melcher, who is fifty-three, with abundant blond ringlets and a warm, husky voice, told me that she loved flower arranging and refinishing old furniture—activities that would be occupying her days more often if there weren't a heroin crisis. Stride, who is forty-seven, wore her hair in a ponytail and had curly bangs; Mayson, who is forty-six, had long, sparkly nails.

At one point, Stride said, "Please don't think I'm rude," as she picked up her phone to read a text.

"He's in!" she cried. "He made it!"

The women cheered.

They had spent the previous day working on behalf of a woman and her twenty-one-year-old son, who is addicted to heroin. He had private insurance, so they had signed him up for a drug rehab program in New Hampshire. "We had a plane ticket ready, and they were ready to go to the airport," Stride said. "I left them, and then the mother called me and said, 'My son's lips are blue—he's overdosed. What do I do?' " Stride became teary. "And I said, 'Call 911. I'm coming right back over.' "

Stride went on, "So he was in the hospital, and then his mom reached out to me late last night and said, 'He's been released.' First question I asked is 'Where is he?,' because we're afraid he's going to run. And she said, 'Instead of putting him on a plane, can we drive him? Because I want to know he makes it.' And I said, 'Yes, you can.' So they are driving eight hours to take him to his detox. Detox was

good to go—so we know for the next seven to ten days he's safe."
After that, the man was set to go to Florida, to attend a thirty-day
program that Stride respected.

Melcher said, "Praise God, he made it," and the women all nodded.

Mayson, who works at the Department of Veterans Affairs and
has two adult children, said that the Hope Dealer women had become like sisters. When one of them has a hard day, she can count
on one of the others to tell her to rest and recharge—or, as Melcher
often says, to "*breeeathe.*"

As mothers, they felt that they had a particular ability to commu-
nicate with women who needed help with their addicted children.
Stride said, "I remember when I first found out my son was an addict. I was devastated. I didn't know who to turn to, who I could
trust. And I worked and worked to find my son a place, and that's
rough. Hearing 'No' or 'We can't take him today, but we can take
him a week from today.' 'No, you need to take him *now*. My son's
gonna *die*.' So now, when moms reach out to us, we're, like, 'We've
got this.'"

Melcher said, "When you're in that space? Oh, my gosh, you can
hardly breathe, you're a cryin' mess."

Stride nodded and said, "So when we come in and say, 'Mom,
we're gonna take care of your child,' I don't care if that child is fifty
years old—you see a relief."

On May 21st, I got an e-mail from Melcher, telling me that Christina, her daughter, had fatally overdosed on heroin. Christina, she
said, had completed rehab several times, and had been clean for
ninety days before relapsing. Melcher refused to hide the fact that
Christina had "lost her battle with addiction," but added, "When
a child passes away, the last thing a mother wants to say is that the
child was an addict." Melcher plans to continue her volunteer work,
in honor of Christina's "beautiful but tortured life."

John Aldis doesn't look like a maverick. He's seventy-one, white-
haired and pink-cheeked, with a neat mustache, half-rimmed specta-
cles, and a penchant for sweater vests and bow ties. You could imagine

him playing the Stage Manager in a production of "Our Town." But two years ago Aldis became the first doctor in West Virginia to offer free public classes to teach anybody—not just first responders and health professionals—how to reverse overdoses with Narcan.

Aldis is a family practitioner with a background in public health and tropical medicine. His mother taught nursing, and his father was an obstetrician. "We never made it through the second feature at the drive-in," Aldis recalled. "He would always be summoned over the loudspeaker to attend a birth." There was no question in Aldis's mind that he would become a doctor, too. He spent most of his career in Asia and Africa, as a U.S. Navy physician and as a medical officer with the State Department. He retired in 2001. He and his wife, Pheny, a medical technologist, bought the house where he'd lived as a small child, in Shepherdstown. They filled it with art and antiques, acquired two Jack Russell terriers, and prepared for a quiet life enlivened by visits from their two daughters and the grandkids.

But Aldis soon became aware of the opioid epidemic in the Eastern Panhandle—several people he'd hired to work on his house were "good fellows" as he described them who were also addicted to drugs. "When I started to see it, I could not look away," he told me. He took a job at the New Life Clinic, in Martinsburg, where he could prescribe Suboxone, one of the long-term treatments for opioid addiction. He found it enormously frustrating that addicts were often urged to quit heroin cold turkey or to stop taking Suboxone (or methadone or naltrexone, the other drugs used, with considerable success, to treat addiction and counteract withdrawal symptoms). In his view, this was wholly unrealistic. Most addicts needed what is known as medication-assisted treatment for a long time, if not the rest of their lives. He found the work at the clinic the most satisfying he'd done since graduating from medical school, forty-six years earlier. Patients struggled, and many of them failed, but when one of them told him, "Doc, I talked to my mom for the first time in three years yesterday," that was, Aldis said, "just the greatest thing."

Aldis is generally a forbearing man, but he can be dismissive of people who don't share his sense of urgency. As he wrote to me in an e-mail, "The lack of understanding of medication-assisted treatment among otherwise reasonably intelligent people at all levels of our community is astounding and (for me) completely unacceptable."

In 2015, West Virginia University's Injury Control Research Center, along with several state and county agencies, started investigating ways to make naloxone—the generic name for Narcan—more widely available, in the hope of saving people in the throes of an overdose. Aldis attended a talk on the subject by the center's deputy director, Herb Linn, and afterward he approached him and urged, "Let's not study this anymore. Let's just start a program." Linn recalls, "I told him, 'Just do it! You could actually prescribe it to your patients.'"

Aldis taught his first class on administering Narcan on September 3, 2015, at the New Life Clinic. Nine days later, a woman who'd attended the class used Narcan to revive a pregnant woman who had overdosed at a motel where they were both living. During the next few weeks, Aldis heard of five more people saved by people who'd attended the class.

In his seminars, Aldis addresses why addicts' lives are worth saving. One might assume that was self-evident, but at this point in the opioid epidemic some West Virginians feel too exhausted and resentful to help. People like Lori Swadley and the Hope Dealer women and John Aldis must combat an attitude that some people I spoke with summed up as "Leave 'em lie, let 'em die." Some frustrated locals worry that making Narcan easily available could foster complacency about overdoses because they could be handled more discreetly.

William Poe, a paramedic, told me, "The thing about Narcan is that it kind of makes it O.K. to overdose, because then you can keep it in your house and keep it private. And a lot of times *we're* the wake-up call. I remember one time, we had a kid who had O.D.'d, and we had him in the ambulance. A call came over the radio—someone about his age had just died from an overdose. And the kid was, like, 'I'm so glad you guys brought me back.'" It was humiliating when an ambulance showed up at your house and carted you out, pale and retching, but it also might push you to change. Then again, Poe mused, when most of your neighbors—not to mention your mom and your grandma—already knew that you used heroin, shaming might not be as much of a thing.

This past winter, I watched Aldis teach two classes in Berkeley Springs, an Eastern Panhandle town, at a storefront church between a convenience store and a pawnshop. The bare trees on the ridge above us were outlined like black lace against the twilight. Inside, a few dozen people, mostly women, sipped coffee from Styrofoam cups in an unadorned room with a low ceiling, tan carpeting, and rows of tan chairs.

Aldis touched briefly on what an overdose looks like, but acknowledged that the attendees probably already knew. ("Oh, Lord, yes," a woman behind me muttered.) He demonstrated how to spray Narcan up a patient's nose—take-home kits come in atomizer form—and announced that at the end of class he'd be writing prescriptions, which those in attendance could get filled at a pharmacy. If they had Medicaid or private insurance, the kit would cost only a few dollars; if they didn't, it could cost anywhere from a hundred and twenty-five to three hundred dollars. At the first meeting I attended, in November, a few women began to cry when they heard that. At the second, in January, Aldis had some good news: the state had agreed to provide a hundred and eighty free kits.

Aldis told me that he'd like to see Narcan "inundating the community." It carried no potential for abuse, and couldn't harm you if someone gave it to you mistaking some other medical emergency for an overdose. "They ought to be selling this stuff next to the peanut butter in the Walmart," he liked to say. And free supplies of Narcan should be everywhere, like fire extinguishers: "kitchen cabinets, your purse, schools, gyms, shopping malls, motels."

Melody Stotler, who ran a local organization for recovering addicts, had been the one to invite Aldis to speak that evening. She said to the class, "Unfortunately, there are people in this community who don't understand addiction, who don't think Narcan should be out there."

"They say we're enablers," Aldis put in. "Somebody who has a heart attack—are we enabling them by giving them C.P.R.? 'But their cholesterol's too high! We shouldn't have saved his life!'" People laughed ruefully.

Aldis introduced Kathy Williams, a former patient of his and the mother of two little girls. She had twice saved people with Narcan. One time, while she was driving, she spotted a car on the side of the road, and a man lying on his back next to it. The other time, a neighbor in her apartment complex knocked on her door and said that a guy was overdosing in the parking lot. "So I grabbed my Narcan kit, and I ran out there," she recalled. She saw a woman tending to the man. "What had happened was that these two had stopped at Kmart. She went in to pick up her layaways, and when she came out he had just done shooting up, and said, 'Please take me home.' Well, he was overdosing from Kmart all the way. By the time I got there, he was in the back of the car, completely blue, and I had another guy help me pull him out—a neighbor, 'cause where I live, I been there almost thirty years now, and I know everybody. A couple people saw me running, and they started running, too, because they said, 'Kathy's running—something must be going on.' We gave him two doses of Narcan, and by the time the E.M.T. got there his eyes were just starting to flicker, and I really thought we were too late." The man began to stir.

A woman named Tara, who was at the January meeting with her teen-age stepdaughter, told me that she had revived a guy who lived in the trailer park where she did some babysitting. He'd refused to go to the hospital, even though he was "puking like he was possessed." I asked Tara—who was thirty, and had a soft, kind face—if the man had said anything to her after she saved him. "Every day, the next four days after that, he thanked me every time," she told me. "He also said it was stupid and he'd never do that again, which wasn't true, because he was arrested for driving under the influence of heroin a few weeks ago. Nodded out in the McDonald's parking lot. Someone called the police."

Tara wasn't judging. She got it. She was a recovering addict herself—seven years now, and studying to be a medical assistant.

Jason Chalmers loved his children, that was for sure. He crawled around on all fours, pretending to be a pony, to amuse his daughter, Jacey, and her younger brother, Liam. He submitted to Jacey whenever she wanted to cover his face with makeup. When Jacey was six months old, Jason wrote a letter to his grandparents in which he described the "absolute, overwhelming" love that he felt for his daughter. "It's not for or about me any more," he wrote. "That's probably for the best because I never did well with myself. She deserves a father who's going to love her unconditionally and so help me God, I'm going to do it. Maybe she's the answer to why I'm still here."

Liam was born in 2009. His mother, Angie, had an opioid problem, and had taken Suboxone to combat it during her pregnancy. She told me that she also "might have used" heroin "a couple of times." At the hospital, Jason felt that something was amiss with his son. His mother, Christine Chalmers, recalled, "He says, 'Mom, this baby is in withdrawal. They can't release him—he's in terrible pain. If we take him home, he's going to scream and scream and scream, and we won't have anything to help him.'" So we called the doctor and, by golly, they checked him over, and he was in total withdrawal. He was on morphine for two solid weeks in the hospital."

Jason, who grew up in Martinsburg, was addicted to heroin for most of his life, a fact that puzzled his family almost as deeply as it saddened them. He grew up in an attractive, wooded development on a country road, with horses and dogs, and a kindhearted mother. His grandparents lived in the development, too, and Jason and his two siblings waited for the school bus together on a wooden bench that a neighbor had carved for them.

There were scraps of an explanation here and there. Jason's parents had divorced when he was eight, and he was a shy, anxious kid; when he was twenty-five, he was given a diagnosis of obsessive-compulsive disorder. His older brother, Michael—the publisher of the Shepherdstown *Observer*—told me, "If you gave us a bag of Reese's peanut-butter cups when we were kids, Jason would eat fifty of them. I'd eat

five. I would've *liked* to eat fifty, but I was, like, 'Nah, I'll eat five.'"
Maybe, Michael suggested, this was evidence that Jason had a genetic
predisposition for addiction. But who knew, really?

In high school, Jason was "smart, good-looking, and athletic,"
Michael recalled, but he became the "king of the stoners." He barely
got his diploma. It was the beginning of a self-destructive pattern.
Jason did things while he was on drugs, or trying to get drugs, that
walloped him with shame; to mute those terrible feelings, at least
for a while, he'd get high again. He got into using heroin, then into
selling it. A friend's father was a dealer, and Jason went to work for
him, driving up to New York to procure drugs and driving back to
Martinsburg to sell them. He introduced heroin to a girlfriend—a
good student who had a scholarship to an excellent university. She
dropped out, overdosed, and died. He got a tattoo of the girlfriend's
initials next to a dove, and a tattoo of Jesus, and a tattoo that represented his addiction: a desperate-looking demon with a gaping
mouth. He went to jail dozens of times (drug possession, credit-card
theft) and had a series of nearly fatal overdoses. In 2002, he stole his
grandfather's checkbook and emptied his bank account. Christine
urged her father to press charges, both because she felt that Jason had
to be held responsible and because she felt safest—and could actually
sleep through a night—when he was behind bars. He lied to her, and
stole from her, and after using heroin he would pass out on her deck,
in her garage, at the end of her driveway.

Jason did not go to college, and he could not keep a job for long;
he worked for a few weeks at a mini-mart, but got fired when the
background check on him came in. He'd get clean in jail, and write
abject letters of apology to his family. Then he'd return to Martinsburg and start hanging out again with his addict friends. Michael
moved to Chicago to start a career as an advertising copywriter, and
their sister, Antonia, got married, bought a house, went to work for
the school system. Jason, now in his thirties, was stuck—walking
everywhere because he couldn't get a driver's license, and showing up
at his mother's house in the middle of the night to beg for milk and
cereal.

In 2008, Jason wrote to his grandparents, "If I was a gambling man, which if you look at my track record my whole life has been a gamble, I'd have to say there's not enough time left in the world to make good on the pain I've caused." He observed, "Damaged people can be dangerous because they know they can survive, but for some reason they don't know quite how to live."

Christine Chalmers had struggled financially to raise three children as a single mother. But in 2002, when Jason was twenty-six, she was doing well as a real-estate agent, and she sent Jason to a month-long rehab program in Colorado that cost ten thousand dollars. She recalled, "I went after a couple of weeks, for parents' weekend, and you know what? It was so worth it. He'd been on heroin for ten years at this point, and it was the first time in all that time I saw him like my boy. He says, 'It's like a new world, Mom—I can see things, I can smell things, I can feel things.'" She paused. "I thought, You know what? If I never have anything else, he had a month, and I had a weekend, and he was my boy."

On April 28, 2014, Jason fatally overdosed. He was thirty-seven. His death did not come as a surprise: he had started telling Christine that the worst part of overdosing was waking up.

After an overdose death, an autopsy is usually performed. Because of the epidemic, coroners in West Virginia are often backed up. It took two weeks before Jason's body was returned to the Chalmers family. Afterward, Christine thought about how consumed she had been by her attempts to save Jason and, later, to protect his children from him. One day, Michael and Antonia had been cleaning up Jason's apartment, and they brought over to Christine the contents of his kitchen cabinet. Christine told me, "There were a couple of cans of peas. And I had never served peas—I didn't like them. I said, 'I didn't know Jason liked peas!' There's your boy, your baby, and you never knew he liked peas. Such a simple thing. But I started crying, because I thought, What did we know about him as a *person*?"

When the man who sold Jason his final dose of heroin went on trial, Christine testified. "But, you know, from that point on I have felt terrible about it," she said. "The guy got ten years. And in some

sense his life was saved, because he would have ended up the same as
Jase. But when I look at him I know he'd just done the same things
Jason did. I mean, who knows who Jase sold to? Who knows who
lived or died because he sold to them?"

Christine, who is now sixty-four, and works full time as a secretary
in the Berkeley County government, has found herself raising Jacey,
who is in the third grade. (Liam lives with his mother, in another
state.) One of the biggest collateral effects of the opioid crisis is the
growing number of children being raised by people other than their
parents, or being placed in foster care. In West Virginia, the number of children removed from parental care because of drug abuse
rose from nine hundred and seventy in 2006 to two thousand one
hundred and seventy-one in 2016. Shawn Valentine, a program director for a nonprofit that helps children navigate foster care in West
Virginia, says that although the goal is to reunite children with their
parents, this happens in "less than twenty-five per cent of the cases
we are involved in." A major reason is that parents often can't get access to recovery programs or medication-assisted treatment, because
of waiting lists and financial obstacles.

Valentine said, "I had a six-year-old once tell me that he had to
hold the stretchy thing on his mom's arm. What would happen if he
just didn't want to do that? He told me, 'Well, she would smack my
head down, so that powdery stuff got all over my face.'"

Christine and Jacey live in Martinsburg, in a pretty bungalow with
a porch swing and a glider, and a front door with bright-yellow trim.
Down the street, there's a couple with five adopted children whose
parents were addicted to opioids. Across the street, a woman named
Melissa lives with her elderly father and her youngest sister's two little
boys. Their mother was addicted to heroin, and lost custody of the
kids two years ago. At the time, Melissa, who is a medical technician
at a nursing home, was working and living in Maryland—she is divorced, and her own children are grown. She rushed home to Martinsburg to care for her nephews, whom I'll call Cody and Aiden.

One afternoon, I sat talking with Melissa and Christine on

Christine's front porch, while Jacey and the boys ran around in a ragged, laughing pack. Christine served some brownies that she had baked. Melissa recalled that, when her sister lost custody, her nephews' caseworker told her that Aiden, who was then a toddler, would be quickly adopted, but that eight-year-old Cody, who bore more obvious signs of trauma, and could be difficult to manage, would probably languish in foster care. Melissa said that she couldn't stand to see them separated. "I was, like, 'What choice do I have?'" she said.

Christine patted her on the knee. "Good girl," she said.

Jacey kept a close eye on Aiden, who kept wandering over to the neighbor's yard, where there was a new Chihuahua puppy.

Christine said, "The sad thing about it is there are so many of these kids."

"Yes!" Melissa said. "Aiden's pre-K teacher told me forty percent of the kids in her class are being raised by somebody other than a parent."

"That means forty per cent have been found out," Christine said. "Who knows what's going on with the other parents?"

Jacey is a bright, curious kid, with pearly pink glasses and a sprinkling of freckles. The first time I met her, she catalogued her accomplishments in gymnastics. "I can do a handstand, a round-off, I'm working on my back handspring," she said. "I can do a front flip. I want to try a back flip, but it's kinda hard. I still have a lot more ahead of me."

Christine has been honest with Jacey about Jason's addiction, in the hope that it will keep her from ending up on a similar path. But in any case, it would be hard to keep the truth from Jacey: she remembers finding her father's needles, and she remembers him getting high. He often dropped into a state of suspended animation—still standing, bent over at the waist, head dangling near his knees. Jacey told me that she and Liam used to think it was a game: "It was, like, he's dead, but he's also alive. You could tap on him and talk to him— he'd just be snoring there. But you could also feel that he was breathing. We would put our hands up to his nose and we could feel the air coming in and out."

Last fall, Jacey won a statewide poster-making contest, called "Kids Kick Opioids," that was sponsored by the West Virginia attorney general's office. Jacey's poster—one of two thousand entries—included a photograph of Jason, in a backward baseball cap and baggy shorts, holding a grinning Liam on one hip and Jacey on the other. She had written a little passage about how much she missed him after he'd "died from taking drugs," and how she wanted to "hug and kiss him every day." She wrote, "It is very sad when kids don't have their daddy to play with."

Christine said of the poster, "I think Jason would have wanted it. Jason wanted so badly for people not to follow him."

One day when I was visiting, Jacey lay on the porch floor, drawing a rainbow with some colored pencils. Christine was telling me she thought that it was wrong to send opioid addicts to prison.

Jacey piped up. "Yeah, but they should take them away from their home town. Also, get them help."

"Yes," Christine said. "Long-term help. A month is not enough."

"But take them away from, say, Martinsburg," Jacey said, looking down at her rainbow. "Maybe take them across the world."

Recently, Martinsburg has begun to treat the heroin crisis more openly as a public-health problem. The police chief, a Chicago transplant named Maurice Richards, had devised a progressive-sounding plan called the Martinsburg Initiative, which would direct support services toward children who appeared to be at risk for addiction, because their families were struggling socially or emotionally. In December, Tina Stride and several other local citizens stood up at a zoning meeting to proclaim the need for a detox center. They took issue with residents who testified that such a center would bring more addicts, and more heroin, to their neighborhoods. "I'm here to say that's already here," a woman in favor of the proposal said. "It's in your neighbor's house, in the bathroom at Wendy's, in our schools." She added, "We're talking about making America great again? Well, it starts here."

That night, the Board of Zoning Appeals voted to allow a detox center, run by Peter Callahan, the psychotherapist, to occupy an unused commercial building in town. People in the hearing room cheered and cried and hugged one another. The facility will have only sixteen beds and won't be ready for patients until December, but the Hope Dealer women were thrilled about it. Now they wouldn't have to drive halfway across the state every time an addict called them up.

John Aldis, who was sitting next to me during the vote, breathed a sigh of relief. He said later, "It's like that Winston Churchill quote: 'This is not the end. It is not even the beginning of the end. But it is, perhaps, the end of the beginning.'"

This spring, Berkeley County started its first needle-exchange program, and other efforts are being made to help addicts survive. The new app that first responders are using to document overdoses allows them to input how many times a patient is given Narcan; when multiple doses are required, it can often mean the heroin was adulterated with potent synthetics, such as fentanyl. The data can help the health department and law enforcement track dangerous batches of drugs, and warn addicts.

Some Martinsburg residents who had been skeptical of medication-assisted treatment told me that they were coming around to the idea. A few cited the Surgeon General's report on substance abuse, released in November, which encouraged the expansion of such treatment, noting that studies have repeatedly demonstrated its efficacy in "reducing illicit drug use and overdose deaths." In Berkeley County, it felt like a turning point, though the Trump Administration was likely to resist such approaches. Tom Price, the new Secretary of Health and Human Services, had dismissed medication-assisted treatment as "substituting one opioid for another." It was also unclear how most addicts would pay for treatment if the Affordable Care Act were to be repealed.

Martinsburg residents, meanwhile, tried to take heart from small breakthroughs. Angel Holt, the mother who'd overdosed at the softball practice, told me that she and her boyfriend had stayed clean since that day, and she was hoping to regain custody of her children. She'd been moved by the kindness of an older couple, Karen and Ed Schildt, who lived in Thurmont, Maryland. A year earlier, the Schildts had lost their twenty-five-year-old son, Chris, to a heroin overdose. They were deeply religious, and when they heard what happened to Angel Holt and Christopher Schildt they decided to reach out to them. The fact that their son had the same name as Holt's boyfriend surely meant that God had put the couple in their path. Karen texted Holt words of encouragement almost daily.

In February, I spent an afternoon with Shawn Valentine, the non-profit program director whom I'd talked to about foster care and the opioid crisis. Valentine introduced me to Shelby, her twenty-five-year-old daughter. Shelby had become addicted to opioids at twenty-one. She'd been depressed, living at home again after a brief stint in Florida, arguing with her mom a lot, waitressing at a Waffle House, falling asleep in the college classes she was trying to keep up with. Her co-workers always seemed to know how to get their hands on pills somewhere or other, oftentimes from a guy who hung out behind the Food Lion. When the meds got too expensive, but she couldn't seem to do without them anymore, Shelby turned to heroin.

Shelby, Valentine, and I were sitting in Valentine's kitchen, along with Shelby's fifteen-year-old brother, Patrick, a sweet kid who was listening closely to her. Shelby said, "People don't realize what the brain goes through when you're addicted—it's like a mental shutdown. Everything is gray. You have these blinders on." As she described it, the constant hunt for heroin imposed a kind of order on life's confounding open-endedness. Addiction told you what every day was for, when otherwise you might not have known.

For close to a year, Shelby had been in a program which required her to place a dissolvable strip of Suboxone on her tongue every day, and attended group and individual therapy. (The word "assisted" in "medication-assisted treatment" indicates the primacy of the need for recovering addicts to undertake therapy as well, to figure out how to restructure their lives and maybe what got them into opioids to begin with.) Shelby said that Suboxone helped curb her craving for heroin, without sedating her. "There are triggers," she said. "But the urge to run a hundred yards down the street and try to find my ex-dealer and pay him, then shove a used rig in my arm real quick? That's gone."

She can now be relied upon not to pilfer the kinds of treasured possessions she once took and sold for drug money: her little brother's video-game console, her mom's four-leaf-clover necklace. When every day was about getting ahold of heroin, she couldn't be bothered to wash or comb her long, auburn hair hardly at all; her mother once spent four hours trying to untangle it, strand by snarled strand. Now her hair is silky and soft.

Valentine told me that, if Shelby had to be on Suboxone all her life, "I'm absolutely on board with that." She turned to Shelby. "Whatever it takes for you to be a healthy, productive human being."

Recently, Shelby's mother had made a big concession that felt sort of like hope in action. She'd told her, "O.K. I'll let you take the truck without me, to take your brother to the movies." Shelby recalled, "I was almost, like, 'Pinch me, wake me up—this can't be true.' Because without her truck there's no working. That's how she makes her living. She said, 'Here's a piece of trust. Don't throw it away.'"

Shelby and her brother drove to the mall and saw a horror movie. It was a pretty dumb one, they agreed, but it didn't matter—Shelby had made it to the mall and back, trust intact. They headed down the long road home in the dark, and the moment they got inside, Shelby put the keys to the truck in her mother's hand.

Margaret Talbot has lightly revised the essay that appears in this volume from the version that appeared in the New Yorker *on June 5, 2017.*

NO FAMILY IS SAFE FROM THIS EPIDEMIC

James Winnefeld

The Atlantic, November 29, 2017

The last photograph of my son Jonathan was taken at the end of a new-student barbecue on the campus green at the University of Denver. It was one of those bittersweet transitional moments. We were feeling the combination of apprehension and optimism that every parent feels when dropping off a kid at college for the first time, which was amplified by the fact that we were coming off a rocky 16 months with our son.

We had moved him into his dormitory room only that morning. I remember how sharp he looked in the outfit he had selected, and his eagerness to start class and make new friends. We were happy, relieved, and, knowing what we thought he had overcome, proud. At lunch, I asked Jonathan whether he thought he was ready for the coming school year. "Dad, I can handle it as long as I continue my recovery," he said. "Everything flows from that."

Only three days later, Jonathan was found unresponsive in his dormitory-room bed, one of several victims of a fentanyl-laden batch of heroin that had spread through the Denver area that week.

Jonathan grew up as the introverted, but creative, younger kid in a career Navy officer's family. He was born a week after I returned from a long deployment, and lived through two deployments before reaching his fourth birthday. During one six-year stretch, he attended school in five different districts due to military moves. The one constant was his big brother, his best friend, whom he followed around like he was a rock star. I remember him grinning from ear to ear when he was asked to play on his brother's soccer team because it was short one kid, and again when the two of them learned to ride a bike on the same day.

It wouldn't be the last time Jonathan proved himself a quick study. When Jonathan was in the second grade, his teacher called to notify us that he was selling school supplies to his classmates, lending them money with interest. In the fifth grade, he made a perfect score on the Virginia Standards of Learning science test. In the ninth grade, he hit a walk-off single in a baseball tournament. A year later, he pitched seven gritty innings of no-hit ball over two consecutive all-star games, with the help of a curveball that seemed to defy gravity.

Jonathan was quiet, but he had a big heart. He helped coach little kids in baseball and laid wreaths at Arlington National Cemetery. He had no enemies, only friends. His baseball coach told us his mind was a gift. "He was a brilliant kid who never laughed out loud that I can remember, but he had a wry and knowing smile," he told me. And Jonathan was humble, only replying "thank you" when complimented, never letting anything go to his head. "Jon didn't brag about what he knew or who he knew," his coach said.

Jonathan's military lineage extended to a grandfather and great-grandfather who also served in the Navy, and a great-great-grandfather who was a Prussian cavalryman. One of the few times I saw Jonathan beam with genuine pride was when he was given his great great-grandfather's sword at my retirement ceremony. The moment was deeply meaningful to him because it signaled equal recognition among family; Jonathan had to pedal hard in the shadow of a successful father and a brother now carrying on the tradition of military service.

On the surface, Jonathan was a handsome, shy, gentle kid with a warm and disarming demeanor. But underneath that exterior he struggled with anxiety and depression, which eventually spiraled into addiction, with all its sickening complexity.

Many people have a simple understanding of addiction. They think it happens only to dysfunctional people from dysfunctional families, or to hopeless people living on the street. But our addicted population is spread across every segment of society: rich and poor, white and black, male and female, old and young.

There are several gateways to opioid addiction. Some people suffer a physical injury, and slowly develop a dependency on prescribed painkillers. Others self-medicate for mental ailments using whatever substance is available. Because the brain is so adaptable while it's still developing, it's highly susceptible to dependencies, even from non-opioids such as today's newly potent marijuana strains. We now understand that early marijuana use not only inhibits brain development; it prepares the brain to be receptive to opioids. Of course, like opioids, marijuana has important medical applications, and it seems to leave less of a mark on a fully matured brain. It's worth examining whether it would make sense to raise the legal marijuana age to 25, when the brain has fully matured.

From an early age, Jonathan lacked confidence and self-esteem. He never seemed comfortable in his own skin. He followed more than he led. Like many of the 40 percent or more of teenagers who have reportedly suffered from one mental-health issue or another, Jonathan started on the road to addiction early. He began by sneaking a bit of alcohol at night in order to bring himself down from the Adderall a doctor had prescribed him, based on a misdiagnosis of attention deficit disorder. By the eighth grade, he was consuming alcohol in larger quantities and beginning to self-medicate with marijuana. Next came Xanax and, eventually, heroin.

We first tried counseling and psychiatry for Jonathan, thinking this was merely a matter of bad friends and worse choices. We figured that he would age out of it and turn away from drugs. Not understanding how addiction progresses, we foolishly hoped, reinforced by his assurances, that every incident would be the last. The incidents worsened after a girlfriend turned away from him and he was disqualified from playing varsity baseball during his senior year due to deteriorating grades. One April night that year, a suicidal gesture and a car accident left him in the hospital and left us with no doubt that we needed to make a radical change.

With no available spaces in treatment facilities in Washington, D.C., Jonathan detoxed in Richmond, Virginia, for a week while we frantically searched for an inpatient center that would accommodate his dual diagnosis of depression/anxiety and addiction. He growled that putting him into treatment was the worst mistake we would ever make. But we stuck with our decision, and sent him away to two sequential state-of-the-art inpatient treatment programs.

According to the treatment professionals with whom we worked, it takes most addicts well over a year of skilled, intense inpatient treatment to even have a *chance* of recovery, and my son is evidence that not even that amount of time is a guarantee. Effective treatment generally requires a combination of craving-reducing drugs (to give recovery a chance), time (for the brain to literally recover), counseling (for the addict to understand what he or she is going through), mutual support (to maintain sobriety), and transition training (to prepare for reentering society).

Even getting people into treatment can be difficult, although some are trying to make doing so easier. In drug courts, for instance, judges are able to suspend drug-offense sentences in favor of an addict entering—and remaining in—a treatment program. But these programs are still terribly expensive. Because the military's Tricare medical system would not adequately cover treatment for a dual diagnosis, we dug in and spent more than the equivalent of four years' tuition at a private college for 15 months of treatment for Jonathan, a sum that would be well beyond the reach of most American families.

It wasn't until our exposure to the parent-education sessions at Jonathan's first treatment center that we awakened to the full horror of addiction's relentless spiral. Unlike cancer, which can be seen under a microscope, addiction works away at the brain much more covertly, using the brain's own flexibility against it.

As Sam Quinones writes in his book *Dreamland*, the morphine molecule has "evolved somehow to fit, key in lock, into the receptors that all mammals, especially humans, have in their brains and spines . . . creating a far more intense euphoria than anything we come by internally." It creates a higher tolerance with use, and, Quinones continues, exacts "a mighty vengeance when a human dares to stop using it." What starts as relief of physical or mental pain transforms into a desperate need to avoid withdrawal.

Treatment was tedious for Jonathan, due to long periods of boredom and his discomfort at being required to reach out to others and talk about himself. But he knew he needed help to recover. Over 16 long months, we saw him almost miraculously begin to pull out of the abyss. We were gradually getting our son back. We watched as his brain recovered and he turned back into his old self. He was more communicative, he was happy to see us when we visited, and he even led a 12-step Alcoholics Anonymous meeting once a week.

In his last few months in treatment, Jonathan sought and earned his emergency-medical-technician qualification. He said he wanted to use it to help others, especially young people, avoid his experience. He was so proud that he had found something he loved to do. It was one of the very few things that would light him up in a discussion, so we brought it up with him whenever we could.

Based on his steady progress in recovery, and his successful completion of the rigorous EMT certification program, we thought Jonathan was ready to reenter normal life, and we believed that he deserved the chance. Together, we decided he would attend the University of Denver, which had granted him a gap year after high school. Thanks in part to a sympathetic admissions counselor who had an experience with addiction in her own family, the school agreed to allow him to enter in the fall.

The members of his incoming class were required to read J. D. Vance's *Hillbilly Elegy* over the summer and to write an essay about a person who had had a profound impact upon their life. Jonathan wrote powerfully about encountering a man in the grip of an overdose-induced cardiac arrest in a McDonald's bathroom during the first ride-along of his EMT training. He said the experience had made him realize how precious life is. "I never found out his name," he wrote, but the experience had made him see his life "in a whole new light."

Sadly, the morphine molecule had burrowed deeper into his brain than we understood. Even as he was writing his moving essay, referring to himself as a *former* addict, his relapse was already one week old. Such is the Jekyll-and-Hyde nature of the disease of addiction.

During the weekend before we dropped off Jonathan at college, we missed the telltale signs of relapse. Feeling the shame of his condition, Jonathan used the addicted person's shrewdness to hide them. As for us, we were blinded by our own optimism. We read his restlessness as an understandable case of nerves about what was coming next, or perhaps too high a dosage of anxiety medicine. In retrospect, it appears that he was experiencing symptoms of withdrawal.

Scientists who study addiction understand how little the disease needs to return at full strength. Even brief flashing images of drug paraphernalia are sufficient to trigger a flood of dopamine in a recovering brain, which can, in turn, cause a relapse. The addict is all the more vulnerable when access to the drug is easy. The location where Jonathan, two weeks away from entering the University of Denver, was taking a nighttime electrocardiogram course is close to one of that city's open-air heroin markets. He told one of his friends back home that he had been offered heroin while walking back to where he was staying, but had refused. This encounter likely provided the stimulus for his relapse and eventual overdose.

Instead of allowing these open-air markets to thrive, we would do well to develop "safe-use zones" like those in Portugal and parts of British Columbia. These areas not only dramatically reduce opioid overdoses (because trained users of the overdose-reversing drug naloxone can be right on the scene); they can offer treatment to addicts who are ready to seek help.

We are hopeful that the exceptional efforts of a determined Denver police detective will lead to the apprehension, prosecution, and punishment of the drug dealer who sold our son that fatal fentanyl-laced dose. Indeed, the deadliest link in the overdose supply chain is the street dealer who looks an addicted person coldly in the eye and sells what he or she knows could be the person's last high. However, much of our prosecutorial apparatus views selling drugs as a "nonviolent crime." Many refuse to prosecute for the small amounts that dealers carry. Some dealers are released overnight, allowing them to move on to another location to resume their deadly work.

Meanwhile, addicts continue to suffer under long-standing stigmas associated with drug use, and are subject to the same punishments as dealers. Data from the FBI's Uniform Crime Reporting Program show that of the approximately 1.2 million people arrested for a drug-related offense in 2016, 85 percent were arrested for individual drug possession, not for the sale or manufacture of a drug. This is no way to solve an epidemic.

Drug overdose, like the one that took Jonathan from us, is now the leading cause of death for Americans younger than 50 years old. The Centers for Disease Control and Prevention reports that more than 64,000 Americans lost their life to a drug overdose in 2016, including 15,446 heroin overdoses. The total is more than 20 times the number of Americans killed on 9/11.

The costs of the opioid epidemic—in terms of health care, its corrosive effects on our economic productivity, and other impacts on society—extend far beyond the loss of life. The White House Council of Economic Advisers just raised its estimate of the epidemic's annual cost from $78.5 billion to a whopping $504 billion. Princeton University's Alan Krueger recently completed a study suggesting that 20 percent of the reduction in male participation in our workforce is due to opioid use, and that nearly one-third of prime-working-age men who are not in the labor force are taking prescription pain medication on a daily basis. I sit on the board of a medium-size industrial company in America's heartland that has had trouble recruiting employees, despite being willing to hire anyone who walks in the door who can pass a drug test.

If America is going to reverse this epidemic, we need to start treating it like the national emergency it really is. We need a call to arms like the one that led to our nation's dramatic decrease in cigarette usage, or to the effective Mothers Against Drunk Driving movement. There are reasons to hope that public awareness of the opioid epidemic is finally beginning to catch up with the facts on the ground, but its defeat will be possible only through a concerted effort that includes full-spectrum prevention, stronger prescription-drug controls, more-robust law enforcement, and far more access to quality treatment. All of this will in turn require major increases in public resources.

The final sentence of Jonathan's University of Denver freshman essay reads, "I now live my life with a newfound purpose: wanting to help those who cannot help themselves." Jonathan was very serious about his recovery. He wanted to live, and was on an upward trajectory, with brand-new hopes and dreams. He fought honorably against the demons of this disease, but, as with so many others, he lost his battle. Losing Jonathan has left us heartbroken, but we are determined to carry his purpose forward. If his story leads to one less heartbroken family, it will have been worth sharing.

KING OF BOISE: THE LIFE AND TIMES OF A TEENAGE OXYCODONE DEALER

Joe Eaton

Pacific Standard, November 21, 2017

Austin Serb mashed the pedal on his 1994 Mazda RX-7 and wound it up way past 100. It was six days before Christmas, 2012, and he was running late. Serb, then 19, had downed gallons of water and vitamin B-12 tablets to flush out prescription painkillers, cocaine, and whatever else might be lingering in his bloodstream.

His girlfriend sat in the passenger seat, clipped into a custom racing harness. It was for her that Serb was taking the drug test, a prerequisite for a tech-support job he'd applied for. She didn't want him to be a drug dealer anymore. And he, too, had been thinking of going straight.

Serb had been selling drugs since he was 14. He was wildly successful, often making more than $100,000 a month off the prescription painkiller oxycodone. The money paid for a diamond-studded Rolex, all-night hotel parties, and his modified RX-7—a 500-horsepower rotary-engine rocket straight out of the *Fast and Furious* film franchise—which was currently hurtling him west out of Boise. It was hard to think of $11 an hour.

Serb floored it and yelled over the howl of the engine: "Watch out for the cops." He had forgotten to put in his contact lenses.

As they raced down Interstate 84, flashing past cars in the slow lane, Serb saw it first: a black Dodge Charger in the right lane, Boise Police in silver letters below the taillights.

He hammered the brakes and felt all four wheels lock up, the rear end fishtailing, everything going slow motion, just like in Xbox *Forza*, his favorite racing game. This wasn't happening, he thought, as he slowed down and slid right next to the police car.

Heart pumping, hands on the wheel, Serb kept the speedometer at 65. The cop fell back, and pulled up close behind the Mazda. Serb's girlfriend yelled at him to pull over. But the cop hadn't flipped on the lights.

At least he had followed his rules for once, Serb thought. There were no drugs in the car.

Serb stole glances in the rearview mirror as the police car followed him for five excruciatingly long miles. As they approached the outskirts of Boise, the officer pulled alongside Serb's car. Serb kept driving. Eventually, he saw the police car's turn signal flashing. He watched as it pulled off at an exit ramp.

It didn't make sense, Serb thought. Maybe the officer didn't notice the RX-7 approaching rapidly from behind? Maybe he didn't see the smoke pouring off the skidding wheels? Nobody gets that lucky. Maybe the cop was calling for back-up?

Serb got off at the next exit and zigzagged down the back roads to the clinic, where he peed in a cup, then pulled out his iPhone and logged on to Facebook.

"Mobbing 130 mph," he wrote. "And blow past a cop. Hahahaha."

Austin Serb got his start at McDonald's. In 2008, his father lost his job making computer chips at Micron Technology, a semiconductor manufacturer based in Boise. Suddenly, money was tight.

Serb, who had been homeschooled by his mom using religious textbooks from Bob Jones University Press, entered public middle school and took a job flipping burgers for $6.50 an hour.

At school, the short and chubby 14-year-old hooked up with kids he knew from summers at the public swimming pool. On weekends, they rode their BMX bikes to a dried-up canal behind a gas station at the edge of town. Down in the canal, hidden away from the city, they drank cans of warm Keystone Light and smoked marijuana his friend Alex stole from his parents.

They called themselves The Dots, a reference to the scars they burned into the bases of their thumbs with glowing cigarettes as an initiation rite of sorts.

One of Serb's co-workers at McDonald's sold weed on the side. In time, he fronted Serb an ounce, and, soon after, Serb quit, having found himself suddenly flush with walking-around money.

In high school, the drugs changed. Marijuana was a constant, but ecstasy and other party drugs were in higher demand. The Dots changed their name to the B.C. (short for Bro Council) and set up a private Facebook page, and the number of kids burning in grew, drawn from the outsiders—kids who didn't fit in with the preppies, jocks, or nerds.

Serb wasn't popular, but he sold drugs to all the cliques at the three Boise high schools he attended as a result of frequent family moves. The selling came easy. It was sourcing drugs that was the problem. He didn't have many connections.

By 11th grade, Serb was coaxing friends to take him to Seattle or Portland to buy ecstasy (he didn't have a driver's license). Often, the trips ended with him getting robbed of his money, his stash, or both.

Boise is a law and order city. Residents walk the streets at night without fear. Teenagers tend to dress in outdoor clothing, as if they are about to go rock climbing or skiing. Serb stood out in gold chains, basketball shorts that hung to his knees, and mismatched $200 Air Jordans.

In 2011, he rented a three-bedroom town house in southeast Boise with his girlfriend and his older brother and went on a shopping spree. He bought a 70-inch flat-screen television for the living room, a 60-inch flat-screen for his bedroom, and a 27-inch for the bathroom.

Serb hung a painting of a seaside Italian village in the bedroom and arranged his T-shirts by color in the walk-in closet. On the floor, he laid out 40 pairs of basketball shoes, mostly Nikes, in every color of the rainbow. He felt like he had made it.

It wasn't long before the Boise police began hearing about him.

Joe Andreoli, a plainclothes detective in the Boise Police Department, first made contact with Serb in 2011. At home on a Monday evening, Andreoli received a call from another detective who'd received a text message from an unknown number advertising "dank buds" at $265 an ounce.

The next day, Andreoli, a recreational boxer who cultivates the scruffy look of a middle-aged drug dealer, used the detective's cell phone to make an appointment to buy 1.5 ounces of marijuana.

Then he tracked the phone number to Austin Serb. Andreoli knew about Serb from several anonymous tips called in to the department. He had heard rumors of the giant safe where Serb kept his money. Andreoli thought he might be an up-and-comer in the Boise drug scene, and this could be an easy chance to take him off the streets.

At around 10 p.m., Andreoli was waiting inside a Jack in the Box when surveillance officers saw Serb arrive in a maroon Pontiac. Andreoli watched as Serb entered, and another officer made the arrest.

Serb's career as a drug dealer might have ended there, but he didn't go to jail. In Serb's account of the night, he made a deal with Andreoli to work as an informant in exchange for having the charge dropped. (Andreoli declined to discuss why Serb wasn't charged that night.)

According to Serb, police interviewed him several times after the bust about a good friend who was also a dealer. Serb says he told them his friend had left the game. He assumed they believed him, and that the fake information he was giving police would keep him out of jail.

Less than a month later, Serb graduated from high school. His career as a drug dealer was about to explode.

To smoke oxycodone, roll up a dollar bill or pull out the insides of a pen to make a "tooter." Tear a rectangular piece of foil, hold it flat in one hand, and place a pill at the top edge. Put the tooter in your mouth. With your other hand, aim a lighter's flame under the pill and tilt the foil at a 45-degree angle.

Suck the smoke into your lungs as the pill slides down the foil leaving a black trail. Hold. Exhale. The first hit burns your throat, but the second will be better because the painkiller will have begun to take effect. Follow the pill up and down the foil until it is gone.

The high comes on fast, a euphoric feeling of life itself slowing down, a calm feeling of absolute contentment. But the feeling is fleeting. Thirty minutes later, an addict will be itching for more.

In Boise, they call them "dirty 30s," or just "dirts," a reference to the 30-milligram oxycodone tablets users prefer.

Prescribed by doctors to treat pain, oxycodone is a strong synthetic opioid, a factory-made version of heroin with an almost identical molecular structure. Medical sales of prescription opioids nearly quadrupled from 1999 to 2014, and the explosion created an easy source for users, many of whom became addicts.

Like elsewhere, many of the earliest users in Boise sourced oxycodone pills from home medicine cabinets or stole them from grandparents.

Today, an opioid addiction epidemic is overwhelming law enforcement, addiction treatment centers, and social services providers across the country. From 1999 to 2015, the number of overdose deaths in the United States from prescription opioids and heroin more than quadrupled. Each year has been worse than the last, and public-health experts say there is no indication that the epidemic is slowing. It's one of the greatest public-health crises of our time.

Serb's personal policy on drug use was no meth, no crack, and no heroin. Everything else, he figured, wouldn't kill you, especially if it came from a prescription pill bottle.

The first time he smoked oxycodone, he didn't really like it. As he sucked the smoke into his lungs, he thought it tasted like burned sugar. Then it hit.

The high wasn't an event, like cocaine or ecstasy. It was like pushing pause, a warm and mellow body high, a feeling the fidgety high-strung kid had never looked for and didn't particularly enjoy.

Oxycodone wasn't easy to come by in Boise. Serb's customers were asking for it, but he didn't have a source.

At a concert of the rapper The Game in Boise, he made the connection that changed everything: Ajellon Dedeaux, a California drug dealer who he called A.J. In the parking lot after the show, a friend of Serb's bought a half-pound of marijuana from A.J.

To Serb, A.J. was just another weed dealer. Maybe a source. But later, when Serb contacted him to ask if he could get prescription painkillers, A.J. mailed him 300 pills stuffed inside a teddy bear. Serb paid him $12 a pill.

When Serb texted his buyers to let them know he had painkillers, his phone lit up. Serb drove from one side of Boise to the other, all day long and into the night, dropping off pills at $40 a pop. Within a week, they were gone. He walked away with more than $8,000. Nothing had ever sold that fast. He put in another order to A.J. and waited for the shipment. Again they sold out.

Within months, Serb was selling 1,000 pills a week, sometimes twice that, shipped inside teddy bears, or hidden inside glass-bowl candles that had been melted and repoured with pill bottles encased inside. Serb stored the pills in a hollowed-out broom handle he kept in his garage.

Selling painkillers was easier than pushing marijuana and other drugs, where strains are different and buyers are picky and always looking for the next best thing. With oxycodone there were never any complaints.

And because the drug is so addictive, Serb's buyers usually came back for more, often with friends. Each week was better than the last, and the money was piling up.

Serb didn't trust banks. He kept money in safes, shoe boxes, and with longtime friends who didn't use drugs—people he thought he could trust.

And he kept much of it in his wallet, a leather Tommy Hilfiger that flopped out of his back pocket, so thick it couldn't be folded. Serb started most days nearly empty. By nightfall, his wallet was packed with thousands of dollars, almost all of it in $20 bills.

His B.C. friends called it the Serb Wallet. It was the thing, but also a concept—the source of the group's fun. It paid for Serb's jewelry, giant televisions, fur coats, and basketball shoes. It paid for sushi dinners for a dozen friends, paintball outings, and endless laps at Fast Lane, an indoor go-kart track.

Serb was generous with his money. He never had much as a kid, and throwing it around felt good. His policy was money was for spending. It was everything for everyone, always on the Serb Wallet.

Not long after he met A.J., Serb rented adjoining rooms at a Holiday Inn and invited the entire Bro Council, as well as his new friends from the drug trade. They pulled the door connecting the rooms off its hinges, set it flat on two chairs in the open doorway, and played all-night beer pong tournaments. Serb set out a bag of cocaine for guests.

Austin Serb wasn't the only dealer in town, but he was the biggest, and the only dealer with consistent supply. By 2012, he had cornered the market for painkillers in Boise, a high-desert city of around 225,000. He employed 11 pushers, each with their own territory, armed them with iPhones, and paid bonuses to top sellers.

Together, they sold painkillers to thousands of customers, mostly men in their early 20s. But they also sold to women, and older people. Everyone, it seemed, had a taste for the drug. For every $9,000 they brought in, Serb's take was $3,000.

After setting up his crew, Serb did less selling. He managed shipments and sent wire transfers to A.J.—sometimes as much as $15,000, which he heard was the cutoff before people got suspicious—using the fake name Austin Knowles. If bankers asked, Serb told them he ran a business importing high-performance car parts from Japan. Usually, they didn't ask.

And he got high. Oxycodone, anticlimactic when he first tried it, quickly became like food—he needed it to get through the day. He didn't like the high, which sapped all his energy, but smoking oxy kept away the dope sickness, an intense nausea followed by a soul-wrenching depression like he had never experienced.

The down, which came on fast, made Serb feel like he was starving, paired with the feelings you get when a girl breaks your heart: hurt, anxiety, and a loss of motivation and hope.

For years, Serb had raided magazine racks, looking for anything he could find on import tuner cars—the sports cars, mostly from Japan, that people modify heavily for optimum performance and style. He could quote the zero-to-60 times and horsepower ratings of a dizzying array of cars, but the closest he'd come to driving one was the racing games he played on his Xbox.

In the spring of 2012, Serb and his friend Devyn loaded a shoe box filled with $12,000 in the trunk of Devyn's Subaru and set out for Tacoma, Washington. Serb had found his dream car—a white RX-7—on Craigslist.

Devyn drove, with Serb smoking in the passenger seat. The old friends planned to buy the car, then drive to Seattle and check out the city. It would be a sort of victory lap for Serb. He packed a few dozen oxycodone pills for the trip.

They drove for eight hours, the length of Oregon and up through Washington, smoke from melting painkillers filling the car. When they arrived at a Walmart parking lot in Tacoma to meet the seller, Serb had already smoked through most of his stash. He was nervous. The seller was late.

Finally, a lowered silver Mitsubishi Lancer Evolution with wide wheels and a snarling exhaust note pulled up. A young Asian guy rolled down his window. But it wasn't the guy Serb talked to on the phone. The guy told Devyn to follow him to the Mazda. It felt weird, Serb thought, almost like a drug deal, as they followed the Evo through town and into a subdivision.

The guy in the Evo stopped in front of a house and waived them into a driveway. Just as Devyn turned off the Subaru, a dozen Asian guys piled out of the house. Something didn't feel right. Suddenly, a brand new Nismo 370Z pulled into the driveway, blocking them in.

"Shit," Serb said to Devyn. "It's a set-up."

He'd told the seller he would be paying in cash. Now they were stuck, two guys from Boise with $12,000 in drug money in the trunk.

Just then, the garage door started inching up in front of them, and Serb saw five-inch exhaust pipes poking out from under the ground effects of the RX-7. Then he saw the driver's door, which opened vertically, like on a Lamborghini. The seller hadn't told him about the Lambo doors.

The car was like a fantasy from one of his car magazines. Serb quickly handed over the shoe box of money to the guy who stepped out of the Nismo and signed the title. Twenty minutes later, they were gone.

Over the next two years, the Mazda would become Serb's calling card, a sign of his success. He treated it like a person, posting a series of photos on social media and dropping tens of thousands of dollars to make it faster and prettier.

But on the day he bought the car, Serb was unable to drive it. He didn't yet know how to operate a stage-5 racing clutch.

Serb's nerves were frayed, and he was nearly out of pills. Continuing on to Seattle was out of the question. The two friends caravanned back to Boise, Devyn driving the Mazda, Serb following in the Subaru, the sickness creeping up in his stomach.

Serb thought the Boise police had given up on the Jack in the Box charges. He was wrong. Almost a year and a half after his arrest, he was upstairs in his apartment when his girlfriend came up looking worried.

"Austin, there's cops downstairs," she said.

"You let them in?" he said, thinking about the $30,000 he had in the safe and hundreds of pills hidden in the house.

He went downstairs, and the police arrested him. Serb didn't even understand the charges. It was about drugs, but which drugs? The police didn't seem to be raiding the house. Instead, they led him to a police car and to jail. Later, when he learned that prosecutors had filed charges from the Jack in the Box bust, he was relieved. It was only a bit of weed—probation at the worst.

Out on bail, Serb hired a criminal defense attorney. And he began to reconsider his future. The charges were minor, but they could have been much worse. He took the bust as a sign.

Altogether, Serb had around $120,000, enough, he figured, to stop selling drugs, fight his charges, and figure out a new life. Over the next five months, he stopped selling and cut back on his drug use, instead spending his days playing the first-person shooter video game *Call of Duty* and preparing for his court appearance.

At the final hearing, Serb got off on a technicality. He remembers walking up to Andreoli with a cocky grin. "Keep doing what you're doing," Serb says he told the detective.

Andreoli doesn't remember the exchange, but he took the loss hard. It was a clean bust, easy even. Serb had come right to him. He was frustrated with a legal system that would put someone like Austin Serb back out on the street. He'd come to believe that Serb was behind the spike in oxycodone in the city, and the chance to take him out had failed.

Though the impact of Serb's dealing on Boise is difficult to quantify with precision, Andreoli says his caseload as a narcotics detective was consumed by opioids during the years Serb sold oxycodone. And uniformed police (the ones who respond to suspicious deaths) noticed a marked rise of young, seemingly healthy men and women overdosing from painkillers.

Serb didn't immediately go back to selling drugs after beating the charges, but attorney fees and his own drug use, which was once again spiking, quickly burned through his savings. Plus, he was bored sitting in his apartment, often by himself. His phone was silent. The Serb Wallet was gone.

Within a few months, he was selling again, and as business ramped up, so did his paranoia.

In late 2012, Serb moved in with Devyn and set up a system of surveillance cameras outside the house. He bought a handheld metal detector and swiped visitors to make sure they weren't wearing a wire. On the telephone, he insisted buyers call him Brody in case the cops were listening in.

He was right to be concerned. After losing in court, Andreoli opened a narcotics-unit investigation into Serb's network, and agents quickly began to learn the scope of Serb's operation. They collected trash outside Devyn's house and found broken candles with voids the size of pill bottles and squares of tinfoil with the telltale tracks of melting oxycodone pills. They knew the pills were coming from out of town, but they didn't know where, or who was sending them.

But before Andreoli could present a search-warrant request to a judge, Serb moved again, holing up in an apartment across town. It would be months before Andreoli could locate him.

On the day after Christmas, 2013, Serb walked through the food court and out the doors of the Towne Square Mall to pass some pills off to a friend who was parked outside. Before he'd left his apartment, he'd hid his stash in his secret spot inside a baseball hat, and packed dozens of painkillers in the pocket of his black fur coat.

Since high school, Serb had grown to over six feet, but he was down to 140 pounds, with deep black circles around his eyes and pasty skin. To offset the oxycodone pills he smoked—as many as 30 a day now—he snorted a gram a day of high-quality flaky cocaine dealers called "fish scale." All his pushers were also addicted by now, and they were making stupid mistakes—taking the drugs they were supposed to sell, losing money.

Serb knew Andreoli was watching him, but he had a more immediate problem. It had been a year since he'd nearly sped past the police car at more than 100 miles per hour on his way to a drug test. (He hadn't gotten the job, and he and his girlfriend had since broken up.)

Boise Police Sergeant Matthew Bryngelson had not missed the speeding white RX-7 in his driver's side mirror. The car was going so fast—perhaps 120 miles per hour, or more, Bryngelson wrote in a police report—that the officer had thought a police car might already be in pursuit. None was.

When Serb slammed on the brakes, Bryngelson saw smoke billow up under the front and rear wheel wells. The officer thought for a moment that the RX-7 might slam into his cruiser.

Bryngelson didn't pull Serb over that day because he had two prisoners in the back seat. But he did record Serb's plate number and called it in to dispatch before exiting the interstate.

Later that day, Bryngelson received a call from Ted Arnold, a Boise Police officer who worked as a school resource officer at Timberline High School, where Serb graduated. Arnold recognized the description of the Mazda, and he helped Bryngelson find Serb's Facebook page.

"Mobbing 130 mph," the officer read. "And blow past a cop. Hahahaha."

When Serb's wanted picture turned up on the Boise Police website a few days later, he turned himself in. But Serb's attorney won continuance after continuance, and the case dragged on for more than a year. Serb put the charges out of his mind. By Christmas, he'd already missed a couple of court dates on the reckless driving charge and had two warrants out for his arrest.

Two plainclothes officers were following him that day as he walked past the Cheesecake Factory, exited the mall, and handed pills to his friend. He lit a Parliament. Someone yelled his name.

Serb turned and saw the officers. He turned away, reached into his coat, and jammed the pill bottle deep in the compression underwear he wore for exactly this purpose.

Next thing Serb knew, he was on the ground in handcuffs, the cops hammering him with questions. He played it cool. Later, in jail, police found 72 pills in his underwear.

Serb woke up the next morning dope-sick in the Ada County Jail. He faced multiple felony drug charges. He downed a large plate of spaghetti at lunchtime, and headed back to a shared cell with an exposed toilet in the center.

He climbed to his top bunk and lay down. Soon he was sweating through his clothes, then freezing, his guts twisted up tight. It was a feeling he knew well. He got himself down off the bed, but didn't make it to the toilet. He barfed the spaghetti right onto the floor.

Serb couldn't stand up. On his hands and knees, he felt like he would black out. A cellmate called to a guard, and they moved Serb to a medical cell.

As he went through withdrawal over the next three days, Serb felt starved. But every time he ate, he threw up. He was sick of being an addict, he thought. When he got out of jail, he planned to take buprenorphine to kill the cravings and try to get clean.

Serb made bail again, and a bondsman drove him to the second-story condo with a view of a lake, where he had moved a year earlier. As they navigated through the streets of Boise, Serb had a bad feeling. Everything seemed wrong, and being off drugs made it worse.

He opened the door to his condo and hit the light.

The spot on the floor where his 70-inch flat-screen sat was empty. Then he saw the balcony door, kicked off its hinges. His favorite oil painting—the one with the Italian ocean view—wasn't on the wall.

Serb ran to his room and shuffled through his hat rack for his pills. Gone. So were his Rolex and gold chains.

Surely it was someone in his crew, he thought. Only someone who knew he had been arrested and knew where he kept his pills could have done it.

He called a dealer friend. He needed pills. But everyone in Boise was seemingly out of everything except heroin. That evening, he tied off a vein in his arm and shot up for the first time.

Serb was out of money. Other dealers were moving in on his business, and he was losing his source. Several months earlier, A.J. had driven to Boise and beat Serb up for smoking though $12,000 worth of pills he'd fronted him. A.J. was now relying on others in Serb's network to push pills in Boise.

Serb had one thing left. He drove his Mazda to the auto shop that had done his engine work and put the car down on an $8,000 loan to buy a shipment of painkillers. He never was able to buy back the car.

Over the next few months, Serb stayed in his condo, often with Andrew Colwell, an expert in manufacturing hash oil, the waxy concentrated cannabis extracted with butane and other solvents. The two dealers smoked and played Xbox *Forza*, often nodding off on the racetrack, leaving only when they had to pick up shipments.

He didn't know it, but the end was already in sight. Two months before Serb's arrest at the mall, Andreoli appealed to the Drug Enforcement Administration for a federal wiretap investigation into Serb's network. By November of 2013, Andreoli, a DEA agent, and members of the Boise Police narcotics unit were listening through the night as Serb set up buys and talked with his pushers. The DEA dubbed the investigation Operation Candle Wax.

Late one evening, as Andreoli sat in the DEA's office with his headphones on, he heard Serb tell a buyer that a girl at a party was overdosing. It was a pivotal moment for the investigation. If the police forced their way into the apartment, they would tip Serb off. If they didn't, the girl could die.

The investigators dispatched a patrol officer to the apartment and waited. By the time the officer arrived, Serb had performed CPR on the girl and she was breathing. Hearing the police radio at the door, Serb snuck to the garage, squeezed through a tiny window, and ran. Later, on the wire, Andreoli heard Serb conclude that someone at the party must have called the police.

That night, Andreoli knew the investigation had to end soon, before more people became addicted, or somebody died. He worried that Serb himself, now 20, couldn't sustain the damage of the drugs he was taking.

By January, less than two months after the wire went live, the DEA operation identified A.J. in Sacramento as the source of the painkillers flooding the valley. They had gathered what they thought was solid evidence on Serb and his network of pushers. They were almost ready to move.

In January, Andrew Colwell traveled to Sacramento to teach A.J.

how to make hash oil. While in California, Colwell sent several packages back to Boise. DEA agents followed him to the post office and snagged several of the packages, finding hundreds of oxycodone pills packed inside teddy bears.

On March 7th, one of Serb's pushers picked Serb up in a Toyota Celica. They got high on the last of Serb's pills and drove to an associate's house to pick up the package from Colwell. The package was late. Serb was anxious. A lot of packages had been turning up late, or not at all. His dealers were smoking their stashes. Everything was falling apart.

Serb called Colwell's cell phone to ask for the tracking number, but Colwell wasn't answering. It didn't take a genius to figure it out. Serb had been ripped off again. Someone had made off with the package.

Serb was coming down and he needed to smoke. One of his pushers set up a meeting to buy some pills in the parking lot of a bookstore. Serb hunkered down in the back seat of the Celica as they drove through town.

Both cars pulled into the bookstore parking lot, but before Serb could get out of the Celica, men in ski masks and sunglasses carrying assault rifles swarmed the car.

Serb thought he was getting robbed. Somebody knew he was supposed to make a pick-up today. He laughed, thinking about how the guys in ski masks would go away empty-handed. Then he heard it.

"DEA! Get the fuck on the ground!"

In the visitation room of a low-security federal prison outside Denver, inmates sit in rows of plastic chairs anchored to the floor.

It is a warm afternoon in April of 2017. Serb, now 24, wears khaki pants, a work shirt, and fashionable plastic-frame eyeglasses. His light brown hair is cropped close on the sides and slicked over in an aggressive part. Gone are the sunken, dark-rimmed eyes and pasty skin. He is up to 195 pounds, thanks to the days spent leading workouts in the prison gym. He is off drugs, which he says are widely available inside the prison, and his fidgety cooped-up energy is back.

In 2016, Serb was sentenced to 10 years in prison after pleading guilty to conspiracy to distribute oxycodone. A.J. also pleaded guilty and was sentenced to 12 years. Ten of Serb's associates were given lesser prison sentences.

As visitors carry plastic bags filled with quarters toward vending machines to buy snacks for prisoners, Serb considers the events that turned him from a homeschooled middle school kid into a major drug dealer. By his own accounting, Serb pushed 5,000 oxycodone pills a month into southwestern Idaho's Treasure Valley. In three years, he made millions of dollars.

Maybe selling drugs made him feel important, he says. He was the plug, as they put it in the drug trade, the guy everyone needed to know—or at least everyone who liked to get high.

He insists he has no money or anything else left from his days of crime.

"You know, even if I had some kind of millions of dollars stashed away somewhere, it still wouldn't be worth it," he says. "I have thought of it. Even if I had a million dollars stashed, I would probably pay that just to get out for a year."

Some of his associates are already out of prison. Some, like Andrew Colwell, have kicked their addictions and are getting their lives back on track. Others have many years yet to serve.

Meanwhile, opioid addiction continues to ravage Boise. Asked about his role in that, Serb fidgets in his seat and stammers. His face turns red.

"I've thought about that a lot," he says. "And . . ."

It's not something he can put words to. There's not really anything to say.

Later, in an email from prison, he revisits the topic.

"You asked me a few times about how I feel about the damage I caused to people. . . . I can't tell you the level of guilt and sorry I feel. I wish there was more I can do. But once given the chance, I will do what I can to help, specifically addicts."

In Boise, the oxycodone epidemic has come and gone, replaced by heroin.

That's the irony of taking down Austin Serb, Andreoli says as he looks through binders of evidence from the case. Putting Serb and his network in prison slowed the flow of oxycodone into the valley. Addicts were forced to adapt.

Like elsewhere in America, they moved from synthetic heroin to the real thing, which is easier to find and less expensive. In 2014, the year Serb was arrested, there were 33 heroin arrests in Boise. In 2016, that number jumped to 178.

Andreoli is conflicted about the dealer he tracked for so long. He knows addiction is a big part of what led Serb into trouble. That, and the hopeless disregard for consequences that is a part of being a teenager.

But the damage he caused is hard to ignore.

"In this valley, I blame Austin Serb and that crew for creating so many opiate addicts to the point that now heroin has such a stronghold," he says.

Serb reads the Bible every day now. He is studying social psychology in college classes at the prison and tutors other prisoners who are studying for their GEDs.

He knows that getting caught saved him. A few months earlier, a good friend in Boise had died of a painkiller overdose. If Serb hadn't ended up in prison on federal drug charges, he says, he'd probably be dead too.

1 SON, 4 OVERDOSES, 6 HOURS: A FAMILY'S ANGUISH

Katharine Q. Seelye

The New York Times, January 21, 2018

The first time Patrick Griffin overdosed one afternoon in May, he was still breathing when his father and sister found him on the floor around 1:30. When he came to, he was in a foul mood and began arguing with his father, who was fed up with his son's heroin and fentanyl habit.

Patrick, 34, feeling morose and nauseated, lashed out. He sliced a love seat with a knife, smashed a glass bowl, kicked and broke a side table and threatened to kill himself. Shortly after 3, he darted into the bathroom, where he shot up and overdosed again. He fell limp, turned blue and lost consciousness. His family called 911. Emergency medical workers revived him with Narcan, the antidote that reverses opioid overdoses.

Throughout the afternoon his parents, who are divorced, tried to persuade Patrick to go into treatment. His father told him he could not live with him anymore, setting off another shouting match. Around 4, Patrick slipped away and shot up a third time. He overdosed again, and emergency workers came back and revived him again. They took him to a hospital, but Patrick checked himself out.

Back at his mother's house and anxious to stave off withdrawal, he shot up again around 7:30, overdosing a fourth time in just six hours. His mother, frantic, tried pumping his chest, to no avail, and feared he was dead. Rescue workers returned and administered three doses of Narcan to bring him back. At that point, an ambulance took him to the hospital under a police escort and his parents—terrified, angry and wrung out—had him involuntarily admitted.

The torrent of people who have died in the opioid crisis has transfixed and horrified the nation, with overdose now the leading cause of death for Americans under 50.

But most drug users do not die. Far more, like Patrick, are snared for years in a consuming, grinding, unending cycle of addiction.

In the 20 years that Patrick has been using drugs, he has lost track of how many times he has overdosed. He guesses 30, a number experts say would not be surprising for someone taking drugs off and on for that long.

Patrick and his family allowed The New York Times to follow them for much of the past year because they said they wanted people to understand the realities of living with drug addiction. Over the months, their lives played out in an almost constant state of emergency or dread, their days dictated by whether Patrick would shoot up or not. For an entire family, many of the arguments, the decisions, the plans came back to him and that single question. Even in the cheeriest moments, when Patrick was clean, everyone—including him—seemed to be bracing for the inevitable moment when he would turn back to drugs.

"We are your neighbors," his mother, Sandy Griffin, said of the many families living with addiction, "and this is the B.S. going on in the house."

In Patrick's home state of New Hampshire, which leads the country in deaths per capita from fentanyl, almost 500 people died of overdoses in 2016. The government estimates that 10 percent of New Hampshire residents—about 130,000 people—are addicted to drugs or alcohol. The overall burden to the state, including health care and criminal justice costs and lost worker productivity, has ballooned into the billions of dollars. Some people do recover, usually after multiple relapses. But the opioid scourge, here and elsewhere, has overwhelmed police and fire departments, hospitals, prosecutors, public defenders, courts, jails and the foster care system.

Most of all, though, it has upended families.

All of the Griffins speak of nonstop stress. They have lived through chaotic days: When the parents called the police on their children (both Patrick and his sister, Betsy, have been addicted to drugs); when Dennis, the father, a recovering alcoholic, worried that every thud on the floor was Patrick passing out; and when Sandy was, by turns, paralyzed with a common parental fear—that she had somehow caused her children's problems—or was out driving around looking for them on the streets.

For much of his adult life, Patrick, who once dreamed of writing graphic novels, has had no job and no prospects. He has a lengthy record of arrests, and the times he has been clean, he has always seemed to be on the verge of derailing his family once again. He got money to buy drugs by selling them at a profit.

Dennis, 66, a retired iron worker who also worked at a light bulb manufacturing plant, spends his days on the phone, trying to assist his addicted son with lawyers, counselors, insurance companies, even politicians—a whole new career he never sought and one he now fears may never end.

Patrick's younger sister, Betsy, 29, who used to shoot heroin with him, is in recovery and has a job, but Patrick's influence is a constant threat.

And Sandy, 59, a waitress, is determined to maintain a sense of peace, even as she is constantly on guard, knowing that her children could at any time pick up a needle. That comes with a question she can never push away—if they did, would it be for the last time?

"It's a merry-go-round, and he can't get off," Sandy said of Patrick and his overdoses. "The first couple of times, I started thinking, 'At least he's not dead.' I still think that. But he's hurting. He's sick. He needs to learn to live with the pain of being alive."

An Intervention

One day in July, Patrick's family staged a spur-of-the-moment intervention in his mother's living room in Pembroke, a pre-Revolutionary town in central New Hampshire not far from the state capital, Concord. In her apartment, up a set of steep, dark steps, the curtains were pulled against a blistering midday heat. Floor fans thrummed but did little more than push around the thick, dead air.

Sandy sat by Patrick on the sofa, a pillow clenched to her stomach. Dennis told Patrick he could no longer live with him and urged him to seek help.

Patrick shot down every suggestion.

"My father would never have put up with any of this," Dennis erupted.

"Your father was from the Stone Age," Patrick shot back. "There are better ways to handle these situations these days."

Dennis turned to his ex-wife.

"Aren't you going to—" he started to say.

"What am I going to make him do?" Sandy said sharply, anticipating a rebuke for being too soft on their son. "Don't put the finger on me, because that's what you're doing."

Dennis told Patrick, who had overdosed once again the night before, that he should turn himself in to the "safe station" program at the fire department, which helps people with addiction find treatment. Patrick scoffed. He did not even look at his parents.

"You've detoxed in jail before," Dennis said, "so it can't be worse than that."

"You have no idea how bad that was," Patrick said.

"Then why are you still using?" his father pleaded. "That makes no sense to me."

"I know it doesn't, Dad," Patrick snapped, "because you're not a heroin addict."

As a young teenager, Patrick had been bullied, and later he was diagnosed with attention deficit hyperactivity disorder, his parents said. He said he started self-medicating at age 14 with beer and marijuana, then moved on to cocaine and crystal meth. "All I wanted to do was get high and forget," he said. The meth made him vomit, so he turned to prescription painkillers that his friends stole from their parents. When the government tightened the supply of painkillers, Patrick sought out heroin and fentanyl.

"I thought, 'Nothing is going to kill me,'" he said.

Years later, he was diagnosed with major depression and borderline antisocial personality disorder, his family said, and more recently, post-traumatic stress disorder, illnesses that often go hand-in-hand with substance misuse. He has worked with mental health counselors for years, his family said, and has been on and off antidepressants.

For anyone in New Hampshire seeking heroin and fentanyl, a ready supply awaits, just over the state line in Massachusetts. The old mill towns of Lawrence and Lowell have long served as hubs of major drug distribution networks that funnel opioids throughout New England. Law enforcement officers say that dealers there often drop baggies of drugs into the open passenger windows of cars stopped at red lights.

Back when Patrick had a job at an auto-parts store and as a banquet server, his morning routine involved driving to Lawrence before work and scoring his daily fix.

Then he would shoot up with heroin or fentanyl at the wheel of the car while driving back to New Hampshire.

"I'd get these looks from people who would see me using," Patrick recalled. "Some guy started yelling at me and honking. They didn't know that I needed to get this in me so I wouldn't be sick anymore."

At one point on that steamy day in July, several hours into the family intervention, the conversation reached a lull. Patrick stepped out of the room and padded down a hallway in his bare feet.

He pulled a box from beneath his sister's bed and disappeared into the bathroom. Ten minutes later, he returned. His eyes drooped. He slouched on the sofa. He twitched and tugged at his goatee and plugged and unplugged his cellphone, an unlit cigarette in his hand.

Yes, he acknowledged a few minutes later. As his parents despaired over his future, he had been getting high.

"Needles All Over"

Patrick was high again a day later when he was arrested at a Burger King with a bag of Xanax bulging from one of his socks. He was charged with possession with intent to distribute, then blacked out.

He awoke in a small, concrete cell, charged with three felonies and two misdemeanors. Bail was set at $10,000 cash.

In jail, he was kept from all drugs, including Suboxone, an opioid substitute that eases withdrawal symptoms and that Patrick had been prescribed by a doctor years earlier as part of an effort to transition him into treatment. New Hampshire is among several states that have banned Suboxone from prisons because inmates often sell it to each other, sometimes leading to overdoses.

Patrick went into an intense withdrawal, with extreme vomiting and diarrhea, in a cramped 6-foot-by-8-foot cell that he shared with another inmate. His cellmate, who stayed on the top bunk, faced the wall and tuned him out, Patrick said. He said a second mattress was placed on the floor next to his lower bunk in case he fell out during a seizure.

"I was sweating," he said. "My eyes wouldn't stop watering. My nose wouldn't stop running. And I was so sleep deprived, I was seeing things." The worst of his symptoms persisted for more than 10 days. The aroma of food made him nauseous. Patrick, who is 5-foot-9, dropped to 133 pounds.

He spent seven weeks in jail, then 28 days in an inpatient treatment program as his legal case made its way through the courts.

By early October, the program was done, he was temporarily released on his own recognizance, and he had been drug-free for almost three months. And yet his family churned with anxiety. Having him locked away in jail was gloomy and unsettling. But it was nothing compared with the dread of having him out.

"He's going to come back and do the exact same thing, and I don't know how to stop it," Dennis said before Patrick was released and moved back in with him.

"That's what happens every time," Dennis said, sitting at his dining room table in his spare, tidy home. "I find needles all over the house. They're in back of the toaster. They're in the bathroom, underneath the vanity. They're upstairs. They're in the basement."

Still, this time, Patrick seemed different.

Patrick and his father joined a gym and began working out together. Patrick muscled up and put on 30 pounds. Color returned to his gaunt face.

But without drugs, Patrick said, he felt lost. He was not in treatment, had no mental health counselor and no job. If he wanted treatment to help him keep his resolve, he could not afford it. He had no insurance—incarceration automatically cost him his Medicaid benefits. His parents had long ago spent their savings to pay for lawyers, counselors and legally prescribed medications.

His stint in jail had also cost Patrick his slot with his mental health counselor, who had taken on so many new patients in Patrick's absence that she had no room for him when he returned.

What he did still have was his family.

Since Dennis retired a few years ago, he has spent much of his time trying to cope with his son's addiction. On many days, he waits for return calls from people like Patrick's public defender to find out the status of his legal case, or from the Medicaid bureaucracy to restart Patrick's benefits. He sometimes calls the offices of New Hampshire's top politicians to urge them to crack down harder on opioids.

"You wait for retirement, you wait for that magic age when your kids are grown and you can actually do something," Dennis said. "All I see is me just dying. I don't want them to die before me."

Diverging Paths

Patrick's sister Betsy has also been in and out of rehab and jail. But she is in recovery now and her life looks far different. She has a job working at an animal rescue shelter. She bought a car and started community college this month, her sights set on becoming a veterinary technician.

All of it raises a question: Why is one person from the same family, the same background, and who has the same attraction to drugs, able to stop, but another cannot seem to?

Sandy and Dennis have an older daughter, Jane, 37, an apprentice carpenter, who is not addicted. She has tried to distance herself from the family drama and has moved out of the area. Although she visits often, moving away has left her with what she describes as survivor's guilt.

"I had to make a conscious effort to put space between myself and them, for my own self-preservation," she said. "I'd already come to terms with the fact that my brother was going to die—I've already mourned him."

Jane has thought long and hard about why some people from the same background become addicted and others don't. She thinks she was spared because she never tried opioids in the first place.

"I don't know anyone who just 'tried' it and then stopped," she said. "Watching Pat do this was heartbreaking, but watching Betsy—who was outgoing, did well in high school and was planning on college—was super frustrating. I wanted to shake her, and say, 'You know how this goes. Knock it off.'"

Sandy said that Betsy, who completed a highly structured treatment program and underwent cognitive behavioral therapy, seemed more motivated than Patrick to quit.

And Betsy, who started using drugs at 19, said she suspected that Patrick had a harder time quitting because he had started when he was 14. A Surgeon General's report in 2016 said that the younger people are when they start taking drugs, the more likely they are to become addicted long-term. "His brain is still that young," Betsy said. "As intelligent as he is, this is his only coping mechanism."

It was especially difficult getting clean while her brother was still using, Betsy said, as she cuddled a frisky mutt outside the animal shelter. Now, Patrick stays with his father and Betsy lives with her mother; everyone is wary that if the siblings lived together, they could drag one another down.

Patrick said Betsy had succeeded where he had not because she had found passion in her work. She saw glimpses of herself in the shelter dogs and their painful pasts; when she was 8, her parents divorced and her father was drinking. She said she sometimes had to take care of him.

"She loves those dogs," Patrick said.

He said that during periods when he has been clean, he tends to take on too much, as he did last year when he signed up for multiple coding courses at community college. He said the heavy caseload left him frustrated, with failing grades. That preceded the relapse in May when he overdosed four times in a single afternoon.

Like many parents in families torn apart by drugs, Sandy has blamed herself. For a time, she wondered if she was too permissive, even as she reported her children to the police and kicked them out of the house.

At Al-Anon sessions for families of alcoholics, Sandy learned what are known as the four C's—"You didn't cause it, you can't control it and you can't cure it, but you can contribute to it." She said she came to understand that she had been an enabler. "Even though you think you're helping them, you're not," she said.

Now, Sandy sounds almost fatalistic about addiction.

"You could be the best parent in the world, but if it's going to happen, it's going to happen," she said. "It doesn't matter what walk of life you come from."

Patrick lives with his father, but he often feels crowded by him and visits his mother a lot, usually for supper.

As a late fall day turned to dusk, Patrick lounged on an overstuffed chair in her living room. He said he had not used drugs since he went to jail in July and had applied for a job at a local packaging plant. But he also said he had no self-confidence and no idea how to break free from his cravings.

"I'm afraid I'm going to screw it up all over again," he said. "That's what happens every time."

He said he knew he was not a sympathetic figure, that people may look at his life and wonder why he cannot pull himself out of this hole, especially with so much family backing.

"I feel like I've got nothing to offer," he said. "I'm depressed all the time, and I'm isolating myself. I don't really know what sober people do."

His eyes welled with tears and he scraped them, hard, with his open palms.

"I don't want people to pity me," he added. "But I don't want to lie to people about my past, either. I have a hard time asking for help. I always say, 'I got this.' But I never got this."

Seeking Solid Ground

On an unseasonably warm night in late October, Sandy attended a support group for parents of addicted children.

On this evening, 17 people showed up at the group, called Families Sharing Without Shame. All had adult children either in the throes of addiction or in recovery. As they sat in a circle, they shared their horror at discovering the drug use going on under their roofs. They drew nods of recognition when they said they finally understood why their teaspoons were vanishing from their kitchens (powdered opioids are heated in a spoon with water to convert them to a liquid that can be injected).

Unlike some of the other parents, Sandy seemed battle hardened, like one who had been immersed in a war for a long time.

"I lost myself 10 years ago," she told the group. "I couldn't go to work, I couldn't get out of bed." She said she was consumed by codependency, in which "you are addicted to this human being to save them."

She said she had realized that she had to save herself. Among her escapes: She learned to play the violin and bought a pair of kayaks.

"Being selfish is not a bad thing," she told the other parents, some of whose children would die in the ensuing weeks.

But if Sandy has gotten better, Patrick still struggles.

"He suffers more than anybody," she said later that night after the group broke up. "He wants to be a man, a man who has a wife and kids and a car and a job. He wants to be that man and he doesn't know how to be that man."

The next morning was a spectacular New England fall day, warm and bright, with leaves ablaze in a kaleidoscope of copper and crimson. Sandy and Patrick took the kayaks to a lake and went for a long paddle.

Out on the water, there was no chance he would relapse because he had not hidden away any drugs. Besides, he was busy paddling, soaking up the sun on his face and watching the light dance on the water. Out there, he didn't have to look back over the ruins of the past or stress about what might come next.

But eventually they would have to return to shore, where life, for both Patrick and his family, would always seem on edge.

Over the next two months, things would look up for Patrick. He got the job at the packaging plant. His Medicaid benefits were restored. He was on antidepressants and was back in counseling.

And at a court hearing earlier this month, his legal case was more or less resolved: In a deal worked out with the prosecution, he planned to plead guilty to two misdemeanors, with the other charges dropped. Any jail sentence would be suspended as long as his good behavior continued and he stayed in counseling.

For drug users and their loved ones, though, the worry never ends. No day can be ordinary. The threat of relapse is constant.

When Patrick recently texted Sandy, saying, "I love you," her first thought was that he was about to kill himself. She frantically called him back. Patrick told her he was fine, he had just been thinking about her.

For a moment, Sandy caught her breath.

THE POISON WE PICK

Andrew Sullivan

New York, February 19, 2018

It is a beautiful, hardy flower, *Papaver somniferum*, a poppy that grows up to four feet in height and arrives in a multitude of colors. It thrives in temperate climates, needs no fertilizer, attracts few pests, and is as tough as many weeds. The blooms last only a few days and then the petals fall, revealing a matte, greenish-gray pod fringed with flutes. The seeds are nutritious and have no psychotropic effects. No one knows when the first curious human learned to crush this bulblike pod and mix it with water, creating a substance that has an oddly calming and euphoric effect on the human brain. Nor do we know who first found out that if you cut the pod with a small knife, capture its milky sap, and leave that to harden in the air, you'll get a smokable nugget that provides an even more intense experience. We do know, from Neolithic ruins in Europe, that the cultivation of this plant goes back as far as 6,000 years, probably farther. Homer called it a "wondrous substance." Those who consumed it, he marveled, "did not shed a tear all day long, even if their mother or father had died, even if a brother or beloved son was killed before their own eyes." For millennia, it has salved pain, suspended grief, and seduced humans with its intimations of the divine. It was a medicine before there was such a thing as medicine. Every attempt to banish it, destroy it, or prohibit it has failed.

The poppy's power, in fact, is greater than ever. The molecules derived from it have effectively conquered contemporary America. Opium, heroin, morphine, and a universe of synthetic opioids, including the superpowerful painkiller fentanyl, are its proliferating offspring. More than 2 million Americans are now hooked on some kind of opioid, and drug overdoses—from heroin and fentanyl in particular—claimed more American lives last year than were lost in the entire Vietnam War. Overdose deaths are higher than in the peak year of AIDS and far higher than fatalities from car crashes. The poppy, through its many offshoots, has now been responsible for a decline in life spans in America for two years in a row, a decline that isn't happening in any other developed nation. According to the best estimates, opioids will kill another 52,000 Americans this year alone—and up to half a million in the next decade.

We look at this number and have become almost numb to it. But of all the many social indicators flashing red in contemporary America, this is surely the brightest. Most of the ways we come to terms with this wave of mass death—by casting the pharmaceutical companies as the villains, or doctors as enablers, or blaming the Obama or Trump administrations or our policies of drug prohibition or our own collapse in morality and self-control or the economic stress the country is enduring—miss a deeper American story. It is a story of pain and the search for an end to it. It is a story of how the most ancient painkiller known to humanity has emerged to numb the agonies of the world's most highly evolved liberal democracy. Just as LSD helps explain the 1960s, cocaine the 1980s, and crack the 1990s, so opium defines this new era. I say era, because this trend will, in all probability, last a very long time. The scale and darkness of this phenomenon is a sign of a civilization in a more acute crisis than we knew, a nation overwhelmed by a warp-speed, postindustrial world, a culture yearning to give up, indifferent to life and death, enraptured by withdrawal and nothingness. America, having pioneered the modern way of life, is now in the midst of trying to escape it.

How does an opioid make you feel? We tend to avoid this subject in discussing recreational drugs, because no one wants to encourage experimentation, let alone addiction. And it's easy to believe that weak people take drugs for inexplicable, reckless, or simply immoral reasons. What few are prepared to acknowledge in public is that drugs alter consciousness in specific and distinct ways that seem to make people at least temporarily happy, even if the consequences can be dire. Fewer still are willing to concede that there is a significant difference between these various forms of drug-induced "happiness"—that the draw of crack, say, is vastly different than that of heroin. But unless you understand what users get out of an illicit substance, it's impossible to understand its appeal, or why an epidemic takes off, or what purpose it is serving in so many people's lives. And it is significant, it seems to me, that the drugs now conquering America are downers: They are not the means to engage in life more vividly but to seek a respite from its ordeals.

The alkaloids that opioids contain have a large effect on the human brain because they tap into our natural "mu-opioid" receptors. The oxytocin we experience from love or friendship or orgasm is chemically replicated by the molecules derived from the poppy plant. It's a shortcut—and an instant intensification—of the happiness we might ordinarily experience in a good and fruitful communal life. It ends not just physical pain but psychological, emotional, even existential pain. And it can easily become a lifelong entanglement for anyone it seduces, a love affair in which the passion is more powerful than even the fear of extinction.

Perhaps the best descriptions of the poppy's appeal come to us from the gifted writers who have embraced and struggled with it. Many of the Romantic luminaries of the early 19th century—including the poets Coleridge, Byron, Shelley, Keats, and Baudelaire, and the novelist Walter Scott—were as infused with opium as the late Beatles were with LSD. And the earliest and in many ways most poignant account of what opium and its derivatives feel like is provided by the classic memoir *Confessions of an English Opium-Eater*, published in 1821 by the writer Thomas De Quincey.

De Quincey suffered trauma in childhood, losing his sister when he was 6 and his father a year later. Throughout his life, he experienced bouts of acute stomach pain, as well as obvious depression, and at the age of 19 he endured 20 consecutive days of what he called "excruciating rheumatic pains of the head and face." As his pain drove him mad, he finally went into an apothecary and bought some opium (which was legal at the time, as it was across the West until the war on drugs began a century ago).

An hour after he took it, his physical pain had vanished. But he was no longer even occupied by such mundane concerns. Instead, he was overwhelmed with what he called the "abyss of divine enjoyment" that overcame him: "What an upheaving from its lowest depths, of the inner spirit! . . . here was the secret of happiness, about which philosophers had disputed for many ages." The sensation from opium was steadier than alcohol, he reported, and calmer. "I stood at a distance, and aloof from the uproar of life," he wrote. "Here were the hopes which blossom in the paths of life, reconciled with the peace which is in the grave." A century later, the French writer Jean Cocteau described the experience in similar ways: "Opium remains unique and the euphoria it induces superior to health. I owe it my perfect hours."

The metaphors used are often of lightness, of floating: "Rising even as it falls, a feather," as William Brewer, America's poet laureate of the opioid crisis, describes it. "And then, within a fog that knows what I'm going to do, before I do—weightlessness." Unlike cannabis, opium does not make you want to share your experience with others, or make you giggly or hungry or paranoid. It seduces you into solitude and serenity and provokes a profound indifference to food. Unlike cocaine or crack or meth, it doesn't rev you up or boost your sex drive. It makes you drowsy—*somniferum* means "sleep-inducing"—and lays waste to the libido. Once the high hits, your head begins to nod and your eyelids close.

When we see the addicted stumbling around like drunk ghosts, or collapsed on sidewalks or in restrooms, their faces pale, their skin riddled with infection, their eyes dead to the world, we often see only misery. What we do not see is what they see: In those moments, they feel beyond gravity, entranced away from pain and sadness. In the addict's eyes, it is those who are sober who are asleep. That is why the police and EMS workers who rescue those slipping toward death by administering blasts of naloxone—a powerful antidote, without which death rates would be even higher—are almost never thanked. They are hated. They ruined the high. And some part of being free from all pain makes you indifferent to death itself. Death is, after all, the greatest of existential pains. "Everything one achieves in life, even love, occurs in an express train racing toward death," Cocteau observed. "To smoke opium is to get out of the train while it is still moving. It is to concern oneself with something other than life or death."

This terrifyingly dark side of the poppy reveals itself the moment one tries to break free. The withdrawal from opioids is unlike any other. The waking nightmares, hideous stomach cramps, fevers, and psychic agony last for weeks, until the body chemically cleanses itself. "A silence," Cocteau wrote, "equivalent to the crying of thousands of children whose mothers do not return to give them the breast." Among the symptoms: an involuntary and constant agitation of the legs (whence the term "kicking the habit"). The addict becomes ashamed as his life disintegrates. He wants to quit, but, as De Quincey put it, he lies instead "under the weight of incubus and nightmare . . . he would lay down his life if he might get up and walk; but he is powerless as an infant, and cannot even attempt to rise."

The poppy's paradox is a profoundly human one: If you want to bring Heaven to Earth, you must also bring Hell. In the words of Lenny Bruce, "I'll die young, but it's like kissing God."

No other developed country is as devoted to the poppy as America. We consume 99 percent of the world's hydrocodone and 81 percent of its oxycodone. We use an estimated 30 times more opioids than is medically necessary for a population our size. And this love affair has been with us from the start. The drug was ubiquitous among both the British and American forces in the War of Independence as an indispensable medicine for the pain of battlefield injuries. Thomas Jefferson planted poppies at Monticello, and they became part of the place's legend (until the DEA raided his garden in 1987 and tore them out of the ground). Benjamin Franklin was reputed to be an addict in later life, as many were at the time. William Wilberforce, the evangelical who abolished the British slave trade, was a daily enthusiast. As Martin Booth explains in his classic history of the drug, poppies proliferated in America, and the use of opioids in over-the-counter drugs was commonplace. A wide range of household remedies were based on the poppy's fruit; among the most popular was an elixir called laudanum—the word literally means "praiseworthy"—which took off in England as early as the 17th century.

Mixed with wine or licorice, or anything else to disguise the bitter taste, opiates were for much of the 19th century the primary treatment for diarrhea or any physical pain. Mothers gave them to squalling infants as a "soothing syrup." A huge boom was kick-started by the Civil War, when many states cultivated poppies in order to treat not only the excruciating pain of horrific injuries but endemic dysentery. Booth notes that 10 million opium pills and 2 million ounces of opiates in powder or tinctures were distributed by Union forces. Subsequently, vast numbers of veterans became addicted—the condition became known as "Soldier's Disease"—and their high became more intense with the developments of morphine and the hypodermic needle. They were joined by millions of wives, sisters, and mothers who, consumed by postwar grief, sought refuge in the obliviating joy that opiates offered.

Based on contemporary accounts, it appears that the epidemic of the late 1860s and 1870s was probably more widespread, if far less intense, than today's—a response to the way in which the war tore up settled ways of life, as industrialization transformed the landscape, and as huge social change generated acute emotional distress. This aspect of the epidemic—as a response to mass social and cultural dislocation—was also clear among the working classes in the earlier part of the 19th century in Britain. As small armies of human beings were lured from their accustomed rural environments, with traditions and seasons and community, and thrown into vast new industrialized cities, the psychic stress gave opium an allure not even alcohol could match. Some historians estimate that as much as 10 percent of a working family's income in industrializing Britain was spent on opium. By 1870, opium was more available in the United States than tobacco was in 1970. It was as if the shift toward modernity and a wholly different kind of life for humanity necessitated for most working people some kind of relief—some way of getting out of the train while it was still moving.

It is tempting to wonder if, in the future, today's crisis will be seen as generated from the same kind of trauma, this time in reverse.

If industrialization caused an opium epidemic, deindustrialization is no small part of what's fueling our opioid surge. It's telling that the drug has not taken off as intensely among all Americans—especially not among the engaged, multiethnic, urban-dwelling, financially successful inhabitants of the coasts. The poppy has instead found a home in those places left behind—towns and small cities that owed their success to a particular industry, whose civic life was built around a factory or a mine. Unlike in Europe, where cities and towns existed long before industrialization, much of America's heartland has no remaining preindustrial history, given the destruction of Native American societies. The gutting of that industrial backbone—especially as globalization intensified in a country where market forces are least restrained—has been not just an economic fact but a cultural, even spiritual devastation. The pain was exacerbated by the Great Recession and has barely receded in the years since. And to meet that pain, America's uniquely market-driven health-care system was more than ready.

The great dream of the medical profession, which has been fascinated by opioids over the centuries, was to create an experience that captured the drug's miraculous pain relief but somehow managed to eliminate its intoxicating hook. The attempt to refine opium into a pain reliever without addictive properties produced morphine and later heroin—each generated by perfectly legal pharmaceutical and medical specialists for the most enlightened of reasons. (The word *heroin* was coined from the German word *Heroisch*, meaning "heroic," by the drug company Bayer.) In the mid-1990s, OxyContin emerged as the latest innovation: A slow timed release would prevent sudden highs or lows, which, researchers hoped, would remove craving and thereby addiction. Relying on a single study based on a mere 38 subjects, scientists concluded that the vast majority of hospital inpatients who underwent pain treatment with strong opioids did not go on to develop an addiction, spurring the drug to be administered more widely.

This reassuring research coincided with a social and cultural revolution in medicine: In the wake of the AIDS epidemic, patients were becoming much more assertive in managing their own treatment— and those suffering from debilitating pain began to demand the relief that the new opioids promised. The industry moved quickly to cash in on the opportunity: aggressively marketing the new drugs to doctors via sales reps, coupons, and countless luxurious conferences, while waging innovative video campaigns designed to be played in doctors' waiting rooms. As Sam Quinones explains in his indispensable account of the epidemic, *Dreamland*, all this happened at the same time that doctors were being pressured to become much more efficient under the new regime of "managed care." It was a fateful combination: Patients began to come into doctors' offices demanding pain relief, and doctors needed to process patients faster. A "pain" diagnosis was often the most difficult and time-consuming to resolve, so it became far easier just to write a quick prescription to abolish the discomfort rather than attempt to isolate its cause. The more expensive and laborious methods for treating pain—physical and psychological therapy—were abandoned almost overnight in favor of the magic pills.

A huge new supply and a burgeoning demand thereby created a massive new population of opioid users. Getting your opioid fix no longer meant a visit to a terrifying shooting alley in a ravaged city; now it just required a legitimate prescription and a bottle of pills that looked as bland as a statin or an SSRI. But as time went on, doctors and scientists began to realize that they were indeed creating addicts. Much of the initial, hopeful research had been taken from patients who had undergone opioid treatment as inpatients, under strict supervision. No one had examined the addictive potential of opioids for outpatients, handed bottles and bottles of pills, in doses that could be easily abused. Doctors and scientists also missed something only recently revealed about OxyContin itself: Its effects actually declined after a few hours, not 12—thus subjecting most patients to daily highs and lows and the increased craving this created. Patients whose pain hadn't gone away entirely were kept on opioids for longer periods of time and at higher dosages. And OxyContin had not removed the agonies of withdrawal: Someone on painkillers for three months would often find, as her prescription ran out, that she started vomiting or was convulsed with fever. The quickest and simplest solution was a return to the doctor.

Add to this the federal government's move in the mid-1980s to replace welfare payments for the poor with disability benefits—which covered opioids for pain—and unscrupulous doctors, often in poorer areas, found a way to make a literal killing from shady pill mills. So did many patients. A Medicaid co-pay of $3 for a bottle of pills, as Quinones discovered, could yield $10,000 on the streets—an economic arbitrage that enticed countless middle-class Americans to become drug dealers. One study has found that 75 percent of those addicted to opioids in the United States began with prescription painkillers given to them by a friend, family member, or dealer. As a result, the social and cultural profile of opioid users shifted as well: The old stereotype of a heroin junkie—a dropout or a hippie or a Vietnam vet—disappeared in the younger generation, especially in high schools. Football players were given opioids to mask injuries and keep them on the field; they shared them with cheerleaders and other popular peers; and their elevated social status rebranded the addiction. Now opiates came wrapped in the bodies and minds of some of the most promising, physically fit, and capable young men and women of their generation. Courtesy of their doctors and coaches.

It's hard to convey the sheer magnitude of what happened. Between 2007 and 2012, for example, 780 million hydrocodone and oxycodone pills were delivered to West Virginia, a state with a mere 1.8 million residents. In one town, population 2,900, more than 20 million opioid prescriptions were processed in the past decade. Nationwide, between 1999 and 2011, oxycodone prescriptions increased sixfold. National per capita consumption of oxycodone went from around 10 milligrams in 1995 to almost 250 milligrams by 2012.

The quantum leap in opioid use arrived by stealth. Most previous drug epidemics were accompanied by waves of crime and violence, which prompted others, outside the drug circles, to take notice and action. But the opioid scourge was accompanied, during its first decade, by a record drop in both. Drug users were not out on the streets causing mayhem or havoc. They were inside, mostly alone, and deadly quiet. There were no crack houses to raid or gangs to monitor. Overdose deaths began to climb, but they were often obscured by a variety of dry terms used in coroners' reports to hide what was really happening. When the cause of death was inescapable—young corpses discovered in bedrooms or fast-food restrooms—it was also, frequently, too shameful to share. Parents of dead teenagers were unlikely to advertise their agony.

In time, of course, doctors realized the scale of their error. Between 2010 and 2015, opioid prescriptions declined by 18 percent. But if it was a huge, well-intended mistake to create this army of addicts, it was an even bigger one to cut them off from their supply. That is when the addicted were forced to turn to black-market pills and street heroin. Here again, the illegal supply channel broke with previous patterns. It was no longer controlled by the established cartels in the big cities that had historically been the main source of narcotics. This time, the heroin—particularly cheap, black-tar heroin from Mexico—came from small drug-dealing operations that avoided major urban areas, instead following the trail of methadone clinics and pill mills into the American heartland.

Their innovation, Quinones discovered, was to pay the dealers a flat salary, rather than a cut from the heroin itself. This removed the incentives to weaken the product, by cutting it with baking soda or other additives, and so made the new drug much more predictable in its power and reliable in its dosage. And rather than setting up a central location to sell the drugs—like a conventional shooting gallery or crack house—the new heroin marketers delivered it by car. Out-side methadone clinics or pill mills, they handed out cards bearing only a telephone number. Call them and they would arrange to meet you near your house, in a suburban parking lot. They were routinely polite and punctual.

Buying heroin became as easy in the suburbs and rural areas as buying weed in the cities. No violence, low risk, familiar surround-ings: an entire system specifically designed to provide a clean-cut, friendly, middle-class high. America was returning to the norm of the 19th century, when opiates were a routine medicine, but it was consuming compounds far more potent, addictive, and deadly than any 19th-century tincture enthusiast could have imagined. The country resembled someone who had once been accustomed to opium, who had spent a long time in recovery, whose tolerance for the drug had collapsed, and who was then offered a hit of the most powerful new variety.

The iron law of prohibition, as first stipulated by activist Richard Cowan in 1986, is that the more intense the crackdown, "the more potent the drugs will become." In other words, the harder the en-forcement, the harder the drugs. The legal risks associated with manufacturing and transporting a drug increase exponentially un-der prohibition, which pushes the cost of supplying the drug higher, which incentivizes traffickers to minimize the size of the product, which leads to innovations in higher potency. That's why, during the prohibition of alcohol, much of the production and trafficking was in hard liquor, not beer or wine; why amphetamines evolved into crystal meth; why today's cannabis is much more potent than in the late 20th century. Heroin, rather than old-fashioned opium, became the opioid of the streets.

Then came fentanyl, a massively concentrated opioid that deliv-ers up to 50 times the strength of heroin. Developed in 1959, it is now one of the most widely used opioids in global medicine, its mi-raculous pain relief delivered through transdermal patches, or loz-enges, that have revolutionized surgery and recovery and helped save countless lives. But in its raw form, it is one of the most dangerous drugs ever created by human beings. A recent shipment of fentanyl seized in New Jersey fit into the trunk of a single car yet contained enough poison to wipe out the entire population of New Jersey and New York City combined. That's more potential death than a dirty bomb or a small nuke. That's also what makes it a dream for traffickers. A kilo of heroin can yield $500,000; a kilo of fentanyl is worth as much as $1.2 million.

The problem with fentanyl, as it pertains to traffickers, is that it is close to impossible to dose correctly. To be injected at all, fentanyl's microscopic form requires it to be cut with various other substances, and that cutting is playing with fire. Just the equivalent of a few grains of salt can send you into sudden paroxysms of heaven; a few more grains will kill you. It is obviously not in the interests of drug dealers to kill their entire customer base, but keeping most of their clients alive appears beyond their skill. The way heroin kills you is simple: The drug dramatically slows the respiratory system, suffocating users as they drift to sleep. Increase the potency by a factor of 50 and it is no surprise that you can die from ingesting just a half a milligram of the stuff.

Fentanyl comes from labs in China; you can find it, if you try, on the dark web. It's so small in size and so valuable that it's close to impossible to prevent it coming into the country. Last year, 500 million packages of all kinds entered the United States through the regular mail—making them virtually impossible to monitor with the Postal Service's current technology. And so, over the past few years, the impact of opioids has gone from mass intoxication to mass death. In the last heroin epidemic, as Vietnam vets brought the addiction back home, the overdose rate was 1.5 per 10,000 Americans. Now, it's 10.5. Three years ago in New Jersey, 2 percent of all seized heroin contained fentanyl. Today, it's a third. Since 2013, overdose deaths from fentanyl and other synthetic opioids have increased sixfold, outstripping those from every other drug.

If the war on drugs is seen as a century-long game of chess between the law and the drugs, it seems pretty obvious that fentanyl, by massively concentrating the most pleasurable substance ever known to mankind, is checkmate.

Watching as this catastrophe unfolded these past few years, I began to notice how closely it resembles the last epidemic that dramatically reduced life-spans in America: AIDS. It took a while for anyone to really notice what was happening there, too. AIDS occurred in a population that was often hidden and therefore distant from the cultural elite (or closeted within it). To everyone else, the deaths were abstract, and relatively tolerable, especially as they were associated with an activity most people disapproved of. By the time the epidemic was exposed and understood, so much damage had been done that tens of thousands of deaths were already inevitable.

Today, once more, the cultural and political elites find it possible to ignore the scale of the crisis because it is so often invisible in their—our—own lives. The polarized nature of our society only makes this worse: A plague that is killing the other tribe is easier to look away from. Occasionally, members of the elite discover their own children with the disease, and it suddenly becomes more urgent. A celebrity death—Rock Hudson in 1985, Prince in 2016—begins to break down some of the denial. Those within the vortex of death get radicalized by the failure of government to tackle the problem. The dying gay men who joined ACT UP in the 1980s share one thing with the opioid-ridden communities who voted for Donald Trump in unexpected numbers: a desperate sense of powerlessness, of living through a plague that others are choosing not to see.

At some point, the sheer numbers of the dead become unmissable. With AIDS, the government, along with pharmaceutical companies, eventually developed a plan of action: prevention, education, and research for a viable treatment and cure. Some of this is happening with opioids. The widespread distribution of Narcan sprays—which contain the antidote naloxone—has already saved countless lives. The use of alternative, less-dangerous opioid drugs such as methadone and buprenorphine to wean people off heroin or cushion them through withdrawal has helped. Some harm-reduction centers have established needle-exchange programs. But none of this comes close to stopping the current onslaught. With HIV and AIDS, after all, there was a clear scientific goal: to find drugs that would prevent HIV from replicating. With opioid addiction, there is no such potential cure in the foreseeable future. When we see the toll from opioids exceed that of peak AIDS deaths, it's important to remember that after that peak came a sudden decline. After the latest fentanyl peak, no such decline looks probable. On the contrary, the deaths continue to mount.

Over time, AIDS worked its way through the political system. More than anything else, it destroyed the closet and massively accelerated our culture's acceptance of the dignity and humanity of homosexuals. Marriage equality and open military service were the fruits of this transformation. But with the opioid crisis, our politics has remained curiously unmoved. The Trump administration, despite overwhelming support from many of the communities most afflicted, hasn't appointed anyone with sufficient clout and expertise to corral the federal government to respond adequately.

The critical Office of National Drug Control Policy has spent a year without a permanent director. Its budget is slated to be slashed by 95 percent, and until a few weeks ago, its deputy chief of staff was a 24-year-old former campaign intern. Kellyanne Conway—Trump's "opioid czar"—has no expertise in government, let alone in drug control. Although Trump plans to increase spending on treating addiction, the overall emphasis is on an even more intense form of prohibition, plus an advertising campaign. Attorney General Jeff Sessions even recently opined that he believes marijuana is really the key gateway to heroin—a view so detached from reality it beggars belief. It seems clear that in the future, Trump's record on opioids will be as tainted as Reagan's was on AIDS. But the human toll could be even higher.

One of the few proven ways to reduce overdose deaths is to establish supervised injection sites that eventually wean users off the hard stuff while steering them into counseling, safe housing, and job training.

After the first injection site in North America opened in Vancouver, deaths from heroin overdoses plunged by 35 percent. In Switzerland, where such sites operate nationwide, overdose deaths have been cut in half. By treating the addicted as human beings with dignity rather than as losers and criminals who have ostracized themselves, these programs have coaxed many away from the cliff face of extinction toward a more productive life.

But for such success to be replicated in the United States, we would have to contemplate actually providing heroin to addicts in some cases, and we'd have to shift much of the current spending on prohibition, criminalization, and incarceration into a huge program of opioid rehabilitation. We would, in short, have to end the war on drugs. We are nowhere near prepared to do that. And in the meantime, the comparison to ACT UP is exceedingly depressing, as the only politics that opioids appear to generate is nihilistic and self-defeating. The drug itself saps initiative and generates social withdrawal. A few small activist groups have sprung up, but it is hardly a national movement of any heft or urgency.

And so we wait to see what amount of death will be tolerable in America as the price of retaining prohibition. Is it 100,000 deaths a year? More? At what point does a medical emergency actually provoke a government response that takes mass death seriously? Imagine a terror attack that killed over 40,000 people. Imagine a new virus that threatened to kill 52,000 Americans this year. Wouldn't any government make it the top priority before any other?

In some ways, the spread of fentanyl—now beginning to infiltrate cocaine, fake Adderall, and meth, which is also seeing a spike in use—might best be thought of as a mass poisoning. It has infected often nonfatal drugs and turned them into instant killers. Think back to the poison discovered in a handful of tainted Tylenol pills in 1982. Every bottle of Tylenol in America was immediately recalled; in Chicago, police went into neighborhoods with loudspeakers to warn residents of the danger. That was in response to a scare that killed, in total, seven people. In 2016, 20,000 people died from overdosing on synthetic opioids, a form of poison in the illicit drug market. Some lives, it would appear, are several degrees of magnitude more valuable than others. Some lives are not worth saving at all.

One of the more vivid images that Americans have of drug abuse is of a rat in a cage, tapping a cocaine-infused water bottle again and again until the rodent expires. Years later, as recounted in Johann Hari's epic history of the drug war, *Chasing the Scream*, a curious scientist replicated the experiment. But this time he added a control group. In one cage sat a rat and a water dispenser serving diluted morphine. In another cage, with another rat and an identical dispenser, he added something else: wheels to run in, colored balls to play with, lots of food to eat, and other rats for the junkie rodent to play or have sex with. Call it rat park. And the rats in rat park consumed just one-fifth of the morphine water of the rat in the cage. One reason for pathological addiction, it turns out, is the environment. If you were trapped in solitary confinement, with only morphine to pass the time, you'd die of your addiction pretty swiftly too. Take away the stimulus of community and all the oxytocin it naturally generates, and an artificial variety of the substance becomes much more compelling.

One way of thinking of postindustrial America is to imagine it as a former rat park, slowly converting into a rat cage. Market capitalism and revolutionary technology in the past couple of decades have transformed our economic and cultural reality, most intensely for those without college degrees. The dignity that many working-class men retained by providing for their families through physical labor has been greatly reduced by automation. Stable family life has collapsed, and the number of children without two parents in the home has risen among the white working and middle classes. The internet has ravaged local retail stores, flattening the uniqueness of many communities. Smartphones have eviscerated those moments of oxytocin-friendly actual human interaction. Meaning—once effortlessly provided by a more unified and often religious culture shared, at least nominally, by others—is harder to find, and the proportion of Americans who identify as "nones," with no religious affiliation, has risen to record levels. Even as we near peak employment and record-high median household income, a sense of permanent economic insecurity and spiritual emptiness has become widespread. Some of that emptiness was once assuaged by a constantly rising standard of living, generation to generation.

But that has now evaporated for most Americans.

New Hampshire, Ohio, Kentucky, and Pennsylvania have over-taken the big cities in heroin use and abuse, and rural addiction has spread swiftly to the suburbs. Now, in the latest twist, opioids have reemerged in that other, more familiar place without hope: the black inner city, where overdose deaths among African-Americans, mostly from fentanyl, are suddenly soaring. To make matters worse, political and cultural tribalism has deeply weakened the glue of a unifying pa-triotism to give a broader meaning to people's lives—large numbers of whites and blacks both feel like strangers in their own land. Mass immigration has, for many whites, intensified the sense of cultural abandonment. Somewhere increasingly feels like nowhere.

It's been several decades since Daniel Bell wrote *The Cultural Contradictions of Capitalism*, but his insights have proven prescient. Ever-more-powerful market forces actually undermine the founda-tions of social stability, wreaking havoc on tradition, religion, and robust civil associations, destroying what conservatives value the most. They create a less human world. They make us less happy. They generate pain.

This was always a worry about the American experiment in capitalist liberal democracy. The pace of change, the ethos of indi-vidualism, the relentless dehumanization that capitalism abets, the constant moving and disruption, combined with a relatively small government and the absence of official religion, risked the construc-tion of an overly atomized society, where everyone has to create his or her own meaning, and everyone feels alone. The American project always left an empty center of collective meaning, but for a long time Americans filled it with their own extraordinary work ethic, an un-precedented web of associations and clubs and communal or ethnic ties far surpassing Europe's, and such a plethora of religious options that almost no one was left without a purpose or some kind of easily available meaning to their lives. Tocqueville marveled at this American exceptionalism as the key to democratic success, but he worried that it might not endure forever.

And it hasn't. What has happened in the past few decades is an accelerated waning of all these traditional American supports for a meaningful, collective life, and their replacement with various forms of cheap distraction. Addiction—to work, to food, to phones, to TV, to video games, to porn, to news, and to drugs—is all around us. The core habit of bourgeois life—deferred gratification—has lost its grip on the American soul. We seek the instant, easy highs, and it's hard not to see this as the broader context for the opioid wave. This was not originally a conscious choice for most of those caught up in it: Most were introduced to the poppy's joys by their own family members and friends, the last link in a chain that included the medical establishment and began with the pharmaceutical companies. It may be best to think of this wave therefore not as a function of miserable people turning to drugs en masse but of people who didn't realize how miserable they were until they found out what life without misery could be. To return to their previous lives became unthinkable. For so many, it still is.

If Marx posited that religion is the opiate of the people, then we have reached a new, more clarifying moment in the history of the West: Opiates are now the religion of the people. A verse by the poet William Brewer sums up this new world:

> Where once was faith,
> there are sirens: red lights spinning
> door to door, a record twenty-four
> in one day, all the bodies
> at the morgue filled with light.

It is easy to dismiss or pity those trapped or dead for whom opiates have filled this emptiness. But it's not quite so easy for the tens of millions of us on antidepressants, or Xanax, or some benzo-drug to keep less acute anxieties at bay. In the same period that opioids have

spread like wildfire, so has the use of cannabis—another downer nowhere near as strong as opiates but suddenly popular among many
who are the success stories of our times. Is it any wonder that something more powerful is used by the failures? There's a passage in one
of Brewer's poems that tears at me all the time. It's about an opioid-
addicted father and his son. The father tells us:

> Times my simple son will shake me to,
> syringe still hanging like a feather from my arm.
> What are you always doing, he asks.
> Flying, I say. Show me how, he begs.
> And finally, I do. You'd think
> the sun had gotten lost inside his head,
> the way he smiled.

To see this epidemic as simply a pharmaceutical or chemically
addictive problem is to miss something: the despair that currently
makes so many want to fly away. Opioids are just one of the ways
Americans are trying to cope with an inhuman new world where
everything is flat, where communication is virtual, and where those
core elements of human happiness—faith, family, community—
seem to elude so many. Until we resolve these deeper social, cultural,
and psychological problems, until we discover a new meaning or rei-
magine our old religion or reinvent our way of life, the poppy will
flourish.

We have seen this story before—in America and elsewhere.

The allure of opiates' joys are filling a hole in the human heart
and soul today as they have since the dawn of civilization. But this
time, the drugs are not merely laced with danger and addiction. In a
way never experienced by humanity before, the pharmaceutically so-
phisticated and ever more intense bastard children of the sturdy little
flower bring mass death in their wake. This time, they are agents of
an eternal and enveloping darkness. And there is a long, long path
ahead, and many more bodies to count, before we will see any light.

Part Two

Treatment and Solutions

THE SOCIAL ROOTS OF ADDICTION

Gabor Maté

Excerpt from *In The Realm of Hungry Ghosts: Close Encounters with Addiction* (North Atlantic, 2010)

I believe that to pursue the American Dream is not only futile but self-destructive because ultimately it destroys everything and everyone involved with it. By definition it must, because it nurtures everything except those things that are important: integrity, ethics, truth, our very heart and soul. Why? The reason is simple: because Life/life is about giving, not getting.
—Hubert Selby Jr., *Requiem for a Dream* (Preface, 2000)

Ralph, the God-starved, pseudo-Nazi poet, said something to me in the hospital that ought to make many of us upstanding, righteous citizens squirm. I was challenging his belief in emancipation through drugs. "You talk about freedom. But how much freedom can there be when you're chasing the drug the whole day for just a few minutes of satisfaction? Where's the freedom in that?"

Ralph shrugs his shoulders. "What else am I going to do? What do *you* do? You get up in the morning, and somebody cooks you bacon and eggs . . . "

"Yogurt and banana," I interject. "I prepare it myself."

Ralph shakes his head impatiently. "Okay . . . yogurt and banana. Then you go to the office and you see a couple of dozen patients . . . and all your money goes to the bank at the end of that, and then you count up your shekels or your doubloons. At the end of the day, what have you done? You've collected the summation of what you think freedom is. You're looking for security, and you think that will give you freedom. You collected a hundred shekels of gold, and to you this gold has the capacity of keeping you in a fancy house or maybe you can salt away another six weeks' worth up and above what you already have in the bank.

"But what are you looking for? What have you spent your whole day searching for? That same bit of freedom or satisfaction that I want; we just get it differently. What's everybody chasing all the money for if not to get them something that will make them feel good for a while or make them feel they're free? How are they freer than I am?

"Everybody's searching for that feeling of well-being, that greater happiness. But I'd rather be a dog out in the street than do what many people go through to find their summation of freedom."

"There's a lot of truth there," I concede. "I can get caught up in all sorts of meaningless activities that leave me only temporarily satisfied, if that. Sometimes they leave me feeling worse. But I do believe there's a greater freedom than either your pursuit of the drug or my pursuit of security or success can provide."

Ralph looks at me as a benign but worldly-wise uncle would gaze upon a naive child. "And what would that freedom of pursuits be? What would be the ultimate freedom to be searching for?"

I hesitate. Can I authentically say this? "The freedom *from* pursuits," I say finally. "The freedom from being so needy that our whole life is spent trying to appease our desires or fill in the emptiness. I've never experienced total freedom, but I believe it's possible."

Ralph is adamant. "If it could be different, it would be. It is what it is. Let me put it to you this way: why is it that some people, through no merit whatsoever, get to have whatever they think will give them happiness? Others, through no fault of their own, are deprived."

I agree it's an unfair world in many ways.

"Then how can you or anyone else tell me that my way is wrong, theirs is right? It's just power, isn't it?"

I've often heard Ralph's worldview espoused by other drug

addicts, if less eloquently. It's clear and obvious that his (and their) rationalization for addiction misses something essential. The defeatist belief that all pursuits arise from a selfish core in all humanity denies the deeper motives that also activate people: love, creativity, spiritual quest, the drive for mastery and autonomy, the impulse to make a contribution.

Although the cracks in his argument are easy to discern, perhaps it would be more worthwhile to consider what *realities* the drug-dependent Ralph might be articulating and what we might learn about ourselves in the dark mirror he holds up for us. Though we pretend otherwise, in our materialist culture many of us conduct ourselves as if Ralph's cynicism reflected the truth—that it's each man for himself, that the world offers nothing other than brief, illusory satisfactions. But from his pinched and narrow perch at the edge of society, the drug addict sees who we are—or more exactly, who we are *choosing to be.* He sees that we resemble him in our frantic material pursuits and our delusions and that we exceed him in our hypocrisies.

If Ralph's view is cynical, it's no more cynical than society's view of drug addicts as flawed and culpable, as people to be isolated and shunned. We flatter ourselves.

And if I'm being honest, I might ask myself to what extent my insistence on that greater freedom is really not just the sentimentality of the privileged, pseudoenlightened addict—a way for me to rationalize my own addictions: *I know I'm hooked, but I'm working on getting free, so I'm different from you.* If I really knew that kind of freedom, would I need to argue for it? Would I not just manifest it in my life and way of being?

"At heart, I am not that different from my patients—and sometimes I cannot stand seeing how little psychological space, how little heaven-granted grace separates me from them"—so I wrote in the first chapter. There are moments when I'm revolted by my patients' disheveled appearances, their stained and decayed teeth, the look of insatiable hunger in their eyes, their demands, complaints, and neediness. Those are times when I would do well to examine myself for irresponsibility in my own life, for self-neglect—in my case not so much physical as spiritual—and for placing false needs above real ones.

When I am sharply judgmental of any other person, it's because I sense or see reflected in them some aspect of myself that I don't want to acknowledge. I'm speaking here not of my *critique* of another person's behavior in objective terms but of the self-righteous tone of personal *judgment* that colors my opinion. If, for example, I resent some person close to me as "controlling," it may be owing to my own inability to assert myself. Or I may react against another person because he or she has a trait that I myself have—and dislike—but don't wish to acknowledge: for example, a tendency to want to control others. As I mentioned in a previous chapter, some mornings I vituperate about right-wing political columnists. My opinion remains more or less constant: their views are based on a highly selective reading of the facts and are rooted in a denial of reality. What does vary from day to day is the emotional charge that infuses my opinion. Some days I dismiss them with intense hostility; at other times I see their perspective as one possible way of looking at things, as an interpretation of their experience of life.

On the surface, the differences are obvious: they support wars I oppose and justify policies I dislike. I can tell myself that we're different. Moral judgments, however, are never about the obvious: they always speak to the underlying similarities between the judge and the condemned. My judgments of others are an accurate gauge of how, beneath the surface, I feel about myself. It's only the willful blindness in me that condemns others for deluding themselves; my own selfishness that excoriates others for being self-serving; my lack of authenticity that judges falsehood in others. It is the same, I believe, for all moral judgments people cast on each other and for all vehemently held communal judgments a society visits upon its members. So it is with the harsh social attitudes toward addicts, especially hard-core drug addicts.

"What characterizes an addiction?" asks the spiritual teacher Eckhart Tolle. "Quite simply this: you no longer feel that you have the power to stop. It seems stronger than you. It also gives you a false sense of pleasure, pleasure that invariably turns into pain."[1]

Addiction cuts large swaths across our culture. Many of us are burdened with compulsive behaviors that harm us and others, behaviors whose toxicity we fail to acknowledge or feel powerless to stop. Many people are addicted to accumulating wealth; for others the compulsive pull is power. Men and women become addicted to consumerism, status, shopping, or fetishized relationships, not to mention the obvious and widespread addictions such as gambling, sex, junk food, and the cult of the "young" body image. The following report from the *Guardian Weekly* speaks for itself:

> Americans now [2006] spend an alarming $15 billion a year on cosmetic surgery in a beautification frenzy that would be frowned upon if there was anyone left in the U.S. who could actually frown with their Botox-frozen faces. The sum is double Malawi's gross domestic product and more than twice what America has contributed to AIDS programs in the past decade. Demand has exploded to produce a new generation of obsessives, or "beauty junkies."[2]

Beauty Junkies is the title of a recent book by *New York Times* writer Alex Kuczynski, "a self-confessed recovering addict of cosmetic surgery." And, with our technological prowess, we succeed in creating fresh addictions. Some psychologists now describe a new clinical pathology—Internet Sex Addiction Disorder.

Physicians and psychologists may not be all that effective in treating addictions, but we're expert at coming up with fresh names and categories. A recent study at Stanford University School of Medicine found that about 5.5 percent of men and 6 percent of women appear to be addicted shoppers. The lead researcher, Dr. Lorrin Koran, suggested that compulsive buying be recognized as a unique illness listed under its own heading in the *Diagnostic and Statistical Manual of Mental Disorders*, the official psychiatric catalog. Sufferers of this "new" disorder are afflicted by "an irresistible, intrusive, and senseless impulse" to purchase objects they do not need. I don't scoff at the

harm done by shopping addiction—I'm in no position to do that—
and I agree that Dr. Koran accurately describes the potential consequences of compulsive buying: "serious psychological, financial, and
family problems, including depression, overwhelming debt, and the
breakup of relationships."[3] But it's clearly not a distinct entity—only
another manifestation of addiction tendencies that run through
our culture and of the fundamental addiction process that varies
only in its targets, not its basic characteristics. Dr. Koran was puzzled and disappointed to find in a recent study that this "biological
disorder" did not respond to treatment with escitalopram, an SSRI
antidepressant.[4]

In his 2006 State of the Union address, President George W.
Bush identified another item of addiction. "Here we have a serious
problem," he said. "America is addicted to oil." Coming from a man
who throughout his financial and political career has had the closest possible ties to the oil industry, this stark admission might have
been transformational. Unfortunately, Mr. Bush framed the problem
purely in geopolitical terms: the United States finds itself dependent
on a resource from abroad; hence, it needs to develop other sources of
energy—drilling for oil in protected nature reserves, for example. So
the problem is not the addiction itself, only that the supply of the substance in question may be jeopardized: typical addict's logic, of course.

Whether we tally health expenditures, loss of human life, economic strain, or any other measure, the "respectable" addictions,
around which entire cultures, industries, and professions have been
built, leave drug addiction in the dust.

We've already defined addiction as any relapsing behavior that
satisfies a short-term craving and that persists despite its long-term
negative consequences. The long-term ill effects of our society's addiction, if not to oil then to the amenities and luxuries that oil makes
possible, are obvious. They range from environmental destruction,
climate change, and the toxic effects of pollution on human health to
the many wars that the need for oil, or the attachment to oil wealth,
has triggered. Consider how much greater a price has been exacted
by this socially sanctioned addiction than by the drug addiction for

which Ralph and his peers have been declared outcasts. And oil is only one example among many: consider soul-, body-, or nature-destroying addictions to consumer goods, fast food, sugar cereals, television programs, and glossy publications devoted to celebrity gossip—only a few examples of what American writer Kevin Baker calls "the growth industries that have grown out of gambling and hedonism." The metropolis of gambling and hedonism, Las Vegas, received nearly 40 million visitors in 2006, and its local population base has increased by 18 percent since 2000. The highest-grossing independent restaurant in the United States is the Tao Las Vegas. It features seminaked women, gaming consoles, poolside plasma TV screens, and preprogrammed iPods all amid a "proliferation of Buddhas, pulsating music, and sensuous decor."[5] I doubt either owners or customers are alive to the absurdity of co-opting the Tao, the ancient Chinese wisdom path of nonattachment and surrender, to support addiction, or of using images of Buddha, the teacher of serene mindfulness, to shill food, liquor, and games of chance.

We need hardly mention legally permissible substance dependencies on nicotine and alcohol: in terms of scale, their negative consequences far surpass the damage inflicted by illicit drugs. And what do the mass marketing and advertising of these often-lethal substances reflect if not addiction? Exactly like drug pushers who are themselves addicted, tobacco companies behave as if they, too, were driven by addiction: in their case, to profit.

In August 2006 U.S. District Judge Gladys Kessler ruled that the big tobacco companies had deceived the public concerning the health effects of their products:

[The] defendants have marketed and sold their lethal product with zeal, with deception, with a single-minded focus on their financial success, and without regard for the human tragedy or social costs that success exacted.[6]

Treating smoking-related illnesses has incurred costs in the multiple hundreds of billions of dollars. According to the *New York Times*, there are currently 44 million adult smokers in the United States, and four out of five are addicted to tobacco. "Tobacco kills 440,000 smokers every year in the United States, and secondhand smoke inhaled by bystanders claims another 50,000."[7] Around the world tobacco kills 5.5 million people annually—claiming roughly the same number of victims each year as were annihilated by the Nazis' genocidal attacks against Jews during World War II. And yet the tobacco manufacturers do not desist, aggressively pushing their products in new markets in the so-called developing countries and, according to a recent study at the Harvard School of Public Health, manipulating menthol levels in cigarettes sold in the United States to youth, a "vulnerable population . . . to promote initiation and dependence."[8]

How can we compare the misdemeanors of my patients—petty dealers thrown against the wall and frisked by police in the back alleys of the Downtown Eastside—with those of their respectable counterparts in corporate boardrooms? In May 2007, Purdue Pharma, a giant drug manufacturer, pleaded guilty to criminal charges that the firm had "misled doctors and patients" in claiming that their product, OxyContin, was less addictive than other opiate medications. "That claim," said the *New York Times*, "became the linchpin of an aggressive marketing campaign that helped the company sell over $1 billion of OxyContin a year. . . . But both experienced drug abusers and novices, including teenagers, soon discovered that chewing an OxyContin tablet—or crushing one and then snorting the powder, or injecting it with a needle—produced a high as powerful as heroin."[9] There have been hundreds of overdose deaths on OxyContin across the United States, devastating entire villages in Appalachia, for example, where the drug became known as "hillbilly heroin" and was illicitly marketed for $40 for a 40-milligram tablet.

We see that substance addictions are only one specific form of blind attachment to harmful ways of being. Yet we condemn the addict's stubborn refusal to give up something deleterious to his life or to the lives of others. Why do we despise, ostracize, and punish the drug addict when as a social collective we share the same blindness and engage in the same rationalizations?

To pose that question is to answer it. We despise, ostracize, and punish the addict because we don't wish to see how much we resemble him. In his dark mirror our own features are unmistakable. We shudder at the recognition. This mirror is not for us, we say to the addict. You are different, and you don't belong with us. Ralph's critique, for all its flaws, is too close for comfort. Like the hard-core addict's pursuit of drugs, much of our economic and cultural life caters to people's craving to escape mental and emotional distress. In an apt phrase, Lewis Lapham[10] derides "consumer markets selling promises of instant relief from the pain of thought, loneliness, doubt, experience, envy, and old age."[11]

According to a Statistics Canada study, 31 percent of working adults aged nineteen to sixty-four consider themselves workaholics who attach excessive importance to their work and are "overdedicated and perhaps overwhelmed by their jobs." "They have trouble sleeping, are more likely to be stressed out and unhealthy, and feel they don't spend enough time with their families," reports the *Globe and Mail*. Work doesn't necessarily give them greater satisfaction, suggested a professor of human resources and management at McMaster University.[12] "These people turn to work to occupy their time and energy"[13]—as compensation for what is lacking in their lives, much as the drug addict employs substances.

At the core of every addiction is an emptiness based in abject fear. The addict dreads and abhors the present moment; she bends feverishly only toward the next time, the moment when her brain, infused with her drug of choice, will briefly experience itself as liberated from the burden of the past and the fear of the future—the two elements that make the present intolerable. Many of us resemble the drug addict in our ineffectual efforts to fill in the spiritual black hole, the void at the center, where we have lost touch with our souls, our spirit—with those sources of meaning and value that are not contingent or fleeting. Our consumerist, acquisition-, action-, and image-mad culture only serves to deepen the hole, leaving us emptier than before.

The constant, intrusive, and meaningless mind-whirl that characterizes the way so many of us experience our silent moments is, itself, a form of addiction—and it serves the same purpose. "One of the main tasks of the mind is to fight or remove the emotional pain, which is one of the reasons for its incessant activity, but all it can ever achieve is to cover it up temporarily. In fact, the harder the mind struggles to get rid of the pain, the greater the pain."[14] So writes Eckhart Tolle. Even our 24/7 self-exposure to noise, e-mails, cell phones, TV, Internet chats, media outlets, music downloads, videogames, and nonstop internal and external chatter cannot succeed in drowning out the fearful voices within.

We avert our eyes from the hard-core drug addict not only to avoid seeing ourselves; we do so to avoid facing our share of responsibility as well.

As we have seen, injection drug use more often than not arises in people who were abused and neglected as young children. The addict, in other words, is not born but made. His addiction is the result of a situation that he had no influence in creating. His life expresses the history of the multigenerational family system of which he is a part, and his family exists as part of the broader culture and society. In society, as in nature, each microcosmic unit reflects something of the whole. In the case of drug addiction, the sins of entire societies are visited unevenly on minority populations.

We know, for example, that a disproportionate number of prisoners incarcerated for drug-related crimes in the jails of the United States are African American males. In 2002, 45 percent of the prisoners in U.S. jails were black, and according to the Department of Justice black males have about a one-in-three chance of being jailed at least once in their lives.[15] In federal prisons, an estimated 57 percent of inmates have been convicted of drug-related crimes, and drug offenders represented the largest source of jail population growth between 1996 and 2002—increasing by 37 percent.[16] The fate of black youth has much to tell us about the larger society in which their stories unfold. Similarly, there is an extraordinarily high ratio of First Peoples among my Portland patients—and in Canada's drug-using population and prisons.

Dr. Robert DuPont, former U.S. drug czar, interprets such facts as flowing from what he calls the "tragic vulnerability" of traditional cultures to alcohol and drug problems. He describes the present susceptibility of Native minority populations to addiction as "one of the sad paradoxes of the world experience with alcohol and drug abuse":

> To see Native Americans suffer from the use of alcohol and other drugs, and even cigarettes, or to see similar suffering among Australian aborigines, is to face the painful reality that traditional cultures are not prepared to withstand exposure to modern drugs and to tolerant values governing drug-taking behaviors.[17]

There is, perhaps, a much more specific and robust cause for minority drug use than "tolerant values" toward drug taking. In fact, given the high incarceration rate of minority members, it's hard to see what these "tolerant values" even are.

As the stories of Serena, Celia, and Angela in the first part of this book illustrated, many women who become injection-drug users were severely abused in childhood—the vast majority, according to the research. Of those three women, two are Native. It is a fact that over the past several generations Native female children in Canada have been more likely to suffer sexual abuse in their families of origin than have non-Natives. That this is so says nothing about the "innate" nature of North American Native peoples. Sexual abuse of young children among tribal peoples living in their natural habitats is virtually nonexistent, and so it was with North American Natives before European colonization. The current dismal statistics say everything about the relationship of aboriginal societies to the dominant culture.

The precursor to addiction is *dislocation*, according to Bruce Alexander, professor emeritus of psychology at Simon Fraser University. By dislocation he means the loss of psychological, social, and economic integration into family and culture—a sense of exclusion, isolation, and powerlessness. "Only chronically and severely dislocated people are vulnerable to addiction," he writes.

> The historical correlation between severe dislocation and addiction is strong. Although alcohol consumption and drunkenness on festive occasions was widespread in Europe during the Middle Ages, and although a few people became "inebriates" or "drunkards," mass alcoholism was not a problem. However, alcoholism gradually spread with the beginnings of free markets after 1500, and eventually became a raging epidemic with the dominance of the free market society after 1800.[18]

Dr. DuPont agrees that in premodern societies, although substance use to the point of intoxication was permitted, "that use was infrequent and managed in families and communities. . . . Stable communities in premodern times were the Golden Age for alcohol and drug use."[19]

With the rise of industrial societies came dislocation: the destruction of traditional relationships, extended family, clan, tribe, and village. Vast economic and social changes tore asunder the ties that formerly connected people to those closest to them and to their communities. They displaced people from their homes and shredded the value systems that secured people's sense of belonging in the moral and spiritual universe. The same process is happening around the world as a result of globalization. China is a prime example. That country's breakneck-speed industrialization has made it an emerging economic superpower, but the accompanying social dislocation is likely to prove disastrous. Entire villages and towns are being depopulated to make room for megaprojects like the Three Gorges Dam. The pressures of urbanization are cutting millions of people adrift from their connections with land, tradition, and community. The social and psychological results of massive dislocation are not only predictable; they're also already apparent. China has had to set up a massive needle-exchange program in an attempt to prevent the spread of HIV and other infectious diseases among its rapidly burgeoning addict population. According to the Ministry of Health in Beijing, nearly half of China's estimated 650,000 people living with HIV/AIDS are drug users who contracted the disease by sharing needles.[20] There can be no doubt that the ravages of social breakdown—alienation, violence, and addiction—will soon make vast and urgent claims on the attention and resources of Chinese authorities, academics, and health professionals. In the rush to emulate the Western world's achievements, many countries are neglecting to learn from the disruptions, dysfunctions, and diseases that Western social models engender.[21]

Of all the groups affected by the forces of dislocation, none have been worse hit than minority populations, such as the Australian aborigines and North American Native peoples mentioned by Dr. DuPont and the descendants of black slaves brought to North America. Among the latter, people were separated not only from their places of origin, their cultures, and their communities but often also from their immediate families. Long after the abolition of slavery, racial oppression and prejudice, along with economic deprivation, have continued to produce intolerable pressures on family life among many African Americans—and the link to addiction is obvious. Equally obvious is the enticement of the drug trade to jobless and undereducated young black men excluded from the economic promises of the "American dream."

The history of dispossession, exploitation, dislocation, and direct abuse of Native peoples on both sides of the forty-ninth parallel is also too well known to require much discussion. Tobacco and other potentially addictive substances were available to North American Natives prior to the European invasions, and even alcohol was available in what are now Mexico and the American Southwest—not to mention potentially addictive activities such as sex, eating, and gambling. Yet, as Dr. Alexander points out, there is no mention by anthropologists of "anything that could be reasonably called addiction. . . . Where alcohol was readily available, it was used moderately, often ceremonially rather than addictively."

With the mass migration of Europeans to North America and the economic transformation of the continent came also the loss of freedom of mobility for Native peoples, the inexorable and still-continuing despoliation and destruction of their habitats, the loss of their traditional livelihoods, the invalidation of their spiritual ways, persistent discrimination, and abject poverty. Within living memory Native children in Canada were seized from their homes, alienated from their families, and, for all intents and purposes, incarcerated in "civilizing" institutions where their lot was one of cultural suppression, emotional and physical maltreatment, and, with distressing frequency, sexual abuse.

The living situations, health conditions, and social deprivation of many North American Natives are abysmal even by third world standards. Under such circumstances—among tormented, dislocated, and, most fundamentally, *disempowered* people—pain and suffering are transmitted from one traumatized generation to the next. It is no accident that both Serena and her mother live in the same Downtown Eastside hotel on Hastings; nor are they the only mother-daughter Native pairing among my patients. Of any group in North America, whether in the United States or Canada, none can be said to be more psychologically and socially oppressed than Native women.[22]

Especially since working in the Downtown Eastside, I have often thought that if society ever apologized to Native peoples for their dispossession and suffering as we have acknowledged the suffering of Japanese Americans and Japanese Canadians for their internment during World War II, our contrition would need to be vast and our willingness to make restitution immensely generous. Perhaps that is why we have never accepted the responsibility.

Dislocation continues to be an ever-accelerating feature of modern living. The disruption of family life and the erosion of stable communities afflict many segments of society. Even the nuclear family is under severe pressure with a high divorce rate and single-parent households or, in many cases, two parents having to work outside the home. For these endemic cultural and economic reasons many children today who are not abused and who come from loving homes have lost their primary emotional attachment with the nurturing adults in their lives, with results disastrous for their development. As children become increasingly less connected to adults, they rely more and more on each other—a wholesale cultural subversion of the natural order of things.

The natural order in all mammalian cultures, animal or human, is that the young stay under the wings of adults until they themselves reach adulthood. This is how under normal circumstances the human young were reared throughout the course of evolution and history, until very recently. Immature creatures were never meant to bring one another to maturity. They were never meant to look to one another for primary nurturing, modeling, cue giving, or mentoring. They are not equipped to act as one another's focus of orientation, to give one another a sense of direction or values. The predictable and widespread consequences of what my friend, psychologist Gordon Neufeld, has termed *peer orientation* are the increasing immaturity, alienation, violence, and precocious sexualization of North American youth.

Another consequence is the entrenchment of addictive behaviors among young people. Research on both humans and animals has repeatedly demonstrated that extensive peer contact and the loss of adult attachments lead to a heightened propensity to addiction. Peer-reared monkeys, for example, are far more likely to consume alcohol than are mother-reared ones.[23] "Peer affiliation," in the words of a review article in the journal *Drug and Alcohol Dependence*, "is possibly the strongest social factor in predicting the onset and early escalation of adolescent substance use."

> Both direct and active peer influence and peer pressure, and active peer affiliation have been shown to cause escalation of affective (emotional), cognitive, and behavioral dysregulation, and early substance use.[24]

It is commonly thought that peer affiliation leads to drug use because kids set bad examples for each other. That's part of the picture, but a deeper reason is that under ordinary circumstances, adolescents who rely on their peers for emotional acceptance are more prone to being hurt, to experiencing the sting of each other's immature and therefore often insensitive ways of relating. They are far more stressed than are children who are well connected to nurturing adults.

Kids are not cruel by nature, but they are immature. They taunt, tease, and reject. Those who have lost their orientation to adults and look to the peer group instead find themselves having to shut down emotionally for sheer protection. As we have seen with children abused at home, emotional shutting down—what Dr. Gordon Neufeld and I, in our cowritten book *Hold On to Your Kids*, call "the dangerous flight from feeling"—greatly increases the motivation to use drugs.[25]

In short, the addiction process takes hold in people who have suffered dislocation, whose place in the normal human communal context has been disrupted—whether they've been abused or emotionally neglected or whether they're inadequately attuned children or peer-oriented teens or members of subcultures historically subjected to exploitation.

To know the true nature of a society, it's not enough to point to its achievements, as leaders like to do. We also need to look at its shortcomings. What do we see, then, when we look at the drug ghetto of Vancouver's Downtown Eastside and similar enclaves in other urban centers? We see the dirty underside of our economic and social culture, the reverse of the image we would like to cherish of a humane, prosperous, and egalitarian society. We see our failure to honor family and community life or to protect children; we see our refusal to grant justice to Native peoples; and we see our vindictiveness toward those who have already suffered more than most of us can imagine. Rather than lifting our eyes to the dark mirror held in front of us, we shut them to avoid the unsavory image we see reflected there.

The Torah says that Aharon, the brother of Moses, was commanded to take two hairy goats and bring them before God. Upon each, he was to place a lot—a marker. On one he was to place the lot of the people's sins "to effect atonement upon it, to send it away to

Azazel into the wilderness." This was the scapegoat—who, cast out, must escape to the desert.

The drug addict is today's scapegoat. Viewed honestly, much of our culture is geared toward enticing us away from ourselves, into externally directed activity, into diverting the mind from ennui and distress. The hard-core addict surrenders her pretense about that. Her life is all about escape. The rest of us can, with varying success, maintain our charade, but to do so, we banish her to the margins of society.

"Do not judge, and you will not be judged," a man of truth once said:

> For the judgments you give will be the judgments you will get, and the amount you measure out is the amount you will be given. Why do you observe the splinter in your brother's eye and never notice the plank in your own? How dare you say to your brother, "Let me take the splinter out of your eye," when all the time there is a plank in your own? Take the plank out of your own eye first, and then you will see clearly enough to take the splinter out of your brother's eye.

In the following chapters [of *In the Realm of Hungry Ghosts*] we'll consider what our stance toward addiction might be if we took Jesus's words to heart. We'll see that his compassion integrates perfectly with what science has taught us about addiction.

Notes

1. Eckhart Tolle, *The Power of Now* (Novato, CA: New World Library, 1997), 18.

2. Joanna Walters, "$15 Billion Spent on Beauty," *Guardian Weekly*, November 3–9, 2006, 7.

3. Paul Taylor, "Shop-till-You-Drop Disorder Taxes Both Sexes," *Globe and Mail*, October 6, 2006, A13.

4. Lorrin Koran et al., "Escitalopram for Compulsive Buying Disorder: A Double-Blind Discontinuation Study," *Journal of Clinical Psychopharmacology* 27(2) (2007): 225–27.

5. Joe Drape, "Setting Restaurant Records by Selling the Sizzle," *New York Times,* July 22, 2007, 1 and 21.

6. "Big Tobacco Lied to Public," *Washington Post,* August 18, 2006.

7. "Ending Our Tobacco Addiction," editorial, *New York Times,* May 30, 2007.

8. "Menthol Dose Manipulated, Study Says," *New York Times,* July 17, 2008, C1.

9. "Narcotic Maker Guilty of Deceit over Marketing," *New York Times,* May 11, 2007, A1.

10. Longtime publisher of and current national correspondent for *Harper's Magazine.*

11. Lewis Lapham, "Time Travel," *Harper's Magazine,* May 2007, 11.

12. Professor Vishwanath Baba, DeGroote School of Business at McMaster University.

13. "Work-Life Balance? Not for One in Three," *Globe and Mail,* May 16, 2007, C1.

14. Tolle, *The Power of Now,* 23.

15. "Facts about Prisons and Prisoners," The Sentencing Project, October 2003, quoted in Amy Goodman, *The Exception to the Rulers* (New York: Hyperion, 2004), 129.

16. U.S. Department of Justice, Bureau of Justice Statistics home page; www.ojp.usdoj.gov/bjs/crimoff.htm.

17. Robert L. DuPont, *The Selfish Brain: Learning from Addiction* (Center City, MN: Hazelden, 2000), 31.

18. Bruce Alexander, "The Roots of Addiction in Free Market Society," *Canadian Centre for Policy Alternatives,* Toronto, April 2001, 12; www.policyalternatives.ca/bc/rootsofaddiction.html.

19. DuPont, *The Selfish Brain,* 31.

20. Agence France Presse, reported in the *Vancouver Sun,* September 30, 2006, A.

21. Dr. Bruce Alexander's soon-to-be published next book is aptly titled *The Globalization of Addiction.*

22. Aboriginal women between the ages of 25 and 44 are five times more likely than all other women of the same age to die as a result of violence, reported a Canadian federal study in 1996, "making them the prime targets and the most vulnerable in our society" (quoted in Stevie Cameron, *The Pickton File* [Toronto: Knopf Canada, 2007], 163). In the United States, according to Department of Justice figures, "more than one in three American Indian and Alaska Native women would be raped in their lifetime, almost double the national average of 18 percent." In the vast majority of cases, the perpetrators are non-Native ("For Indian Victims of Sexual Assault, a Tangled Legal Path," *New York Times*, April 25, 2007, A15).

23. Harold H. Gordon, "Early Environmental Stress and Biological Vulnerability to Drug Abuse," *Psychoneuroendocrinology* 27 (2002): 115–26.

24. Michael A. Dawes et al., "Developmental Sources of Variation in Liability to Adolescent Substance Use Disorders," *Drug and Alcohol Dependence* 61 (2000): 3–14.

25. For this key dynamic of peer orientation, crucial in the initiation of addictions among youth, see *Hold On to Your Kids: Why Parents Need to Matter More Than Peers*, by Gordon Neufeld and Gabor Maté (New York: Ballantine Books, 2006).

THE LIKELY CAUSE OF ADDICTION HAS BEEN DISCOVERED, AND IT IS NOT WHAT YOU THINK

Johann Hari

Huffington Post, January 20, 2015

It is now one hundred years since drugs were first banned—and all through this long century of waging war on drugs, we have been told a story about addiction by our teachers and by our governments. This story is so deeply ingrained in our minds that we take it for granted. It seems obvious. It seems manifestly true. Until I set off three and a half years ago on a 30,000-mile journey for my new book, *Chasing The Scream: The First And Last Days of the War on Drugs*, to figure out what is really driving the drug war, I believed it too. But what I learned on the road is that almost everything we have been told about addiction is wrong—and there is a very different story waiting for us, if only we are ready to hear it.

If we truly absorb this new story, we will have to change a lot more than the drug war. We will have to change ourselves.

I learned it from an extraordinary mixture of people I met on my travels. From the surviving friends of Billie Holiday, who helped me to learn how the founder of the war on drugs stalked and helped to kill her. From a Jewish doctor who was smuggled out of the Budapest ghetto as a baby, only to unlock the secrets of addiction as a grown man. From a transsexual crack dealer in Brooklyn who was conceived when his mother, a crack-addict, was raped by his father, an NYPD officer. From a man who was kept at the bottom of a well for two years by a torturing dictatorship, only to emerge to be elected President of Uruguay and to begin the last days of the war on drugs.

I had a quite personal reason to set out for these answers. One of my earliest memories as a kid is trying to wake up one of my relatives, and not being able to. Ever since then, I have been turning over the essential mystery of addiction in my mind—what causes some people to become fixated on a drug or a behavior until they can't stop? How do we help those people to come back to us? As I got older, another of my close relatives developed a cocaine addiction, and I fell into a relationship with a heroin addict. I guess addiction felt like home to me.

If you had asked me what causes drug addiction at the start, I would have looked at you as if you were an idiot, and said: "Drugs. Duh." It's not difficult to grasp. I thought I had seen it in my own life. We can all explain it. Imagine if you and I and the next twenty people to pass us on the street take a really potent drug for twenty days. There are strong chemical hooks in these drugs, so if we stopped on day twenty-one, our bodies would need the chemical. We would have a ferocious craving. We would be addicted. That's what addiction means.

One of the ways this theory was first established is through rat experiments—ones that were injected into the American psyche in the 1980s, in a famous advert by the Partnership for a Drug-Free America. You may remember it. The experiment is simple. Put a rat in a cage, alone, with two water bottles. One is just water. The other is water laced with heroin or cocaine. Almost every time you run this experiment, the rat will become obsessed with the drugged water, and keep coming back for more and more, until it kills itself.

The advert explains: "Only one drug is so addictive, nine out of ten laboratory rats will use it. And use it. And use it. Until dead. It's called cocaine. And it can do the same thing to you."

But in the 1970s, a professor of Psychology in Vancouver called Bruce Alexander noticed something odd about this experiment. The rat is put in the cage all alone. It has nothing to do but take the drugs. What would happen, he wondered, if we tried this differently? So Professor Alexander built Rat Park. It is a lush cage where the rats would have colored balls and the best rat-food and tunnels to scamper down and plenty of friends: everything a rat about town could want. What, Alexander wanted to know, will happen then?

In Rat Park, all the rats obviously tried both water bottles, because they didn't know what was in them. But what happened next was startling.

The rats with good lives didn't like the drugged water. They mostly shunned it, consuming less than a quarter of the drugs the isolated rats used. None of them died. While all the rats who were alone and unhappy became heavy users, none of the rats who had a happy environment did.

At first, I thought this was merely a quirk of rats, until I discovered that there was—at the same time as the Rat Park experiment—a helpful human equivalent taking place. It was called the Vietnam War. *Time* magazine reported using heroin was "as common as chewing gum" among U.S. soldiers, and there is solid evidence to back this up: some 20 percent of U.S. soldiers had become addicted to heroin there, according to a study published in the *Archives of General Psychiatry*. Many people were understandably terrified; they believed a huge number of addicts were about to head home when the war ended.

But in fact some 95 percent of the addicted soldiers—according to the same study—simply stopped. Very few had rehab. They shifted from a terrifying cage back to a pleasant one, so didn't want the drug any more.

Professor Alexander argues this discovery is a profound challenge both to the right-wing view that addiction is a moral failing caused by too much hedonistic partying, and the liberal view that addiction is a disease taking place in a chemically hijacked brain. In fact, he argues, addiction is an adaptation. It's not you. It's your cage.

After the first phase of Rat Park, Professor Alexander then took this test further. He reran the early experiments, where the rats were left alone, and became compulsive users of the drug. He let them use for fifty-seven days—if anything can hook you, it's that. Then he took them out of isolation, and placed them in Rat Park. He wanted to know, if you fall into that state of addiction, is your brain hijacked, so you can't recover? Do the drugs take you over? What happened is—again—striking. The rats seemed to have a few twitches of withdrawal, but they soon stopped their heavy use, and went back to having a normal life. The good cage saved them. (The full references to all the studies I am discussing are in the book.)

When I first learned about this, I was puzzled. How can this be? This new theory is such a radical assault on what we have been told that it felt like it could not be true. But the more scientists I interviewed, and the more I looked at their studies, the more I discovered things that don't seem to make sense—unless you take account of this new approach.

Here's one example of an experiment that is happening all around you, and may well happen to you one day. If you get run over today and you break your hip, you will probably be given diamorphine, the medical name for heroin. In the hospital around you, there will be plenty of people also given heroin for long periods, for pain relief. The heroin you will get from the doctor will have a much higher purity and potency than the heroin being used by street-addicts, who have to buy from criminals who adulterate it. So if the old theory of addiction is right—it's the drugs that cause it; they make your body need them—then it's obvious what should happen. Loads of people should leave the hospital and try to score smack on the streets to meet their habit.

But here's the strange thing: It virtually never happens. As the Canadian doctor Gabor Mate was the first to explain to me, medical users just stop, despite months of use. The same drug, used for the same length of time, turns street-users into desperate addicts and leaves medical patients unaffected.

If you still believe—as I used to—that addiction is caused by chemical hooks, this makes no sense. But if you believe Bruce Alexander's theory, the picture falls into place. The street-addict is like the rats in the first cage, isolated, alone, with only one source of solace to turn to. The medical patient is like the rats in the second cage. She is going home to a life where she is surrounded by the people she loves. The drug is the same, but the environment is different.

This gives us an insight that goes much deeper than the need to understand addicts. Professor Peter Cohen argues that human beings have a deep need to bond and form connections. It's how we get our satisfaction. If we can't connect with each other, we will connect with anything we can find—the whirr of a roulette wheel or the prick of a syringe. He says we should stop talking about "addiction" altogether, and instead call it "bonding." A heroin addict has bonded with heroin because she couldn't bond as fully with anything else.

So the opposite of addiction is not sobriety. It is human connection.

When I learned all this, I found it slowly persuading me, but I still couldn't shake off a nagging doubt. Are these scientists saying chemical hooks make no difference? It was explained to me—you can become addicted to gambling, and nobody thinks you inject a pack of cards into your veins. You can have all the addiction, and none of the chemical hooks. I went to a Gamblers' Anonymous meeting in Las Vegas (with the permission of everyone present, who knew I was there to observe) and they were as plainly addicted as the cocaine and heroin addicts I have known in my life. Yet there are no chemical hooks on a craps table.

But still, surely, I asked, there is some role for the chemicals? It turns out there is an experiment which gives us the answer to this in quite precise terms, which I learned about in Richard DeGrandpre's book *The Cult of Pharmacology*.

Everyone agrees cigarette smoking is one of the most addictive processes around. The chemical hooks in tobacco come from a drug inside it called nicotine. So when nicotine patches were developed in the early 1990s, there was a huge surge of optimism—cigarette smokers could get all of their chemical hooks, without the other filthy (and deadly) effects of cigarette smoking. They would be freed.

But the Office of the Surgeon General has found that just 17.7 percent of cigarette smokers are able to stop using nicotine patches. That's not nothing. If the chemicals drive 17.7 percent of addiction, as this shows, that's still millions of lives ruined globally. But what it reveals again is that the story we have been taught about The Cause of Addiction lying with chemical hooks is, in fact, real, but only a minor part of a much bigger picture.

This has huge implications for the one-hundred-year-old war on drugs. This massive war—which, as I saw, kills people from the malls of Mexico to the streets of Liverpool—is based on the claim that we need to physically eradicate a whole array of chemicals because they hijack people's brains and cause addiction. But if drugs aren't the driver of addiction—if, in fact, it is disconnection that drives addiction—then this makes no sense.

Ironically, the war on drugs actually increases all those larger drivers of addiction. For example, I went to a prison in Arizona—"Tent City"—where inmates are detained in tiny stone isolation cages ("The Hole") for weeks and weeks on end to punish them for drug use. It is as close to a human recreation of the cages that guaranteed deadly addiction in rats as I can imagine. And when those prisoners get out, they will be unemployable because of their criminal record—guaranteeing they with be cut off even more. I watched this playing out in the human stories I met across the world.

There is an alternative. You can build a system that is designed to help drug addicts to reconnect with the world—and so leave behind their addictions.

This isn't theoretical. It is happening. I have seen it. Nearly fifteen years ago, Portugal had one of the worst drug problems in Europe, with 1 percent of the population addicted to heroin. They had tried a drug war, and the problem just kept getting worse. So they decided to do something radically different. They resolved to decriminalize all drugs, and transfer all the money they used to spend on arresting and jailing drug addicts, and spend it instead on reconnecting them—to their own feelings, and to the wider society. The most crucial step is to get them secure housing, and subsidized jobs so they have a purpose in life, and something to get out of bed for. I watched as they are helped, in warm and welcoming clinics, to learn how to reconnect with their feelings, after years of trauma and stunning them into silence with drugs.

One example I learned about was a group of addicts who were

given a loan to set up a removals firm. Suddenly, they were a group, all bonded to each other, and to the society, and responsible for each other's care.

The results of all this are now in. An independent study by the *British Journal of Criminology* found that since total decriminalization, addiction has fallen, and injecting drug use is down by 50 percent. I'll repeat that: injecting drug use is down by 50 percent. Decriminalization has been such a manifest success that very few people in Portugal want to go back to the old system. The main campaigner against the decriminalization back in 2000 was Joao Figueira, the country's top drug cop. He offered all the dire warnings that we would expect from the *Daily Mail* or Fox News. But when we sat together in Lisbon, he told me that everything he predicted had not come to pass—and he now hopes the whole world will follow Portugal's example.

This isn't only relevant to the addicts I love. It is relevant to all of us, because it forces us to think differently about ourselves. Human beings are bonding animals. We need to connect and love. The wisest sentence of the twentieth century was E.M. Forster's—"only connect." But we have created an environment and a culture that cut us off from connection, or offer only the parody of it offered by the Internet. The rise of addiction is a symptom of a deeper sickness in the way we live—constantly directing our gaze towards the next shiny object we should buy, rather than the human beings all around us.

The writer George Monbiot has called this "the age of loneliness." We have created human societies where it is easier for people to become cut off from all human connections than ever before. Bruce Alexander—the creator of Rat Park—told me that for too long, we have talked exclusively about individual recovery from addiction. We need now to talk about social recovery—how we all recover, together, from the sickness of isolation that is sinking on us like a thick fog.

But this new evidence isn't just a challenge to us politically. It doesn't just force us to change our minds. It forces us to change our hearts.

Loving an addict is really hard. When I looked at the addicts I love, it was always tempting to follow the tough love advice doled out by reality shows like *Intervention*—tell the addict to shape up, or cut them off. Their message is that an addict who won't stop should be shunned. It's the logic of the drug war, imported into our private lives. But in fact, I learned, that will only deepen their addiction—and you may lose them altogether. I came home determined to tie the addicts in my life closer to me than ever—to let them know I love them unconditionally, whether they stop, or whether they can't.

When I returned from my long journey, I looked at my ex-boyfriend, in withdrawal, trembling on my spare bed, and I thought about him differently. For a century now, we have been singing war songs about addicts. It occurred to me as I wiped his brow, we should have been singing love songs to them all along.

ADDICTION, CONNECTION, AND THE RAT PARK STUDY

Adi Jaffe

Psychology Today, August 14, 2015

Recently, I was bombarded with Facebook Messenger messages and posts about an addiction story everyone got really excited about! This story followed Johann Hari's *Chasing the Scream* book and follow-up TED talk. (See my own TEDx here.)[1]

In the talk, Johann mentioned the Rat Park experiment conducted by Bruce Alexander—an experiment I already mentioned in a previous article. In this experiment rats, who are participating in drug studies, are given a large cage with free food, access to sex and toys and many playmates (the childhood kind, not Hugh Hefner's). As Hari talks about in his talk, more a Rat Heaven than Rat Park, but still. . . . Under such conditions, Dr. Alexander found that rats actually refused drug cocktails, unlike their solo-caged study-mates. The conclusion—it's not the drugs that are addiction but rather the environmental stressors that are placed on the rats we are studying. Eliminate the stress and you get rid of the addiction!

How amazing is that?!?!

If only things were really that simple . . .

Dealing with the Real World

Let's ignore for a moment the methodological issues with Dr. Alexander's study. (More on that here.)[2] Assuming that what we are aiming for is not a world free of addicted rats, but rather a world free of addicted people, I have been wondering for quite a few years how we could translate these findings into real life. The decriminalization efforts in Portugal, which Hari mentioned as well, are also something I've written about years ago and I agree that arresting drug users for their crimes leads to more, not less, addiction in the world.

The issue I am struggling with is this—marriages are imperfect, children are abused (physically and psychologically), wars affect citizens and soldiers and bad luck brings about traumatic loss. Our environment, unlike the environment created for the rats in Rat Heaven, is far from stress free. Worse still, as far as I can tell, we will, for the foreseeable future, be unable to create such a Utopia for most people on earth. If this is so, there is little doubt that some of the people affected by negative circumstances, traumatic experiences, or biological disturbances will be led down the path towards struggles with drugs and such.

To make matters more complicated, we know that biological influences related to genetic differences, neonatal (birth-related) circumstances and early nutrition can alter brain mechanisms and make people more, or less, susceptible to the effects of trauma. For instance, we now know that early life trauma alters the function of the hypothalamic-pituitary-adrenal axis, making individuals who have been exposed to trauma at an early age far more susceptible to stress, anxiety and substance use; or that hypoxia during delivery (certainly a form of trauma) can increase the chances of mental health defects later in life. Like the Rat Heaven experiment, it should be somewhat obvious that without these early traumas, the individuals in question would experience less "need" for heavy-duty coping strategies like, let's say, opiates. So biology is important here at least in this regard.

So trauma and stress are not at all objective truths but rather individually determined patterns of influence. I am fully on board with making sure that the treatment system we use does not exacerbate the problems that stress and trauma bring about (so no shaming, breaking-down, or expulsion of clients for their struggles), but I think that the picture this TED talk and the related book present is far too simplified to be as helpful as we want it to be. I believe that more focus should be given to improved prevention efforts in order to reduce the likelihood of these early traumas and therefore of later drug seeking experience in the first place. I also know that significant efforts are already being put into this sort of work through a multitude of social-services organizations and government agencies. Needless to say, the demand for drug use has not abated despite these efforts. The work must be more difficult than setting children up with a big box, water and some chew toys . . .

How Oversimplification Hurts Us

And this brings up a question for me—what if humans are not like rats? I know it's a shocking suggestion but just stay with me for a second. What if human life is somewhat more complicated than rat life, science-lab or not. What if Rat Heaven is not a recipe for success in eradicating human addiction because our own internal struggles, social networks and consciousness-seeking drive us farther in seeking mind-alteration than they do rats? Isn't it possible that even if we were somehow able to make earth a Utopia, and I would argue we are moving farther from such a reality and not closer, we would still be dealing with substance use? It's been happening for at least 8000 years already and I'm thinking it's here to stay.

So while I agree that social connection is very important for dealing with substance use problems (that is why we don't shame our clients at IGNTD and don't expel them for using when the program doesn't call for it), it also matters who we're connecting to and that, unfortunately, is something we control only to a limited extent. We have to deal with the circumstances we are born into—dysfunctional marriages, depression, dietary limitations and gang violence—and sometimes substances are the solution, not the problem.

So let's keep moving towards a shame-free way of looking at addiction but let's not pretend that wishing the struggles away will make it so.

An earnest hug is great, but it is not a panacea.
We have a lot of hard work to do.

Notes

1. Adi Jaffe, "Rebranding Our Shame," TEDxUCLA, https://youtu.be/A9xFJ_hqzDQ.

2. Katie MacBride, "This 38-Year-Old Study Is Still Spreading Bad Ideas About Addiction," *The Outline*, September 5, 2017, https://theoutline.com/post/2205/this-38-year-old-study-is-still-spreading-bad-ideas-about-addiction.

H.: ON HEROIN AND HARM REDUCTION

Sarah Resnick

n+1 Issue 24, Winter 2016

There is a photo of you standing outside the house in Borough Park, grin wide, head back, laughing. Slender in faded blue jeans against the brick and white stucco, your hair a mass of thick black curls, a little unkempt. This was you: "the fun one." On our summer visits to New York, after the long drive south from Ontario, it is you I want to see most of all.

When your daughter was born, I was 5. As I grew older I envied her for having you as a father. We rode the F train to Coney Island, surveying the city through painted windows; ate frankfurters on the boardwalk.

When I was 12, your mother, my grandmother, passed. We stopped visiting New York. I didn't see or speak to you for fifteen years. By the time I went to college, it was apparent that no one knew where you were.

Suddenly in 2007 you call.

I am living in New York now. You tell your brother, my father, that you are living at a shelter on the Bowery. He comes to town soon after, and the three of us go out to dinner. We don't speak much of the past. You say you are doing well, and we agree to meet again soon. Your hair is cropped short and you are thin, very thin.

What surprises me most: you have no teeth.

———

You are not there when I stop by after work. The man at the desk gives me this news, not for the first time. I am tired of relying on luck in order to see you. On my next visit I bring you a prepaid cell phone so we can make plans in advance. This makes you happy.

We walk to B&H Dairy, where I order cold borscht and you cherry blintzes. I show you how to use the phone.

My father calls, tells me he has urgent news to share. *I always thought it was cocaine,* he says. *But it was heroin.* He repeats the last word, drawing out the first two syllables. He is wounded, disbelieving. The way his sibling foundered was worse than he had believed. Cocaine is nefarious, sure, but heroin is depraved. He is waiting for me to interrupt—to affirm that I, too, am appalled.

The first time we meet just the two of us, you tell me you have been diagnosed with bipolar disorder. I hardly believe it. You do not conform to any idea I have of a person with bipolar disorder, though the ideas I do have are received, not based on experience. It's just that you seem to me all right, not terribly different from the way I remember you, though your affect is flatter, hollowed. You wear your defeat.

You complain of ceaseless fatigue, a haze in your head. You list your medications: lithium, Topamax, prazosin, Thorazine, lorazepam, also methadone, more I am forgetting, they are always changing. Frankly I am astonished at, worried by, the number of medications you are taking. The lithium concerns me most. I know that it has dangerous side effects. I know that it is used in batteries. Never once does it occur to me that you seem all right because of the meds and not despite them. You are impressionable and take what I say seriously. The only people you talk to are social workers, counselors, medical doctors, psychiatrists, and you do not seek to inform yourself about your own condition. You are not a skeptic. You do not read. You trust what others tell you. The source is of no relevance.

Within weeks—or is it months?—your behavior seems to me more erratic. You are quick to anger. You demand things of me in your text messages. Usually money. I put fifty dollars' worth of minutes on your phone; the next day you've run out, ask for more. Three, four times in a week, you run out of minutes. I tell you it's too expensive to be using the phone in this way, and who are you talking to all of a sudden in any case? You say it is your friend Lenny. He is agoraphobic, you add. He rarely leaves the house. By now you think that I am trying to control you, to do you harm, and you begin making accusations. I get you a better phone plan, and for a few weeks, we do not speak.

Later you explain that you adjusted the dosage of your lithium without first telling your doctor. That was you in a manic phase.

I know better now.

Mostly we talk about your daughter, Sophie. She is 21 now and the mother of a boy, 18 months. The father is a young naval officer with whom she has parted ways, but his parents take care of the baby often. You have not seen or spoken to Sophie since long before her son was born. She wants nothing to do with you. You have tried phoning her, you tell me, but she will not take your calls.

You know of her whereabouts, though, because you are in touch with the naval officer's parents. You call them regularly, hear the latest on Sophie and the baby. They must empathize with you, perceive good intentions. One day they allow you to visit when Sophie is not around. You meet your grandson and you are ecstatic. You talk about it for weeks.

Then one day you phone and they say they will no longer take your calls. They ask you not to call again, hang up.

I am optimistic. This phase will pass; Sophie will come to see that you have changed. I think I know you will be reunited.

We like eating at B&H Dairy and return there often. Today I bring you *Tompkins Square Park*, a recent book of black-and-white photographs by Q. Sakamaki. In 1986, Sakamaki moved from Osaka, Japan, to the East Village. Throughout the 1980s and '90s, he documented the park and its surrounding streets, then a gathering place for the city's marginalized and homeless and a stronghold of the anti-gentrification movement.

We turn the pages, examine the pictures. I ask you what it was like. You tell me about when you loitered outside an abandoned building turned shooting gallery, waiting in line to buy your next fix. Police officers approached you, but you were neither questioned nor arrested. Instead, they emptied your pockets, took your money. They took everyone's money. Then they left.

It is difficult to know whether your memory is reliable, whether you can be relied on. But I have no reason not to believe you.

Today is a good day for you. You get new teeth. You are more confident.

July 2013. My eye lands on a headline in the New York Times: "Heroin in New England, More Abundant and Deadly." I can't recall the last time I saw heroin in the news. Media coverage of drug use had shifted, or so it seemed to me, to meth.

Officials in Maine, New Hampshire, and Vermont, from "quaint fishing villages" to "the interior of the Great North Woods," are reporting an "alarming comeback" of "one of the most addictive drugs in the world." What's remarkable about the story, according to its authors, is where the comeback is taking place: not in urban centers, but in the smaller cities and rural towns of New England. Experts offer observations. A police captain in Rutland, Vermont, states that heroin is the department's "biggest problem right now." A doctor, an addiction specialist, says, "It's easier to get heroin in some of these places than it is to get a UPS delivery."

Most of the heroin reaching New England originates in Colombia and comes over the US-Mexico border. Between 2005 and 2011, the number of seizures jumped sixfold—presumably in part because of increased border security—but plenty of heroin still got through. In May 2013, six people were arrested in connection with a $3.3 million heroin ring in Springfield and Holyoke, Massachusetts.

The article describes two addicts in particular, both young women. They sell sex for drug money. One overdosed and died after injecting some very pure heroin. The addiction specialist tells us that he is "treating 21-, 22-year-old pregnant women with intravenous heroin addiction." The lone man identified is the companion of one of the women. Beyond his name and age, nothing about him or his circumstances is mentioned. All three are white.

I stop when I read, "Maine is the first state that has limited access to specific medications, including buprenorphine and methadone." I open a new tab, search for what the writers mean by the vague phrase, "has limited access to." Earlier that year, the state enacted legislation to limit how long recovering addicts could stay on metha-done, or similar drug-replacement therapies, before they had to start paying out of pocket. Medicaid patients will receive coverage for a maximum of two years.

I know that for some people, like you, this is not enough time.

Moving to the United States from Canada was, for me, eight years earlier, an easy enough transition. Much is shared between the two countries, and the culture shock was minimal. Yet even after all this time, I still find that certain ideas I'd taken for granted throughout adolescence and early adulthood—ideas about what a good society tries to make available for its citizens—are here not to be taken for granted at all.

At the Bowery shelter you are a model resident. You participate in group. You see a counselor. You follow the methadone program. You are friendly with others. It is on account of this that you are recom-mended for Section 8 housing, and before long you are moved into a 200-square-foot studio with a single bed, a private bathroom, a tiny kitchen. The facility, a four-story building, is designated for people living with psychiatric disabilities. Your share of the rent is $260. You are also responsible for your own utilities. These are subsidized based on your income.

For a time you find yourself in a vexing predicament. The state has deemed you "unfit to work." But each of your applications for disability benefits is denied. It is not at all clear how you are meant to survive.

November 2013. The front page of the Saturday paper features a story on buprenorphine under the headline "Addiction Treatment with a Dark Side." Buprenorphine is an opioid used for maintenance therapy like methadone, but is available by prescription. This is new. Since the 1970s, methadone has been distributed through clinics. People participating in methadone programs must go to the clinic at least once a week, and in some cases every day. This is obstructive, even oppressive. A similar drug that can be had by prescription seems like an improvement. But doctors must receive federal certification to be able to prescribe buprenorphine. Federal law limits how many patients a physician can help with the drug at one time. This means that only people with good insurance, or the ability to pay high fees out of pocket, can access it. "The rich man's methadone," the article calls it.

But this—the part that interests me—isn't what the article is about. The article is about how the drug gets "diverted, misused and abused"; how, since 2003, the drug has led to 420 deaths. (By comparison, there are more than 15,500 deaths from opioid overdose each year.) The article is not about the drug's demonstrated efficacy at helping people with opioid dependencies that negatively impact their lives. Or about how restricted access to the drug is likely contributing to its diversion and misuse in the first place. Studies report that at least some people are self-treating their dependencies and withdrawal symptoms. I read elsewhere that medication-assisted treatment with an opioid agonist, such as buprenorphine, is the most effective treatment available for opioid dependencies.

This is what you tell me: From the time you were young, you possessed an antiauthoritarian streak. This disposition did not emerge from any particular maltreatment, by family members, say, or teachers; it was your natural orientation toward the world. You were enthralled by the neighborhood kids who attracted trouble even as you yourself did not act out. You desired proximity to danger and rebelliousness. Unlike your brother, you attempted to differentiate yourself from your family not by transcending your class, but by assuming

a posture of nonconformity. You liked drugs because you weren't supposed to like them. For a long time—more than a decade—you were
able to manage your use, to keep it, for the most part, recreational.

One time your father found your needle and other supplies for
shooting up. He was furious. You wouldn't hear it. When he died
years later his heart was still broken.

I have difficulty reconciling all this with what else you have told
me of your past. I know that you worked for the police as a 9-1-1
dispatcher. You were good at your job, liked and respected, and soon
you found yourself in a supervisory position. You enjoyed the night
shift, especially, and for a long stretch the Bronx was your district.
The position is notoriously stressful, but you were sharp, capable,
levelheaded, and you excelled.

You were fired when your fidelity to heroin was stronger than it
was to your job.

You love your new apartment, can't believe your good fortune. When
I stop to consider it, neither can I.

Sometimes I imagine what you will do with your time. I picture you
as a volunteer—with other people who use drugs, maybe, or at a food
kitchen or shelter. I feel certain that you will want to do this, that
you will do something good, in the way that others did good for you.
That maybe we will do something good together. Once, when I am
volunteering on American Thanksgiving, I invite you to come along.
I know that you have nowhere else to go. You tell me you'd prefer
to stay home. A few months later, I make the suggestion once more.
Again you decline.

Later I come to recognize this as my own bizarre fantasy, a projection of my savior complex, perhaps. I laugh, not for the first time, at
the naïveté of my younger self.

December 2013. Two articles command my attention. The first, a few
weeks old, is about a radical clinical trial in Canada comparing the ef-
fectiveness of diacetylmorphine—prescription heroin—and the oral

painkiller hydromorphone, i.e., Dilaudid, in treating severe heroin dependency in people for whom other therapies have failed. An earlier study in Canada had demonstrated that both diacetylmorphine and hydromorphone are better than methadone at improving the health and quality of life of longtime opiate users. An unexpected finding was that many participants couldn't tell the difference between the effects of diacetylmorphine and hydromorphone. But the sample group receiving hydromorphone wasn't large enough to draw scientifically valid conclusions. So the study investigators created a new trial to test this finding.

If hydromorphone were to be found as effective as diacetylmorphine, it could mean offering people the benefits of prescription heroin without the legal barriers and associated stigma. The study results have yet to be published.

Larry Love, 62, a longtime dependent: "My health and well-being improved vastly" during the trial. Love's doctor applied to Health Canada for permission to continue prescribing heroin to Love and twenty other patients after their year in the trial was up. The applications were approved, although renewal was required after ninety days. The federal health minister responded by creating new regulations to prevent such approvals. He insisted Ottawa would not "give illicit drugs to drug addicts." Love, four additional patients, and the health-care center that runs the hospital that oversaw the trial are suing the government in turn. The doctor who submitted the applications, Scott MacDonald: "As a human being, as a Canadian, as a doctor, I want to be able to offer this treatment to the people who need it. . . . It is effective, it is safe, and it works. . . . I do not know what they are thinking."

The second is an editorial about a Canadian bill that, if passed, would set new guidelines for opening supervised-injection facilities. Like syringe-distribution programs, supervised-injection facilities act as a frontline service for people who use drugs intravenously, giving out sterile needles and other paraphernalia. But they go one step further: users may bring in drugs procured elsewhere and inject them under the watchful eye of trained nurses. Staff members offer instruction on safer technique ("Wash your hands," "Remove the tourniquet before pushing the plunger," "Insert the needle bevel up") and monitor for overdose, which they counteract with naloxone. They do not directly administer injections.

The new law would erect application hurdles so onerous it would effectively prevent the establishment of any new sites. The columnist attacks the government for acting on ideological rather than scientific grounds. "Supervised injection sites are places where horrible things take place." I cringe a little. "The fact is, however, that these activities are even more horrifying when they take place in the streets, and strict prohibition has never been even remotely successful."

There is, I know, only one such facility in all of North America. It's called Insite, and it's in Vancouver.

It is a fall evening and we are on our way to a movie. We pass a small group of Chabad men on the street. It is Sukkot and they are trying to identify secular Jews by sight, inviting them to perform the ritual with the date-tree fronds (*lulav*) and lemonlike fruit (*etrog*), shaking them together three times in six different directions. They have a small truck nearby (the Sukkahmobile). You tell me how a Chabad man befriended you once, how you almost became religious. He wanted to help you, and you had no one else. You went to dinners at his house. He would call to ask how you were. You say that he and his family were some of the kindest people you had ever met. But you couldn't stick with it, and one day you stopped responding.

I take you to see *Ballast*, that film of austere, understated realism about a drifter boy and a grieving man in the Mississippi Delta. It's more about tone than narrative, and I am moved by the beauty and sadness of its barren landscapes. I worry that you are bored, you nod in and out; but afterward you tell me how much you liked it. I decide I will take you to movies often.

Within weeks of Philip Seymour Hoffman's death, a surfeit of reporting:
    Why heroin is spreading in America's suburbs

How Did Idyllic Vermont Become America's Heroin Capital?
New England town ripped apart by heroin
Today's Heroin Addict Is Young, White and Suburban
Heroin's New Hometown: On Staten Island, Rising Tide of Heroin Takes Hold
When heroin use hit the suburbs, everything changed
Heroin in the Suburbs: A Rising Trend in Teens
Heroin reaching into the suburbs
Heroin Scourge Overtakes a "Quaint" Vermont Town
Heroin-gone-wild in Central New York causes jumps in overdoses, deaths
Actor's heroin death underscores scourge closer to home
Heroin scourge begs for answers
New Wisconsin laws fight scourge of heroin
The scourge of heroin addiction
Heroin scourge cuts across cultural and economic barriers
Colombian, Mexican cartels drive LI heroin scourge
Senate task force hears from Rockland on heroin scourge
Report shows heroin use reaching epidemic proportions in NH
America's heroin epidemic: A St. Louis story
Heroin: Has Virginia Reached an Epidemic?
United States in the grips of a heroin epidemic
Cheap, Plentiful, Deadly: Police See Heroin "Epidemic" in Region
How Staten Island Is Fighting a Raging Heroin and Prescription-Pill Epidemic
A Call to Arms on a Vermont Heroin Epidemic
Fighting Back Against the Heroin Epidemic
Ohio struggles with "epidemic" of heroin overdoses
Cuomo Adds 100 Officers to Units Fighting Heroin
Governors Unite to Fight Heroin in New England
Police Struggle to Fight America's Growing Heroin Epidemic
DuPage officials suggest laws to fight heroin
Taunton Launches Plan to Fight Heroin After Dozens of Overdoses
There are many more I don't write down.

Your disability application is finally approved. You will receive monthly Social Security payments of $780. You are also entitled to the disability that has accrued from the time of your first denied application, which, because it was several years ago, now amounts to several thousand dollars.

There is one condition, however. The state has decided that, given your history, you are unfit to oversee your own finances. You will need someone who can demonstrate gainful employment, preferably a family member, to tend to the money on your behalf.

On a winter morning, early, I take the bus from Prospect Heights to the Social Security office in Bushwick. We have an appointment but we wait a long time. I sign where I am asked to. I attest to my reliability. I assume responsibility.

Soon after I set up a bank account where I am your "representative payee." Your money is deposited to it on the first of each month. From this account I pay your rent, your utilities. We meet every week or two, for food, for a movie, but always so that I can provide you with cash for provisions.

This works for a while.

On the phone one day you tell me you hurt your arm, a man on the street walked right into you, knocked you down to the ground. When I call a few days later to see how you are feeling, you tell me how strange it is, nearly every guy you pass on the street is eyeing you as if he wants to start a fight. These men, they are always brushing up against you on purpose.

Within a week, maybe two, you begin to ramble about the lock on your door, how it's broken, and how you're sure someone is breaking into your apartment to spy on you. You tell me that one day you came home to find a syringe on the floor. Someone planted it there for a supervisor to find, you're certain of it, other residents want your apartment, they want you gone.

I suggest various ways you might resolve these issues. You have excuses, explanations for why each of my recommendations won't work. I ask a lot of questions. Your paranoia does not involve state secrets, the CIA or FBI, tinfoil hats or aliens, the twin towers or global-government conspiracy theories, but the elevation of small anxieties and fears to delusions of persecution. I try reasoning with you, but sometimes, in order to empathize, I must suspend my desire to be rational and take part in your fantasy world. I learn there is nothing I can do for you; you are autonomous in overseeing your own health care. I encourage you to see your psychiatrist and wait. Once your medication is adjusted, you are no longer afraid.

Not long after your disability payments kick in, the debt collectors send notices to my apartment. One is on behalf of an old landlord who, years ago, sued you for rent payments you never made. It has been more than a decade, but this debt has not been forgotten. I mail a check.

Here are some things you might do on a given day: Walk to the methadone clinic to pick up your dose (you are required to go three times a week). Wait in line. Take one bus to the Medicaid office (when your pension kicked in, your monthly benefits went up, pushing you just slightly over the minimum income requirement). Wait in line. Take one bus to see your psychiatrist (you live in Bushwick; your psychiatrist is in Crown Heights). Wait. Take one bus to the Supplemental Assistance Program office (you lost your EBT card and need to request a new one). Wait in line. Take two trains to see your hepatologist at NYU Langone Medical Center. Wait. Walk to the post office (to pick up the check my father has sent you). Wait in line. Walk to the nearest Western Union (where you would cash checks before you had a bank account). Wait in line. Take the bus and two trains to Maimonides Medical Center in Borough Park (you need a colonoscopy). Wait.

I write down statistics, try to make sense of what I'm reading. In 2012, US physicians wrote 240.9 million prescriptions for painkillers, an increase of 33 percent since 2001. The growth can be attributed to a few related factors: patient-advocacy groups calling for better pain treatment; patients, perhaps influenced by pharmaceutical marketing, requesting drugs from their doctors; doctors, some with questionable ethics, overprescribing drugs.

The US government responded in a predictable way. It introduced more stringent prescription guidelines, authorized DEA investigations and closures of "pill mills." State governments began to use databases to track "doctor shoppers," patients who sought out prescriptions from multiple physicians.

In 2010, Purdue Pharma, the producer and patent holder of Oxy-Contin, introduced an abuse-deterrent version of the drug ostensibly impervious to crushing, breaking, chewing, and dissolving, and therefore more difficult to inhale or inject.

That same year, the number of US drug poisoning deaths involving any opioid analgesic (oxycodone, methadone, or hydrocodone) accounted for 43 percent of the 38,329 drug poisoning deaths, a fourfold increase from 1999, when opioid analgesics were involved in 24 percent of the 16,849 drug poisoning deaths.

Following the government crackdown, supply of pharmaceutical opioids decreased sharply. Demand did not. The street price of prescription painkillers inflated, and many pharmaceutical opioid users opted instead for heroin. A rising supply of heroin kept prices low.

According to one study, more than 81 percent of recent heroin users say they switched after first trying prescription painkillers.

You say that one day, out of the blue, you decided to give it up. Just like that.

You call at around eleven on a weeknight to tell me you are going to call an ambulance—you are in pain. Ten days earlier you had surgery on an abdominal hernia. The procedure was supposed to have been minimally invasive, performed with a scope, a few hours all told, and I waited to take you home. But there were complications. They had to cut you open. You were admitted to the hospital, stayed seven nights. Now you are home again but certain that you are not healing properly. When I arrive at your place in Bushwick, the paramedics are helping you into the back of the ambulance. I get in with you. We sit opposite each other. I ask you questions. You are lucid. I expected you to be doubled over, but you are not. The paramedics confirm that your vitals are good. You have no fever. At this point, I am confident that this trip is unnecessary; that there is nothing to worry about except that you are alone, and you understand what that means. But I stay silent as you tell the paramedics to take you to where you want to go.

When we arrive at the emergency room, the triage nurse evaluates you. You tell her about your pain, your recent surgery. Soon you are wearing a bracelet and gown, sound asleep in a bed. It is past midnight. I sit in the vinyl sled-base chair to read, but am more interested in the ER nurses shuffling through the ward, the gurneys wheeling by, bodies and machines, the perverse game of observation and diagnosis. Who among the patients holds the fate worse than all the others? I know that if you're asleep the pain is not as bad as you said it was.

Not far from your bed, just outside the curtain, a young man in a wheelchair, his neck slackened, his chin drooping close to the chest, vomits. It's viscous, like cake batter. It pours out of his mouth and covers the front of his gown. He is unconscious and makes barely any sound. Now is a good time for a walk. I head outside, buy some chips from the gas station.

When I return, the young man has been moved to the center of the ward, where, shuddering now, he continues to vomit. The former contents of his abdomen pool and spread on the floor. A nurse approaches. I point to the man and ask whether something might be done for him. The nurse frowns, tells me that the man is getting what he deserves; he has done this to himself. She walks away. Several nurses pass the gurney, but no one looks at the man.

It is 4 AM by the time the doctor sees you. Everything is fine, he tells us. By now the chaos of the ER has quieted. You slept right through it.

Tomorrow, I will get up early and go into work at an office.

For the first time, I resent you.

The morning I visit Insite I awake to a winter sun, a rare reprieve from Vancouver rain. It is still early when I take the bus downtown. The buildings glimmer gold and red under the warming light.

I decided to come here, to make the long trip to Vancouver, because I wanted to see Insite for myself. I wanted to see the place where people who use drugs intravenously can go to inject more safely, the place where, according even to the supportive editorial I'd read earlier, "horrible things take place." By then I had read enough about supervised injection to know that I thought it less horrible than humane. There is much else for which I would reserve the word *horrible*, including the treatment by law enforcement of people who use drugs.

Between 1992 and 2000, more than 1,200 fatal overdoses were recorded in Vancouver. Many of these took place in the Downtown Eastside, a neighborhood of ten or so square blocks where more than 4,600 people who inject drugs intravenously were known to live. The HIV conversion rate was the highest in the Western world. (This was due in part to the popularity in Vancouver of using cocaine intravenously: cocaine has a very short half-life, and people injecting the drug habitually might do so as many as forty times a day, as compared with heroin, which tends to be injected one to four times a day.) The city, recognizing that American-style prohibition had failed to bring about any improvement, undertook a kind of crash course on drug policy. A succession of public forums, meetings, demonstrations, and conferences with experts from all over the world brought together drug users and their families, service providers, academic researchers, police, and policymakers to examine alternative approaches—heroin-prescription programs, supervised-injection sites, decriminalization.

In 2003, Insite opened as a pilot research program, exempt from the criminal code. It was not the only new service offered in the city, and it was "no silver-bullet solution," a disclaimer Canadian policymakers, activists, and other supporters used often to describe its alternative approaches. But because it seemed to stand at the threshold of what progressive-minded people deemed acceptable—because, for many, it seemed intuitively *wrong*—it received the most attention, and was widely discussed both province- and nationwide. This, too, interested me. Most Vancouver residents initially opposed the facility but came to support it; this took a lot of convincing, and a shift in the way people understand illegal drugs and those who use them. I wanted to know how this had happened.

In 2006, the Conservative Party in Canada won the national election, ousting the Liberals. For the first time since 1993, Canada had a Conservative prime minister; from the start, he began dismantling the country's social programs. Early on, Insite became a battleground for drug policy across the country. The government tried to shut it down, but the Portland Hotel Society (now PHS Community Services Society), the nonprofit group that runs Insite, mounted a human rights case and took it to the Supreme Court. In 2011, Insite won the right to stay open.

Still, I wondered how long it could last. I wanted to know, too, if something like it could ever exist in the United States.

At 9 AM, five men and women sit on the sidewalk on flattened cardboard boxes, first in line to enter when the doors open in an hour. Outside I meet Russ Maynard, Insite's program coordinator. He's with several college students from a health-administration program, there on a class visit.

As a group, we walk through the reception area into the injection room. At first glance, it reminds me of a hair salon. The room is wide and bright, lined on one side by mirrors and a row of numbered bays, thirteen in all. Each has a stainless-steel counter, a sink for hand washing, a sharps container, a plastic chair, and an extraction hood to collect smoke and vapors.

A platform with a curvilinear counter, the kind you see in hospitals, is raised behind the booths. Lining the countertop are bins that contain all the supplies a person would need to inject drugs—a syringe, a cooker for mixing the drug with water, a sterilized-water capsule for flushing the needle, a tourniquet to tie off a vein. There is, too, a tool for crushing pills.

In the injection room, we arrange our chairs in a loose semicircle around Russ, who stands. Russ begins his introduction. Insite is operated by Vancouver Coastal Health, the regional health authority, and PHS Community Services Society, a neighborhood nonprofit that focuses on the hard to house. PHS started in 1991, after a residents association converted a hotel into housing for the homeless. Today it provides residences for 1,200 people across sixteen buildings.

PHS also provides a range of community-based programs, including a credit union, a community drop-in center, medical and dental services, a syringe exchange, and an art gallery. Users of Insite can access all this simply by coming in, and to get them to come in is Insite's goal. Making contact is the first step toward connecting people, at their request, to vital services they might need. They call the people who use their services "clients."

Russ presents the group with a moral dilemma. "Imagine you're working at the front desk and a woman walks in and she's eight months pregnant, and she wants to come in and inject. You have to make a quick decision. If the line starts getting backed up, there's going to be an argument, or maybe worse. So what's going to happen?"

The room is silent.

I try to visualize the scenario, but it tests the limits of my open-mindedness. It is difficult to imagine supporting a pregnant woman's injection-drug habit.

"Is she going to leave and the clouds will part and the sunshine will hit her face and she'll see the error of her ways and never use again? Or is she going to take some equipment and go use in an alley or a doorway or a hotel room or something like that? If you do take her in, you can connect her with the nursing staff. You can have her housed by the end of the day. You can connect her with food, with services, all kinds of things. And you forgo all of that if you turn her away."

Someone asks about the mirrors. They are a critical design feature, says Russ. Staff use them to monitor clients while maintaining a respectful distance. Clients use them to ensure a certain amount of caution when injecting—to pay more attention to doing it properly.

Russ: "You want it in your veins. Because there's a big wash—imagine a wave coming to hit you—and you won't feel anything for a little while. And if you make a mistake, it means that you have to go back out and perform sex work, or beg, or steal, or whatever it is you do to get the ten dollars you need. And that is stressful."

Since 2007, the staff at Insite has been able to refer visitors to Onsite, a detox center on the building's second floor. There are twelve private rooms, each with its own bathroom. Insite connects between 400 and 450 people each year to detox, which, Russ claims, is more than any other project in Canada.

The students leave. One at a time, men and women, young, old, homeless, ordinary, are called in from the waiting room. As they enter, they announce the drug they will be injecting: "down," "dillies," "crystal" (heroin, Dilaudid, methamphetamine). The receptionist records their answers in a database, in case of emergency or overdose.

I watch the mirrors from across the room. A stately man in a wool sweater, navy with white snowflakes, drags a fine-tooth comb through his silvery hair, from the top of his forehead back to his nape. He does this twenty or thirty times before tending to his mustache with the same fastidiousness, never breaking focus. Then he pulls a woolen cap over his head and walks out into the sun.

A young nurse examines the arms of a fiftysomething woman. The woman looks afraid. The nurse speaks in soft tones as she runs her hands along the woman's forearms, helps her to locate a vein that isn't damaged, scarred, or collapsed. The nurse ties a tourniquet around her biceps. They both pause. The woman, hand trembling, inserts the needle. The nurse removes the tourniquet. The woman pushes the plunger.

Hours later, I see the same woman on the bus, traveling along Hastings Street. I want to speak to her, consider doing so, even as I know it's not right (privacy). But the woman is with a friend. Instead I watch her, imagine where she's going, how she will spend her time, what her home is like. If anyone awaits her there.

The woman gets off the bus.

———

I ask Russ whether he knows any clients who might be willing to speak with me. He hesitates. Donovan Mahoney is doing well, he says. He puts me in touch. Now I am in Donovan's living room. We sit opposite each other, on separate couches. A series of photographs he has taken hangs on the wall above his head. Today Donovan is a talented photographer. His apartment, the garden level of a house in a middle-class neighborhood, is spacious, with a chef's kitchen and newly laid blond hardwood floors. He wears khaki pants and a gray sweater, slim-fitting with an overlapping V-neck. A baseball cap covers his partially shaved head of thick black hair.

Donovan tells me the story of his twenties: he followed a girl to Vancouver, fell into coke, then rock cocaine, then heroin. He'd always thought heroin was dirty, but after trying it for the first time he felt its reputation was undeserved.

For a while he made money as a dealer. When he wanted to binge, he would go to the Downtown Eastside, stay in an SRO hotel where no one would find him. Then one time he didn't go home. He let his monthly rent payments pass, grew paranoid. He left behind all his belongings, including his car. This was in 2001. He lived on the streets, mostly. He didn't like to feel closed in by walls, especially when he was high. He shoplifted, was caught often, spent many nights in jail.

He was wary of Insite when he first heard about it. On the street, he knew that everyone was working an angle. There's a forthrightness to interactions that doesn't exist elsewhere. He found it freeing. But he couldn't understand what would motivate the staff at Insite.

Now he credits them for helping him to achieve all that he has.

Donovan: "They're inadvertently showing you that there's another way of life. You start to have normal conversations. You say to them, 'What do you do?' They reply, 'I don't know, I'm in a band.' Of course they are. And then they tell you stuff about what they do with their girlfriend. Or how they went away for the weekend and saw their parents. To me, to an addict, they're showing me something. There's a whole other world out there that I don't even understand. They're showing you what it looks like to be a normal human being. Which is incredible, because if I'm shooting dope in an alley, I may bump into somebody who's been through recovery, and they may be able to guide me. But they're not going to be around when you need them.

"Addiction isn't nine to five. It's not like, 'OK, tomorrow at ten o'clock I'm going to go into recovery.' It happens and you don't really see it coming. It's like, *I think right now, if you guys got me in, I think I could go.*"

You want to be in charge of your own money. It is frustrating to have to travel to me every time you run out of cash. Together we visit your social worker, talk about how this could work. He needs to make a recommendation to your psychiatrist, to the state, before this can happen. We review your history. For the first time it is affirmed to me that you are likely to take methadone all your life. The social worker mentions your dose—120 mg—says it's high, that you haven't decreased it since beginning the therapy. You acknowledge as much. Still, it has been stabilizing, and the social worker is not concerned.

I tell the social worker that I will share the bank account with you, monitor your spending. Satisfied, he makes the recommendation. We open a joint account. Your monthly checks will be deposited and you will be responsible for paying your bills, for making sure you have enough to get through the month. I will check on the account through online banking. I keep your savings, a few thousand dollars left over from the disability back payments, in a separate account in your name.

For a year, at least, you manage all right.

I know that, in the late '80s and '90s, the rapid spread of HIV through needle sharing galvanized US activists to challenge state laws and distribute hypodermic syringes for free, without a prescription; that the rate of new HIV cases in Vancouver among intravenous drug users persuaded even conservative politicians to consider opening a supervised-injection site; that were it not for the HIV epidemic, many drug-policy reforms in the US and elsewhere might not have occurred.

I find it curious how few articles on the emerging "epidemics"—heroin, opioid—mention the disease. I wonder whether it is because, with antiretrovirals so widely available, HIV is perceived to be less threatening than it once was. I chase the question for a time. I print out medical papers, underline findings. I call an epidemiologist at a prestigious university, who answers my questions patiently. He tells me that some of the best research is being done by an epidemiologist in Kentucky, who has been following a cohort of intravenous drug users since 2008. (Appalachia has disproportionately high rates of nonmedical prescription-opioid use and overdose-related deaths.) No one in the cohort had yet been diagnosed HIV positive, but 70 percent have hepatitis C. I ask why this matters, and he says that rising hepatitis C rates often forecast HIV outbreaks, because the viruses spread through the same behaviors—unprotected sexual intercourse and needle sharing—and both require a certain density of drug users to sustain transmission. But hep C is ten times more infectious, can live outside the body longer, and is extremely difficult to kill; it spreads more easily. A hepatitis C outbreak indicates that all the factors are present for an HIV outbreak.

In many ways, it's a ticking time bomb, the epidemiologist says, especially since, in rural Appalachian communities, knowledge about HIV tends to be minimal; these populations have not previously had to deal with the disease.

I hang up the phone, look up the data set that tracks syringe-distribution programs by state. Kentucky, 0; Tennessee, 0; Georgia, 1; South Carolina, 0; North Carolina, 6; Alabama, 0; Mississippi, 0; Ohio, 2; Virginia, 0; West Virginia, 0; Pennsylvania, 2; New York, 22; Maryland, 1.

You are weak and exhausted, have been for months. Every time we make plans, you cancel. Months pass and I don't see you. When by routine appointment you see your hepatologist, he sends you to the emergency room. You will need a blood transfusion to give you the hemoglobin that you need. By the time I arrive, the blood has been ordered from the bank, is being warmed. We wait for hours. The transfusion itself will take hours, too. I leave you there alone.

Before I go, the doctor tells me that what you are experiencing is a complication from hepatitis C.

We sit at your kitchen table beside the four-drawer wooden dresser, its surface lined with pill vials and bottles of methadone. I tell you about Insite. You appear bewildered, shocked even. "How can that possibly help anyone get off drugs?"

Your first reaction resembles most people's, but it's not what I want you to say. I want you to argue that getting people off drugs need not be the primary goal. I want you to be critical of the status quo—of the morass of law and policy in which you and millions of others are entangled. But you are not. You have only ever been exposed to one idea, one approach: abstinence.

I explain it to you this way: that the most serious harms that arise from drug use—HIV, endocarditis, tetanus, septicemia, thrombosis— come not from the drugs but from external factors. Of all the ways to administer drugs, injecting carries the most risks. The drug solution bypasses the body's natural filtering mechanisms against disease and bacteria. Access to sterile equipment and hygienic injection conditions can mean the difference between living and dying.

I say, thinking you might relate, that policing has an especially devastating effect on people who use drugs intravenously and are entrenched in street life. When they fear the police, they don't stop using, they just move elsewhere—to neighboring areas, where they may create new syringe-sharing networks, or to hidden or indoor locations. In such places, needle sharing is more common, because access to clean needles is cut off. When police are around, users avoid carrying clean needles, for fear of being identified as addicts and harassed. Overdoses increase. Precarious witnesses, fearful that police will follow medical personnel to the scene, fail to seek help.

I have stats at the ready. Nearly 500,000 Americans are incarcerated on drug charges. Another 1.2 million are supervised on probation or parole. Overwhelmingly, those affected are black, and not because they use and sell drugs at higher rates—on the contrary. I say that prison is no place for people who use drugs, help does not await them there. Maintenance therapies using methadone and buprenorphine are not available for people with opioid dependencies. Often an incarcerated person will continue to use drugs throughout a prison stay, and the clandestine nature of his use means that he is now more at risk than he might otherwise have been, using unsterile needles and sharing syringes among multiple inmates. Overdose rates peak in the first few weeks after release from prison, with mortality rates higher than what would be expected in similar demographic groups in the general population.

You begin to understand. You agree none of this is good. But still you are uneasy. You maintain it would be better to encourage people to stop using altogether.

A year has passed since I spoke with the epidemiologist. I read in the newspaper that more than eighty people in Scott County, Indiana, have tested positive for HIV, most of them from a small town called Austin. The outbreak can be traced to intravenous use of the drug Opana, an opioid analgesic. The transmission rate has been around 80 percent.

Meanwhile a woman in Austin buys a license to carry a handgun because she fears for her young children. The woman takes pictures of "all this stuff going on" and calls the tip line. "I do nothing but," she says. On her lawn is a sign: NO LOITERING OR PROSTI-TUTING IS ALLOWED IN FRONT OF THESE PREMISES.

You resent me now. I am trying to help you budget your money. You are spending your entire monthly payment within the first week. When your next deposit comes, I transfer it into the account you cannot access. Every week, I allow you one quarter of your stipend, after deducting your bills and rent. But you won't stop texting me, asking for more money. I try to reason with you, explain why you need the budget. I try putting my foot down, which amounts to ignoring your texts. You say you are buying a lot of $5 bootleg DVDs (Hitchcock is your favorite), but you forget that I know how to do math. And you are not interested in any of the solutions I come up with—a cheap computer, an internet connection, Netflix.

Every time I say no, I know I am passing judgment on you, on the things you desire for yourself (your collection of Adidas sneakers is by now substantial), what you prioritize. I am measuring you against an ethic of responsibility, a conception of the good life, that I do not want to force you to share. I can recognize this, but I can't hew my way out of the irony that accepting your irresponsibility only shifts the burden onto me, and this too seems unjust.

You were lucky once. You and my father sold your childhood home for $300,000. You never risked going to prison to support yourself. But before long, your half was gone, and you started spending my father's share. He cut you off, begged you to stop, but you said no, you had never felt so alive, you were having the time of your life.

We go to the bank and close the joint account, transfer your savings. You have total control.

I feel light.

Your savings vanish within a month.

You show up to an appointment with your psychiatrist, but it is the wrong day. You are confused, delirious. You travel by ambulance to the psychiatric emergency room at a nearby hospital. Your social worker calls to report what has happened. He says you may be showing signs of early-onset dementia. He says you may be abusing your methadone. I tell him about our recent conversation, the one where you told me you were taking Klonopin to sleep at night; the one where you guardedly suggested you may not be taking it as directed.

Two weeks later the social worker calls me again. You have terminated your services with their facility. You are within your rights to do so, and by phoning to let me know, the social worker is breaking protocol. But he is worried, thinks you lied when you said you found a psychiatrist closer to home. He believes you may no longer be fit to take care of yourself. He wants to call Adult Protective Services, would I be all right with that, and might he provide them with my phone number? He says to me, Please, you are the only person H. has.

It takes a few days, but I reach you. I come over with pastries from the Doughnut Plant. You seem all right—lucid, lively. You want to know how I know about it all. You are annoyed that someone would call me. You tell me that you like your new facility, that you are happy not to travel to Crown Heights to see your psychiatrist. Getting around the city is hard now. Scoliosis has you bent in two. You are not lying about the existence of this new facility. But when I ask whether you have a new social worker, someone who can help manage your various appointments, who knows what services you are eligible for, who can connect you with the things you need, who you can talk to about your private thoughts, it occurs to you, for the first time, that you do not. I tell you to look into it.

A few weeks later, I hear from my father that you have started traveling to Crown Heights again.

I met R. through a dating app. Now I am sitting with him in a wooden booth in a dark bar drinking Campari with soda and lime. We talk, and it's clear he knows a lot of things. He refuses to say much about it, but for years he studied Kabbalah. He also lived in India, studied Buddhism. Now he works as a professor. We share some ideas about politics, enough to make him stand out among the other dates. We seem to be getting along all right.

Recently he has been to Vancouver. I tell him that I've also been there. We talk about the Downtown Eastside, and he tells me he knows and respects the work of Gabor Maté, whom I interviewed on my trip. Maté is a physician and harm-reduction advocate, a proponent of safe injection sites, who worked in the Downtown Eastside for twelve years. He's also a proponent of the healing powers of ayahuasca, which is how R. knows of him. I enjoy this conversation, the overlaps in our knowledge. I tell him about *Da Vinci's Inquest*, the Canadian television program based on Vancouver's chief coroner

turned mayor, the same mayor who was in office when Insite opened.
R. tells me that he has done, still sometimes does do, heroin. A casual
user.

It's like a test. I can recall the many times I have pointed out, in
abstract conversations, that heroin's reputation does not align with
scientific evidence; that although it can be devastating for some, it
is not, in itself, any more dangerous than a lot of other drugs, and
people who use heroin are unduly stigmatized. But here it is no longer abstract. Will I hold it against R.?

Later, when I mention this detail to a friend, she frowns. "I like
the other guy better."

You are cured of your hepatitis after a course of Sovaldi, a new pill
that clears the disease in 95 percent of cases. The price of this near-
certain cure: $84,000. Each pill costs $1,000. You are fortunate to
live in New York, the state where Medicaid coverage of the drug is
the most generous. Many states pay for only the sickest patients. You
are, relatively speaking, not that sick.

For the first time I come across an article in the popular press that
challenges the accepted narrative. A professor of psychology and
psychiatry named Carl Hart says the heroin public health crisis is a
myth. He claims the attorney general is overstating the problem. The
commonly cited metrics are insufficient and misleading: the number
of people who have tried heroin doesn't tell you how many people
have dependency issues.

Weeks later, I underline a sentence in *Drug War Heresies*, a book
that attempts to project and evaluate the consequences of various legalization regimes and drug-policy reforms: "One million occasional
drug users may pose fewer crime and health problems than 100,000
frequent users."

There are more interviews to transcribe. I've been procrastinat-
ing. Today I am listening to my conversation with Gabor Maté. My
friends have been trying ayahuasca, going on retreats, and they all
seem to know of him, to hold him in high regard.

I know the quote I want, am waiting for him to say it, fast-forward through my own voice.

He says: "Abstinence is just not a model you can force on everybody. There's nothing wrong with it for those for whom it works. But when it comes to drug treatment there's an assumption that one size fits all. And if you're going to wash your hands of people who can't go the abstinence route, then you're giving up."

He says: "Harm reduction means you give out clean needles, you give out sterile water, you resuscitate people if they overdose. You help people inject more safely. You're not treating the addiction. You're not intending to. You're just reducing the harm."

We decide to see a movie in Williamsburg. In the back of a livery car, you tell me that one thing you really miss, one thing you think you should try to do, is find a female companion. I agree that this would be ideal, but I'm not sure how to help. I say that maybe you should go online. I show you the dating app on my phone and we laugh at its absurdity. I say there must be sites for older people. But you don't have a computer, and you don't have a smartphone. I'm certain you could count the times you've used the internet on one hand.

You tell me about the woman in the apartment below you. Whenever you try to shower, she immediately turns on all her faucets and uses up the hot water before you even have time to undress.

I explain the unlikelihood of this—hot-water distribution in a multi-unit building just doesn't work that way. You seem reassured, but the next time we speak, you complain that the problem continues.

Weeks later, you call in a panic. Con Edison is threatening to cut off your service, and you can't afford to pay. The bill is several hundred dollars, despite the subsidy you receive. You tell me you had been running your space heater all day, every day, for weeks—the building had kept the heat on low. You either underestimate my intelligence or the shame is too great.

I call Con Edison, take care of your bill. You haven't sent a payment in six months. When I confront you with this, you insist on your version of the story.

You call a car and ride over to my place because you don't have money to get you through the month. My father says that if I lend it to you, he'll pay me back.

"You know what happened?"

You are sitting at my dining table. You are smiling, and you tell me that when you finally met the hot-water villain, you found her beautiful and fell in love.

You gave her a holiday gift: a note and $30. You stuffed it under her door. She kept the money, of course, but she never acknowledged you.

When you leave I give you extra cash for your car ride home.

A week later, you call to apologize for lying to me about the Con Ed bill. This is a first.

The Canadian government releases details of a damning audit. The audit alleges that PHS Services, which runs Insite and in 2013 received provincial-government funding worth approximately $18 million, misused corporate credit cards and reimbursed improper expenses:

$8,600 for limousine rides in 2013

almost $900 per night for a stay in a British hotel

more than $2,600 for a stay in a Disneyland resort for two adults and two children

$5,832 for a Danube cruise

The article reveals many other missteps.

I wince. I know how hard these people have worked, how much they've done for the hard-to-house in Vancouver. I know this scandal will taint them forever. To open a facility like Insite, to set up crackpipe vending machines (as they have also done)—to challenge the status quo in this way—you can't make mistakes. It's like being a politician. Someone will always want to drag you down.

Even as the media narrative continues to focus on heroin use among middle-class youth in suburban neighborhoods and rural towns, I know that other populations are in need of resources and services. A study by the Centers for Disease Control and Prevention shows that rates of heroin use remain highest among males, 18- to 25-year-olds, people with household incomes below $20,000, people living in urban areas, and people with no health insurance or on Medicaid.

I take the subway up to the Bronx to BOOM!Health, a peer-run harm-reduction organization. With a small grant from the Drug Policy Alliance, BOOM! is trying to open the first legal supervised-injection facility in the US. They've even set up a model site, a single injection booth fashioned after those at Insite. I meet with the organization's president and chief programming officer. He tells me that they want to create a pilot study, much like the one in Vancouver. I know that when advocates in San Francisco tried to set up a facility, the opposition was too great. But BOOM! is optimistic; having Bill de Blasio in the mayor's office presents an opportunity.

I speak with a lawyer specializing in public-health law who argues that a pilot study is not the best strategy. "The people who are moved by evidence are not necessarily legislators. Insite was evaluated every which way. There were so many papers. Most of them are some variation on the theme that it did pretty much what we thought it would do, and it didn't do anything that its detractors thought it might do. Has that proven very persuasive, either in Canada or the US? Not really!"

Framing the facility as an incremental extension of services already available, he suggests, could prove more effective. "Almost do it under the radar." He is not sure that he is correct, but claims that, at least to his knowledge, the federal government never busted a single syringe-exchange program; it was always the local cops and sheriffs.

He adds, hesitantly: "But then the question is: Is that model"—i.e., an unsanctioned facility—"exportable to other cities and states?"

When I began to follow the media coverage of the new "heroin scourge," I didn't have strong ideas about "addiction," except that I knew it when I saw it. I believed it was a disease, and that it should be treated as such. But the more I read, the more people I speak with, the more I begin to question this framework. It is clear that no one—no neuroscientist, psychologist, psychiatrist, or physician—can explain what addiction is or account for its contradictions. Tobacco, cocaine, heroin, alcohol, MDMA, amphetamines—are they inherently addictive? Common knowledge suggests they are. But all around me I see exceptions more than the rule, my friends who use, have used, some or all of these drugs, including heroin, casually. I, too, am one of the exceptions.

I conclude that my own point of view is now best represented by the more radical strands of the harm-reduction movement and by legalization; I can argue, morally, intellectually, why these alternatives are better than what we have now.

Following the lead of those in harm-reduction and drug-users' rights groups, I decide to scrub the word *addict* from my vocabulary, to avoid using the term *drug abuser*. The alternatives can be awkward on the page, in a sentence, but it is more important not to reduce a person to this one aspect of her life, not to ascribe all the negative valences carried by these words.

person with a substance-misuse disorder

person experiencing a drug problem

person who uses drugs habitually

person committed to drug use

I try carrying these over into speech. This, too, is challenging.

I meet Judith in her studio. She is 75, a painter of Indian peafowl, roseate spoonbills, reddish egrets, and other birds of refined plumage and delicate bills. Earlier in the winter, her son, Spencer, died of a methadone overdose. We face each other, seated in chairs, a small table and a glass of water between us. Judith looks the part of a painter. She is poised, like her subjects, and speaks of her son's death with surprising ease.

"Having a son die this way is not the absolute worst thing a mother can experience. I can think of circumstances far worse."

Her stoicism is not an act. Despite countless visits to detox programs and rehab centers, a frightening prison stay, longtime family support, and the benefit of resources unavailable to most, Spencer was unable to stop using drugs in a dangerous way. Judith understands that she's not to blame.

I examine a framed photograph of Spencer that Judith has pulled out on my behalf. He's tall and fit-looking, blue-eyed, sensitive.

Spencer binged. Methadone maintenance never worked for him. Taking anything at all, including methadone, triggered a dangerous cycle. When Spencer overdosed, it was with methadone he received through a program. He had been trying to give up drugs. Judith believes that Spencer was torn between the life he wanted for himself and the life he seemed fated to have. "He had the right to let himself go if he couldn't be happy."

Judith tells me that methadone-maintenance therapy is without a doubt a terrible thing. I want to say: Maybe for some people, like your son, but it has also helped many others. But I can't say it.

Judith says that a person on methadone still has that "all about me" attitude. What she means is that there is a kind of heroin mind, a way of behaving particular to a habitual drug user. The person may prioritize access to heroin above all else, including relationships with loved ones. Lying and stealing are constants in the repertoire of behavior. A person on methadone, Judith is saying, is still in heroin mind.

I make an intellectual case for methadone, say that for some people it can help to stabilize their lives. But Judith stares at me blankly. She is not interested. I want to appeal with a personal example, but I find it hard to come up with one.

She compares those who rely on methadone with those who seek help, and support others, through Narcotics Anonymous, as her son did. The people who commit to these programs, she explains, commit to a life of service. Spencer may have given up on his own life, but he helped save innumerable others. Judith claims the people she met through NA are among the saintliest she knows.

"You should disconnect from your uncle, leave him behind, drop him. He is taking from you without ever giving back."

I feel defensive, uncomfortable, on your behalf and my own. I feel

I'm being perceived as weak for deciding that you, while difficult, are still a person worth knowing.

I say I appreciate the advice.

Judith apologizes, tells me what I really need to do is to find a boyfriend who will treat me like a queen.

I am mistaken. Sophie never does come around. I can't remember the last time you mentioned her name. Two years, maybe more. By now your grandson must be 8 or 9.

With the right login credentials and some basic biographical information—first and last name, an approximate age, a residential state past or present, a relative's given name—there's a lot you can find out about a person, even when Google and Facebook turn up little. When I decide, finally, that I will look for Sophie this way, through databases I can access through my job as a fact-checker, it takes me no more than sixty seconds to locate where she is living.

A trail of email addresses with varying domain names (aol.com, comcast.com, yahoo.com) reveals a few of the websites she's created accounts on: a daily-horoscope generator, a payday-loan provider (cash4thanksgiving.com). Presumably these sites have lax privacy policies. My heart sinks a little when I think of her needing a payday loan; it suggests her life has not been an easy one.

I will write to her, I think.

COULD THIS CONTROVERSIAL TREATMENT HELP MORE PEOPLE BEAT HEROIN ADDICTION?

Maia Szalavitz

Women's Health, June 2017

This is a story of addiction . . . and recovery . . . and relapse. Legions of women are entering rehab to kick opioids and heroin, but the majority of them will fail, largely because they're being denied the treatment most likely to help them succeed. WH investigates how the system got so broken, why women are being exploited at their most vulnerable moments, and where the root of true recovery lies.

I met "the one" when I was 20 years old. It was the mid '80s, and I had just been suspended from Columbia University for selling drugs. I was sitting in a crooked little room in a dingy, run-down Manhattan hotel with some friends when my then-boyfriend, a cocaine dealer, introduced me to my new love: heroin. It wasn't my first affair with drugs—I'd used marijuana, LSD, mushrooms, cocaine—but with one snort of the euphoria-inducing white powder, I was filled with the acceptance, comfort, and love I'd been chasing for what felt like forever, first as an extremely geeky child, then as a suburban high school outsider so obsessed with gaining approval that my entire life's purpose became cracking an Ivy League school. Within a few months, I was injecting.

Back then, I wasn't the stereotypical junkie. These days, however, I would be a proper poster child for opioid addiction. In recent years, there's been an epidemic of women, the majority of them like

me—white, middle class or working class—using and abusing opioids. That includes heroin, which, between 2002 and 2013, increased
in use among women at twice the rate of men—and prescription
painkillers, which about 1.5 million misuse each month. The problem is literally killing them. Between 1999 and 2015, opioid overdose
rates quadrupled among men but *sextupled* among women.

The statistics are sobering. But more distressing is that if and when
these women seek help, the most common treatment—a 28-day stint
in rehab based on the 12-step, abstinence-only model—rarely works
and can even be dangerous. A large-scale study found that with this
practice, which is the basis for 80 percent of treatment for all substance abuse in the U.S., few people receive effective care. I saw this
during my own stay in rehab, where counselors told me that only 1
in 27 people would end their addiction through the program. I met
many women there who had "failed" rehab multiple times.

In my three decades as a journalist specializing in covering addiction, I've also seen people reclaim their lives through a different,
science-backed approach called maintenance therapy, or medication-
assisted treatment (MAT). It has been around since the 1960s and
has more recently been endorsed by recovery experts and government agencies. And yet the approach has been marginalized—vili-
fied, really—by traditional treatment centers, and even some doctors.
The principle behind MAT is this: Because opioid addiction permanently alters the brain receptors, taking the drug completely out
of someone's system can leave them less able to naturally cope with
physical or emotional stress, says Sarah Wakeman, M.D., medical director at the Massachusetts General Hospital Substance Use
Disorder Initiative in Boston and an assistant professor at Harvard
University. So doctors prescribe steady doses of legal opioids (buprenorphine or methadone) that act on the same parts of the brain
as illicit opioids. "With regular use, at the right dose, the drugs don't
produce a high, but they do prevent withdrawal symptoms, reduce
cravings, and, because they create a tolerance to other opioids, reduce
the odds of a deadly overdose if someone relapses," says Wakeman.
The treatment slashes relapse and death rates, yet it's so stigmatized

as "just replacing one drug with another"—something I heard count-less times in rehab—that fewer than 35 percent of people addicted to opioids have access to these medications. With the opioid crisis at an all-time high, it's time to end that.

Programmed for Pain

To truly understand the heroin epidemic, you have to understand how opioids became broadly available through simple supply and demand. In the 1970s, doctors started recognizing that chronic pain was widely undertreated. They responded by prescribing re-cently FDA-approved opioids (like Percocet and Vicodin) in high numbers, believing they were less addictive than they are. Between 1999 and 2014, sales of the drugs nearly quadrupled; in 2012 alone, health-care providers wrote 259 million prescriptions for painkillers, enough for every adult in the country to have a bottle. The majority of the prescriptions went to, and continue to be written for, women, since we're more likely than men to experience chronic pain condi-tions (like multiple sclerosis and fibromyalgia), more apt to visit an M.D. to treat them, and more likely to be given a long-term Rx to match the long-term ache.

Fewer than 10 percent of people treated for chronic pain with opi-oids become hooked on the meds. But those odds increase exponen-tially when you add in other factors that disproportionately affect females: mental illness, and having a history of physical, emotional, or sexual abuse. More than two-thirds of women with prescription opioid addictions have mood or anxiety disorders, which can lead them to self-medicate with the drugs. Worse, some antianxiety meds women use to treat their mental health conditions increase the risk of dying from an opioid overdose if they're taken together. And up to 95 percent of women seeking treatment for opioid addiction have experienced childhood abuse. "A woman who initially took an opi-oid for physical pain may discover it helps her escape from the flash-backs and panic attacks caused by a past trauma, which can lead her to abuse the drugs to cope," says psychologist Carrie Wilkens, Ph.D., cofounder of the Center for Motivation and Change, an addiction treatment center in New York City.

Broken Systems

Eventually, many women addicted to opioids need—and want—help. The majority of them will end up in a 28-day rehab program that requires them to abstain from the drug. In theory, it makes sense—closely monitor people in a safe place so they can get the narcotics out of their systems. In reality, there's little rhyme or reason (or science) behind this treatment. For starters, the time frame isn't research-backed; it was determined largely by insurance companies who decided 28 days was the standard length they would pay for, according to Marvin Ventrell, executive director of the National Association of Addiction Treatment Providers. There's no basis for forgoing opioids altogether either. In fact, data points to the opposite. "Repeated attempts at detox *without* using maintenance therapy actually decreases the odds of success and increases the risk for overdose," says Wakeman.

And then there's the faith factor. While doctors and agencies like the National Institute on Drug Abuse recognize addiction as a disease, there's no other illness for which meeting and prayer are considered mainstream medicine. The majority of rehab programs use the 12-step model created by Alcoholics Anonymous (AA) despite a large-scale international review that found little evidence that it's effective. And it might be damaging: Steps like taking a moral inventory, making amends, and examining character defects can disparage women with addictions, who likely have, and may be ashamed of, a history of trauma or mental illness, says health and medical writer Anne Fletcher, author of *Inside Rehab*.

Surrendering to a "higher power" can be undermining as well—because the implication is that you cannot beat an addiction on your own—especially for the growing number of women who say they're not religious. (There are non-12-step support groups like SMART recovery, an evidence-based program without the spirituality requirement, and Women for Sobriety, a group that aims at empowerment. But they're not as widely studied as MAT.) Even worse, 12-step programs can also put women in direct peril because some men in the groups use the trust established to prey on women sexually. Seducing a newcomer is, disgustingly, joked about as being the "13th step."

When 28-year-old Minnesotan Danielle entered residential rehab, she faced another common obstacle: She was a single mom. She first got hooked on painkillers prescribed after her C-section and progressed to heroin given to her by her then-boyfriend. It's a common path in that 80 percent of new heroin users misused prescription pain medications first. Like roughly 90 percent of people who become addicted to Rx painkillers, Danielle had a history of substance use in her teens and twenties; she'd smoked pot, drank heavily, and dabbled with opioids. Finding a treatment center where she could bring her toddler daughter was a struggle. Few outpatient programs offer affordable day care, and less than 7 percent of residential ones have room to accommodate children. This puts moms like Danielle in a gut-wrenching position—stay with their kids or temporarily put them into foster care so they can get treatment.

Danielle eventually found a rehab that allowed her daughter to stay with her, but later relapsed after giving birth to her second child. She was desperate and decided to try something she'd learned about in rehab: methadone.

A Fair Trade?

Danielle was wary of methadone, having heard treatment medications were just substitute addictions. It's a common, and damaging, misconception. People who take methadone or buprenorphine are told by peers, counselors, and some doctors that they're still hooked, or not "really recovered."

But addiction, by definition, is compulsive drug use despite negative consequences. Taking a daily medication to improve your health doesn't meet this definition. "Maintenance therapy brings a person who is addicted to opioids back to equilibrium the same way that insulin restores normal blood sugar levels for someone with diabetes," says Wakeman. With it, patients are able to go to work, build a family, and socialize. It's safe, even recommended, for pregnant women since quitting opioids during pregnancy can kill the fetus.

Still, that widespread stigma has kept MAT as a "last stop" treatment, despite four decades of conclusive evidence backing its use. Research shows the approach reduces relapse and cuts the death rate by 50 percent compared with those who attend abstinence-only rehab; other findings show up to 90 percent of people on methadone maintenance are successful at beating their opioid addiction. Danielle is one of them. Every day, she goes to a clinic to get an individually tailored dose of methadone (buprenorphine, because it was introduced under less restrictive federal regulations, can be taken at home). After almost a year, she tried coming off the meds due to the side effects (constipation and drowsiness, the two most common) and lingering stigma, but her cravings quickly returned. She realized avoiding relapse was much more important than some vague idea that medication is "bad." With two years of recovery behind her, she says, "I'll be on methadone as long as I feel like it is helping."

How long *should* that be? Doctors don't know. Some patients can taper off after a few months, others may need to take the meds for years, even the rest of their life, says Wakeman, though what is clear is that many people will relapse if they stop MAT after six months or less. And like insulin for someone with diabetes, MAT works best when combined with lifestyle changes, which is why patients are often urged to combine the meds with cognitive behavioral therapy, where they learn to identify and change self-defeating thoughts ("I'll never beat this") and behaviors (e.g., hanging out with friends who are still misusing opioids) that often drive addiction.

Personal Paths

In an ideal world, MAT would be an option for everyone with an opioid-abuse problem, and experts are trying to dispel stigma so the treatment can become more accessible—something that U.S. surgeon general Vivek Murthy backed late last year in a landmark report on drug addiction.

Until then, mounting evidence suggests another drug could also help end the opioid epidemic: pot. Cindi, a 45-year-old native of Orange County, California, has been to 12-step rehab four times to treat her painkiller addiction (it started with a script written for a severe sore throat). But she ultimately recovered in a much less conventional way, by replacing opioids with medical marijuana. Although addiction experts stress more research is needed, several studies link medical marijuana availability to lower risk for opioid use, addiction, and overdose deaths. One California rehab now uses medical marijuana for opioid addiction treatment.

Ultimately, most successful recoveries, like my own—I recovered *despite* going to 12-step rehab, not because of it—involve finding new passions in work, relationships, hobbies, spirituality, or all of the above. Because as surgeon general Murthy wrote in his report, "We must help everyone see that addiction is not a character flaw—it is a chronic illness that we must approach with the same skill and compassion with which we approach heart disease, diabetes, and cancer." To overcome opioid addiction, women need a life we can embrace. And a treatment system that doesn't ignore the evidence.

FINDING A FIX: EMBEDDED WITH THE SUBURBAN COPS CONFRONTING THE OPIOID EPIDEMIC

Julia Lurie

Mother Jones, January/February 2018

At first glance, it looked like Greg Perdue was stretching. The 58-year-old sat cross-legged on the matted wall-to-wall carpet in his Aberdeen, Maryland, apartment, a head of shaggy, graying hair bent toward his knees. But when medical examiners gingerly turned him over, they found his bloated face was a deep purple, his nose and mustache covered with crusted blood. Next to a pack of cigarettes on the kitchen table were three clear pill capsules: two empty, one containing an off-white powder that was later identified as heroin.

In a former life, Perdue was a mechanic, an avid hunter, a drinker, and a romantic who often drove to the tops of the hills nearby to watch the sunset. After being prescribed painkillers to treat a work injury, he started snorting heroin and became estranged from his friends and family. When the cops found him in April, they determined he'd likely been slumped in his apartment for a couple of days. His was the 113th overdose of the year in Harford County, a white, working-class suburb a half-hour up Interstate 95 from Baltimore. There was no funeral; his ashes sit uncollected at the morgue.

After Perdue's quiet death, a lanky, affable 38-year-old cop named Brandon Underhill was assigned to investigate the dealer who had sold the fatal dose to Perdue. Underhill, a clean-cut churchgoer who grew out his wavy blond hair and got his ears pierced when he started doing undercover work 10 years ago, quickly zoomed in on a suspect: Zack Carter, a 35-year-old with a rap sheet including several drug charges and an attempted murder. As spring turned to humid summer, he tracked Carter's cellphone data, talked to "friendlies," or informants, and met Carter behind the yellow home in J&K Mobile Home Park in Aberdeen, where Carter, whose name I have changed, would lean into Underhill's car window and exchange glass vials of heroin for cash.

Underhill was surprised to find that Carter was likable, whether he was confidently breaking up neighborhood tiffs or laying into his underlings, whom he paid in drugs or money, if they tried to steal business. After hiding a GPS tracker under the bumper of Carter's BMW 750, Underhill was able to track the car on his iPad as it traveled to Baltimore a few times a week and then back to Harford to flit among a handful of homes in the county's housing developments and trailer parks. Meanwhile, overdoses kept mounting: In the wake of Perdue's death, cops traced 11 back to Carter, none of which were fatal.

The investigation came to a head in predawn darkness four months after Perdue's overdose, when about 60 officers wearing body armor assembled in an elementary school parking lot for a briefing about the morning's operation. The high beams of dozens of police cruisers cast an eerie light on the officers—nearly all men—who gathered around Underhill as he laid out the plan: Because Carter spent time in five homes nearby, there would be five simultaneous raids at 5:30 a.m. on the dot. "Everybody in the communities all know each other," Underhill explained to me as we drove to one of the raid locations. "When noise starts happening, everybody knows."

The operations that took place a half-hour later looked like a movie scene: the calm of early morning in the trailer parks was interrupted by flash-bang grenades, yelling, the ramming in of doors, cops in perfect V formations with guns drawn. Masked men woke up whoever was sleeping inside and led them out in handcuffs. One resident complained that it was the third time his home had been raided. A half-asleep Carter was hauled out of bed and booked in the Harford County Detention Center.

That morning's raids were part of a Harford County Sheriff's Office initiative to go after the dealers involved in every single overdose in its jurisdiction, fatal or nonfatal. In each case, the county sends a drug investigator, who treats the place of overdose—be it a car in the Home Depot parking lot or a bedroom in a million-dollar home—as a crime scene with a culprit to track down. The task is monumental: In the first 11 months of 2017, there were 78 fatal and 333 nonfatal overdoses in the county of just 250,000 people. "We're gonna come at you with the full force of effective law and every resource we have available to us," said the county's lead narcotics officer, Lee Dunbar, in a *Baltimore Sun* video titled "Capt. Dunbar's Message to Harford's Drug Dealers." The county, one of the first in the nation to investigate every overdose case, has served as "a model of what you can do and what you should do," said Buck Hedrick, supervisor of the Drug Enforcement Administration's intelligence team in Baltimore.

This approach contributes to the already steep price of the epidemic. The average fatal overdose takes more than 40 man-hours for the county's narcotics team to investigate, though that number is highly variable: Underhill worked almost exclusively on the Carter case for more than two months. The cost to the Sheriff's Office of investigating a typical fatal overdose runs between $10,000 and $15,000 once things like salaries, overtime, personal protective gear, and travel to interview witnesses are taken into account. But the spending doesn't stop there: Transporting, cremating, and burying an unclaimed body costs about $700. Medical treatment runs $13,700 for the average inpatient visit after an overdose in Maryland. Add that to the cost of jail or prison for the dealers (about $81 per inmate per night at the Harford County Detention Center), lawyers representing the dealers (at any given time, roughly half of the county's public defenders are working on drug possession or distribution cases), and lawyers representing the state (the state's attorney's office spends about $500,000 a year prosecuting drug cases). And

then there's the crime fueled by addiction: Harford County State's
Attorney Joseph Cassilly estimates that more than half of all thefts,
robberies, and frauds in the county are related to efforts to acquire
cash for drugs.

For all the time, energy, and money Harford cops spend cracking down on dealers, overdoses in Harford are skyrocketing. Then
again, there's no blueprint for cops to follow when it comes to an
epidemic of these proportions, says David Kennedy, a criminologist
who directs the National Network for Safe Communities. After decades of a failed war on drugs, many cops know that arresting users
doesn't work, so they're focusing on dealers, he says. "The sheriffs are
so desperate to try *something*. There are people dying every day, and
they're on the front lines, and we don't have anything to offer them
right now."

The truth is that Harford—along with every other US county hit
hard by the opioid epidemic—is winging it. "I'll go anywhere to try
and get best practices," said Harford County Sheriff Jeff Gahler at a
press conference announcing the opening of the "H.O.P.E. House,"
a model of a drug user's bedroom on wheels aimed at educating the
public about telltale signs of drug abuse. "I don't mind putting it in
reverse if it doesn't work and backing it up and trying again."

Both the Obama and Trump administrations have repeatedly acknowledged the need for treatment for drug users. "We're going to
take all of these kids—and people, not just kids—that are totally addicted and they can't break it," Donald Trump promised at a Colum-
bus, Ohio, town hall meeting just before the election. "We're going
to work with them, we're going to spend the money, we're gonna get
that habit broken." He also promised to declare a national emergency,
which would free up federal money to support afflicted communities. Nothing of the sort has happened. Instead, in October Trump
declared a public health state of emergency, which opened up a fund
containing a grand total of $57,000—or about $1 per fatal overdose
victim. As of this writing, neither the Department of Health and Human Services nor the Office of National Drug Control Policy have
permanent leaders. Repealing Obamacare or enacting the proposed

GOP tax bill would cause millions of Americans with substance abuse and mental health disorders to lose coverage. Meanwhile, the White House Council of Economic Advisers recently estimated that the epidemic cost the nation $504 billion in 2015.

In the absence of federal leadership and funding for social services, police have become the de facto responders, says Keith Humphreys, a Stanford psychiatry professor who advised the Obama administration on drug policy. "If you don't have health care dollars, what else can you do? Put people in jail."

Carter was released on bail three days after the raid, charged with 11 counts of drug offenses, and given a court date in December. The state is also considering charging two of his henchmen with second-degree manslaughter. Since the raid in August, there have been five more overdoses in the trailer parks where police suspect the men operated. The cops are, for the most part, used to this game of cat and mouse, but sometimes, Underhill confessed to me, the process can seem futile. "I feel like we're just playing whack-a-mole," he said, sounding exhausted. "Sometimes you feel like you're just banging your head against a wall—because somebody else is going to pop up and take that business."

Harford County sits squarely between Baltimore and Philadelphia, but it more closely resembles the Pennsylvania Dutch countryside to its north: cornfields and dairy farms dotted with strip malls and cookie-cutter housing developments. The area has long been home to white, middle-class Republicans—lots of cops, military families, and people who commute to Baltimore. The place can have a small-town feel, with high school football and holiday festivals making front-page news in the local paper. On #WantedWednesday, the Sheriff's Office Facebook account features mug shots of people they're looking for, typically for things like not showing up in court or failing to pay child support, against Wild West-themed backgrounds.

While Harford's overdose epidemic is fairly recent, opioids aren't new to Baltimore. For decades, heroin has plagued the city—especially poor communities of color—inspiring HBO's *The Wire* and giving the city the unwanted title of the "heroin capital" of America. "It's been an epidemic in my town since I can remember," a Baltimore dealer known as Doc told me. "Growing up, I didn't even know what dope was, but I knew everybody that sold dope had money."

Opioids started seeping into the surrounding counties in the mid-'90s, when Purdue Pharma introduced OxyContin and dramatically underplayed its addictive qualities. Thanks to pharmaceutical lobbying, years of liberal painkiller prescribing—the United States consumes more than 70 percent of the world's opioid painkillers—planted the seeds for widespread addiction to both painkillers and heroin, which is chemically similar to the prescription pills but far cheaper and more potent.

As the demand for opioids grew in suburban areas, capillaries sprang up from the main drug trafficking artery of Interstate 95, which runs from Florida to Maine, bringing opioids to small towns like Bel Air and Aberdeen. But the turning point in Harford—and much of the country—came in 2015 after fentanyl, an opioid up to 50 times more powerful than heroin that is typically manufactured in illicit labs in China, started making its way into the heroin supply. Complicating matters is the fact that, by the time drugs get to Baltimore or Harford County, they have likely changed hands so many times—and mixed with fentanyl and other additives along the way—that dealers often don't know what they are dealing. Indeed, the customary drug in Baltimore is "scramble": an amalgamation of heroin and other drugs, sold in gel capsules. "We knew [fentanyl] was coming; we were trying to brace for it," said Dunbar. He recruited officers to do nothing but heroin investigations, because "we knew we were gonna see this surge."

And they did. From 2015 to 2017, overdose deaths in Harford County nearly tripled. Today, the Sheriff's Office displays the number of fatal and nonfatal overdoses in real time on signboards with running tickers at the county's police stations and courthouse.

Of course, the epidemic is much bigger than Harford. In Ohio, coroners' offices use refrigerated trucks to store bodies. In

Connecticut, medical examiners' autopsy caseloads have quadrupled in one year. In West Virginia, 1 in 20 infants are born in withdrawal from opioids. And in Maryland, two-thirds of people in jail have a diagnosed substance abuse disorder, according to a 2016 analysis by the governor's office. Harford County Sheriff's Office cops are no longer allowed to test seized drugs suspected to contain opioids on the spot, because of reports that interacting with some variants of fentanyl can be deadly. When the drugs are sent to DEA labs, "while one person is testing, another person is ready to treat them with [the overdose reversal drug] naloxone in case they fall while they're testing," says Hedrick, the DEA supervisor.

As the wave of fatal overdoses hit Harford in early 2015, county officials sprang into action. Police officers are now equipped with naloxone and trained that addiction is a disease. Cops on the Narcotics Task Force rarely charge users for drug possession in quantities that seem intended for personal use. After every overdose, cops give victims a "help card" with addiction treatment resources. "We're not going to solve the problem by putting addicts in jail," said Underhill. "If they're not going to get effective treatment, it's not going to change anything."

Another part of Harford's response is aggressively tracking down dealers. In 2016 alone, the county arrested and charged 240 people with felony drug offenses. As Dunbar sums up the strategy, "We need to lock up the bad guys—the dealers and traffickers putting out stuff on the street—but we also play a role in getting the victims help."

Yet as the opioid crisis continues to metastasize, the line between bad guys and victims is increasingly blurred. "These aren't two distinct sets of people," says District Public Defender Kelly Casper. She estimates that 80 percent of the cases represented by her office are drug-related—whether it's people dealing or stealing to get a fix—and that "darned near 100 percent" of her clients are using. "They want to charge all of these people with drug dealing, when in fact the core of the problem is that they're users."

I saw the user-dealer problem play out a few days after Carter was arrested. I was tagging along with Ryan Wolfe, a friendly, middle-aged cop wearing jeans and a *Voltron* T-shirt who has seen what drugs can do to people—his brother is addicted to heroin. For an hour, Wolfe and I trailed two alleged dealers who appeared to have filled the void left by Carter's absence. When Wolfe's team finally pulled them over, he said into his radio, "Let's hope they still got something, guys."

Back at the station, five cops wearing masks, rubber gloves, and holsters with guns searched the dealers' beat-up Mercury Montego. They pulled out a child's car seat, a Hello Kitty tricycle, a 60-pack of Play-Doh, an Orioles fidget spinner, and an air mattress. One cop slowly poured out family-sized boxes of Froot Loops; another flipped through a child's drawings of flowers. I noticed, for the first time, a bumper sticker: "My child makes Lisby-Hillsdale a great place to learn." The dealers, it turns out, were two women I'll call Vanessa and Tina, a homeless couple, living out of the car and motels, selling to support their own drug addiction.

Later, the women told me how they get by, squeezing an air mattress into the sedan at night, parking in lots where cops won't arrest them, and occasionally getting a room at the Super 8 to take a shower. Sometimes they pick up odd jobs, cleaning houses or painting. Most weeks, they see Tina's three young daughters, who stay with their grandmother and believe Mommy's saving up money for a new house. They take the girls on trips to the park or the library or IHOP—anything cheap.

Both women have been using for the better part of a decade, going through cycles of clean time, relapse, and prison for drug charges. "You use some and sell some—I make my money back to do it for free," said Vanessa, who started snorting heroin after she was prescribed Percocet for an injury. Tina started just after high school, when a boyfriend introduced her to pills. "It feels like you're superwoman," she said of the first time using. "You can run around, get the whole house cleaned, go to work, come home, clean more. And without it you don't want to do anything. You're sick."

It was dark outside by the time the five men, working overtime, had finished searching the Montego. Wolfe's wife was texting him, wondering if he would be home for dinner. In the end, the cops found a dime bag of weed, and a strip search revealed that Vanessa had slipped a little fold of heroin—enough for a single person to use—in her bra. The officers didn't press charges. As they were leaving, Vanessa asked Wolfe whether he knew of any local programs that would help her, a felon with a history of drug charges, find a job. She didn't want to keep living this life, she said. He told her none came to mind.

"Sometimes chalk one up for us; sometimes chalk one up for them," Wolfe said. "They'll get another day to do their thing, and we'll get another day to do ours."

It's not that Harford cops don't empathize with user-dealers. The guy who gets in a car accident is prescribed painkillers, becomes addicted, and then starts selling to support his own habit—"I've seen that story 150 times," Underhill told me. But where do you draw the line? "They're selling just enough to get theirs," he said of user-dealers, "but they're killing people with what they're bringing back." He gets most worked up when he talks about the kids: the toddlers strapped in car seats as he pulls parents over for drugs, the children he terrifies when breaking open front doors with Halligan bars in predawn raids, the teens who come home from school to find that cops have gone through their bedrooms looking for drugs.

When it comes to reforming user-dealers, evidence strongly suggests that prison time isn't very effective. Instead, stable housing, support services, and employment have been shown to promote long-term recovery. Law Enforcement Assisted Diversion, a Seattle program that has been replicated in dozens of jurisdictions across the country, demonstrates the research in action: Rather than jailing people for low-level drug crimes, police divert them to programs offering treatment, housing, and job training. Participants are nearly 60 percent less likely to be rearrested.

The treatment approach also saves money: According to the National Institute on Drug Abuse, part of the National Institutes of Health, "Every $1 invested in addiction treatment programs yields a return of between $4 and $7 in reduced drug-related crime, criminal justice costs, and theft alone."

"Supply follows demand, not the other way around," says Lindsay LaSalle, a senior staff attorney at the Drug Policy Alliance. "The war-on-drugs tactics have been wholly ineffective at curbing sales or use—drugs are more available and pure than ever before."

Attorney General Jeff Sessions is one of the leading advocates for traditional punitive policies, like increasing mandatory minimum sentencing to stop the "thugs and gangs who bring this poison into our communities," as he told DEA employees in May. "It's going from today to the 1980s," says Humphreys, the Stanford professor and former Obama adviser.

Meanwhile, Trump has proposed gutting the social services that act as a safety net for users and dealers—from job training programs to child care to food stamps. "This is a lot of chicken and egg," says Marc Schindler, executive director of the Justice Policy Institute. "We need effective substance abuse treatment. People also need jobs. They need adequate education. They need housing." All of this is, of course, much harder to provide than a prison cell.

Take Doc, the 30-year-old Baltimore dealer who spoke with me under the awning of a McDonald's across from a corner where he sells drugs. He'd been working these corners for the better part of his life but hadn't tried opioids himself until he was shot in a drug-related turf war a few years ago and got addicted to Percocet. He found that the drug numbed his pain—of not just the gunshot wound, but also the childhood trauma of growing up on Baltimore's streets. "Some people done lost their best friend, their brothers, over these fucking corner wars," he told me. "This shit's like Iraq."

When we spoke, he was living in the suburbs with his two kids—daughter loves ballet, son is into football—and waking up at 5:30 a.m. to sell drugs to the early-morning users in the city. He could get a minimum-wage job, he said, but it's far easier to support his family as a drug dealer than as a McDonald's cashier. Doc told me he knows how he appears to an outsider: " 'Look at that guy. Gold teeth, pants hanging off his ass.' You look at us like we're some kind of monster. Well, look at my school system. If you're not going to educate me, where am I gonna work?" In August, he told me he had gotten out of prison just a couple of months before. "You think that my kids aren't fucked up when I'm sitting over in that jail and I'm missing birthday parties?"

Next to Doc under the McDonald's awning was his friend Dre Jackson, a quieter 39-year-old who's known Doc for years. Dre, too, had grown up in Baltimore's rough neighborhoods and had cycled between drug use and prison and recovery. Now, he told me, he was ready to leave the streets behind. He had done a job training program in Pennsylvania—he raved about the peacefulness of the country-side, the lack of violence and drugs—but had come back to Balti-more to take care of his mom. He had a job at a supermarket and a girlfriend who wasn't into drugs. For the moment, life was good. "I didn't wanna be out here homeless where all I wanted to think about was getting high."

When I returned from my trip to Harford County, I called Under-hill and asked what had happened to Carter when he was released on bail. After a brief silence, Underhill admitted he had no idea. He'd just come back from a church mission trip to Romania, he told me, and now he was busy preparing for another raid. "It would be nice to try to keep tabs on people," he said with a sigh, "but we just don't have time."

Once or twice a year, Underhill hears from dealers he caught, who call or text or recognize him on the street and tell him that the day of their arrest was their rock bottom, and that they haven't dabbled in drugs since. "It's infrequent," he admitted, but "if it takes all this manpower and two and a half months of effort to get somebody to say, 'I'm clean, and I'm doing well, and I'm trying,' then, okay, we'll keep doing it."

More often, though, he finds out what happens to the people he's busted another way: by busting them again. In early October, two months after their arrest, Underhill saw Vanessa and Tina hang-ing out in the trailer park, meeting with the same known drug us-ers they'd been seen with before. When the cops pulled the women over, they found cocaine, a bottle of methadone with the label pulled off, and more than $700 in cash. A strip search found that Vanessa had stored a gram of heroin in her anal cavity. The cops seized the cash, which they suspected was earnings from dealing. The money was "all of our savings to be able to get a place and get off the streets," the women countered. Once again, because of the small quantities of drugs, the cops let them go.

"It's very frustrating," said Underhill. "But I don't know what to do differently. We can't just stop."

And sometimes, dealers disappear. A couple of months after I spoke with Doc and Dre at McDonald's, I called Doc to check in and kept getting a busy tone. So I called Dre, who told me the news: Doc had been shot and killed in an apparent robbery in September, just a block from where we'd spoken. "I'm still fucked up over it," said Dre. "I went to the viewing but couldn't go to the funeral." It was just too much.

When we spoke a week later, Dre's words were slurred. He stopped midsentence to start humming. It was his night off, and he and his girlfriend were watching a movie at home. He'd just popped a couple of Percocets, he admitted—my call woke him up from nodding off in the bathroom. "I can't say I got an excuse," he said, "but after [Doc] passed away, I've been doing it more and more." This was the same guy I'd spoken to just two months before—the one who had worked so hard to turn his life around. Now it seemed like he was careening off a ledge. Before we hung up, as if he were reading my mind, he said, "Don't forget about me, okay?"

GRATITUDE LIST

In my limited experience, the process of writing and publishing a book is a bit more gratifying and prideworthy than editing one. But I'm happy to say that I've enjoyed working on this collection, and I am pleased by how it turned out.

I am grateful to:

- Marc Favreau, The New Press's executive editor, for his longstanding friendship, kindness, and expertise. (This is the third book we have collaborated on.)
- Will Hodge, my outstanding graduate research assistant, for tracking down authors and copyright holders, negotiating permissions and fees, and performing various other chores, while also being exceedingly enjoyable to know.
- Pat Bowen, my previous GRA, for helping me launch this project.
- Emily Albarillo, for cheerfully and conscientiously guiding this book through production.
- Angus Johnston, for his outstanding copyediting work on this book.
- Tom Couch, for his friendship, thoughtfulness, and daily support.
- Jason Appelman, for his longstanding friendship, and regular check-ins.
- Jeremy Varon, for his durable friendship, and wise and trusted council.

- Tim McCarthy and Mike Foley, also for their friendships and advice.
- The informal GSU writing group that I belong to, led by Doug Blackmon, and including Julia Gaffield, for helpfully critiquing an early draft of the introduction to this book.
- Dr. Alex Williamson, also for looking over part of the manuscript.
- David Forehand, Stephen and Teresa, Paul Herrgesell, Martin Chen, Jeremy Galen, Lee and Deb Gehrke, High Noon, Back on My Feet, Christine Wolff, and Bill Higgins (for various reasons).
- Cousins Mike and Dan, for helping me stay sane in the Trump Era.
- Eric Foner, Michael Kazin, and Alex Bloom, for their supportive letters.
- Frank Rich, for his unusual kindness.
- Leslie Jamison, for her warmth and generosity, and for writing the terrific foreword to this book.
- The contributors to this volume, for their cooperation, for their diligence and sense of purpose, and for raising awareness about the most vulnerable among us.
- My family—and especially my parents, Harlon and Judy McMillian—for their loving support.

CONTRIBUTORS

Christopher Caldwell is a contributing editor at the *Claremont Review of Books* and the author of *The Age of Entitlement: America Since the Sixties*.

Susan Dominus joined the *New York Times* as a Metro columnist in 2007. She has been a staff writer with the *New York Times Magazine* since 2011. She was also part of a team that won a Pulitzer Prize in 2018 for public service for reporting on workplace sexual harassment issues.

Joe Eaton is a writer in Missoula, Montana. He is an associate professor of journalism at the University of Montana and a former staff writer at the Center for Public Integrity in Washington, DC.

Eric Eyre is a statehouse reporter for the *Charleston Gazette-Mail*. In 2017, he was awarded the Pulitzer Prize in investigative reporting that uncovered massive shipments of prescription painkillers to small towns in West Virginia's coal-mining region. He is writing a book based on that coverage to be published by Scribner.

Johann Hari is the *New York Times* bestselling author of *Chasing the Scream*, which is being adapted into a feature film. He is also the author of *Lost Connections*.

Dr. **Adi Jaffe**, PhD, is a nationally recognized expert on mental health, addiction, and stigma. He is most recently known as the founder of IGNTD Recovery and author of *The Abstinence Myth*, published in 2018.

German Lopez has written for *Vox* since it launched in 2014, with a focus on criminal justice, guns, and drugs. Since 2017, he's dedicated much of his time to covering the opioid epidemic and solutions to the crisis. Previously, he worked at *CityBeat*, a local newspaper in Cincinnati, covering politics and policy at the local and state level, and he graduated from the University of Cincinnati in 2012.

Julia Lurie is a reporter at *Mother Jones*, in San Francisco, where she covers addiction. Here stories have also appeared in *The Atlantic*, the *Washington Post*, and elsewhere.

Beth Macy is the author of three *New York Times* bestselling books, including *Dopesick: Dealers, Doctors, and the Drug Company That Addicted America*. A longtime reporter who specializes in outsiders and underdogs, Macy has won more than a dozen national journalism awards, including a Nieman Fellowship for Journalism at Harvard in 2010.

Tom Mashberg is an independent investigative reporter and editor. In 2014, he and Rebecca Davis O'Brien were finalists for the Pulitzer Prize in Local Reporting for their coverage of the drug trade and opioid epidemic in northern New Jersey in *The Record*, in Bergen County, New Jersey.

Dr. Gabor Maté has written several bestselling books including the award-winning *In the Realm of Hungry Ghosts: Close Encounters with Addiction*; *When the Body Says No: The Cost of Hidden Stress*; and *Scattered Minds: A New Look at the Origins and Healing of Attention Deficit Disorder*, and co-authored *Hold on to Your*

Kids. His works have been published internationally in twenty languages.

Rebecca Davis O'Brien covers white-collar law enforcement at the *Wall Street Journal.* Rebecca previously worked at *The Record,* in Bergen County, New Jersey. In 2014, she and Tom Mashberg were finalists for the Pulitzer Prize in Local Reporting for their coverage of the drug trade and opioid epidemic in northern New Jersey.

Sam Quinones is a journalist, author, and storyteller whose two acclaimed books of narrative nonfiction about Mexico and Mexican immigration made him, according to the *SF Chronicle Book Review,* "the most original writer on Mexico and the border." His book *Dreamland* won the 2015 National Book Critics Circle Award for General Nonfiction.

Sarah Resnick lives in New York. Her writing has been published in a variety of venues, including *The Best American Essays 2017.* She is the recipient of a 2019 Pushcart Prize.

Eli Saslow is a reporter at the *Washington Post* who won the Pulitzer Prize for Explanatory Reporting in 2014 for his series about food stamps in America.

Katharine Q. Seelye has covered national news and politics for the *New York Times* since 1994. She has served since 2012 as the paper's New England bureau chief, based in Boston.

Andrew Sullivan is writer-at-large at *New York* magazine and former editor of *The Dish* and the *New Republic.*

Maia Szalavitz is author of the *New York Times* bestseller *Unbroken Brain: A Revolutionary New Way of Understanding Addiction.*

Margaret Talbot is a staff writer at the *New Yorker* and the author of *The Entertainer: Movies, Magic and My Father's Twentieth Century* (Riverhead, 2012).

Admiral **James A. Winnefeld Jr.** (U.S. Navy, retired) is the co-founder of S.A.F.E. Project, whose mission is to contribute in a tangible way to overcoming the addiction fatality epidemic in the United States.

Publishing in the Public Interest

Thank you for reading this book published by The New Press. The New Press is a nonprofit, public interest publisher. New Press books and authors play a crucial role in sparking conversations about the key political and social issues of our day.

We hope you enjoyed this book and that you will stay in touch with The New Press. Here are a few ways to stay up to date with our books, events, and the issues we cover:

- Sign up at www.thenewpress.com/subscribe to receive updates on New Press authors and issues and to be notified about local events
- Like us on Facebook: www.facebook.com/newpressbooks
- Follow us on Twitter: www.twitter.com/thenewpress

Please consider buying New Press books for yourself; for friends and family; or to donate to schools, libraries, community centers, prison libraries, and other organizations involved with the issues our authors write about.

The New Press is a 501(c)(3) nonprofit organization. You can also support our work with a tax-deductible gift by visiting www.thenewpress.com/donate.

31901066019599